New Hampshire is bounded on the South by the Province of Massachusets, beginning at a Mark ‡ three Miles North from the Mouth of Merrimack River; from thence running Westward on a similar curved Line with the River, at three Miles distance to a Pitch Pine Tree, Three Miles due North (allowing 10 Degrees Variation) from Pantucket Falls, and from thence on a due West Line, untill it meets his Majesty's Government of New York about Twenty Miles East from Hudsons River.

This Province is bounded Eastward by the Atlantic Ocean, as the Coast runs from said Mark to the Mouth of Piscataqua Harbour from thence up the Middle of the River, into the River Nywichwannock (part of which is called Salmon Falls) and thro the Middle of yᵉ same to the furthest Head thereof, and from thence N. 2 Degˢ And then Westerly untill 120 Miles be finished from the mouth of Piscataqua Harbour, or till it meets with his Majestys other Governments.

See Geo: II order in Council for Settling the Line between this Province and the Massachusetts Bay.

N B. Those Towns and Parishes which are so well settled as to be able to support the Gospel among themselves, which is not generally the case till they have at least 60 or 70 Families, have this Character ♂ for their Churches.

Those without that Mark are either newly granted or thinly Inhabited.

Many single Branches of Rivers in the ungranted parts of the Country, are laid down from the Information of Hunters and others.

The Falls on Rivers which obstruct the navigation are markt thus

And the Double prickt Lines point out the carrying Place.

Revolutionary New Hampshire

Whereas it now Appears an Undoubted Fact, That Notwithstanding all the Dutiful Petitions and Decent Remonstrances from the American Colonies and the Utmost Exertions of their best friends in England on their Behalf, The British Ministry, Arbitrary & Vindictive, Are yet Determined to reduce by Fire and Sword our Bleeding Country, to their Absolute Obedience: And for this Purpose, in Addition to their own forces, have Engaged great Numbers of Foreign Mercenaries, who may now be on their Passage here, Accompanied by a Formidable fleet to Ravage and Plunder the Seacoast; From all which we may reasonably expect the most Dismal Scenes of Distress the ensuing Year, unless we Exert ourselves by Every means & Precaution Possible. And Whereas We of this Colony of New Hampshire have the Example of Several of the most Respectable of our Sister Colonies before us for Entering upon that most Important Step of a Disunion from Great Britain, and Declaring ourselves Free and Independent of the Crown thereof, being Impelled thereto by the most violent & Injurious Treatment; And it Appearing absolutely Necessary in this most Critical Juncture of our Public Affairs, that The Honble the Continental Congress, who have this Important Object under their Immediate Consideration Should be also Informed of our Resolutions thereon without loss of Time — We do hereby Declare that it is the Opinion of this Assembly that our Delegates at the Continental Congress Should be Instructed, and they are hereby Instructed to Join with the other Colonies in Declaring The Thirteen United Colonies, a Free & Independent State: Solemnly Pledging our Faith & Honor That we will on our part Support the Measure with our Lives and Fortunes — and that in Consequence thereof they The Continental Congress, on whose Wisdom, Fidelity & Integrity we rely, may Enter into and Form Such Alliances as they may Judge most Conducive to the Present Safety, and Future Advantage of These American Colonies — Provided the Regulation of our Internal Police be under the Direction of our own Assembly — — Entered Acording to the Original.

Pr Noah Emery Cl D Assy

Resolution of the New Hampshire General Assembly on Independence,
June 15, 1776. From the manuscript journal of the
House of Representatives.

REVOLUTIONARY NEW HAMPSHIRE

An Account of the Social
and Political Forces Underlying the
Transition from Royal Province
to American Commonwealth

By RICHARD FRANCIS UPTON

KENNIKAT PRESS
Port Washington, N. Y./London

KENNIKAT AMERICAN BICENTENNIAL SERIES
Under the General Editorial Supervision of
Dr. Ralph Adams Brown
Professor of History, State University of New York

F
38
U68

61078

REVOLUTIONARY NEW HAMPSHIRE

First published in 1936
Reissued in 1970 by Kennikat Press
Library of Congress Catalog Card No: 70-120896
ISBN 0-8046-1289-7

Manufactured by Taylor Publishing Company   Dallas, Texas

KENNIKAT AMERICAN BICENTENNIAL SERIES

Foreword

A FEW years ago, the President and Trustees of Dartmouth College instituted the Senior Fellowships, which are annually awarded to students of proved ability and initiative in order that they may for one year at least enjoy the fullest and freest opportunity to develop the qualities of self-reliance and originality which they are assumed to possess. While the most varied of interests and talents have been recognized in the awarding of these fellowships, there has naturally been a hope that a few at least of those appointed may choose to devote themselves to the study of problems of human society, either in the present or in the past, a better understanding of which will be of value to them later when they face the ever-increasing social responsibilities of our contemporary world.

In the spring of 1934, one of these Senior Fellowships was awarded to Mr. Richard F. Upton, of the class of 1935, the author of this volume. He held the fellowship during the academic year 1934-1935, and for reasons which he states in the author's preface, chose to devote his year of study to an investigation of the developments which took place in New Hampshire during the course of the American Revolution. Upon first thought it might seem that a field for a year's intensive study, thus restricted in time and place, would be unduly narrow, affording little opportunity for the realization of the broader possibilities which have been mentioned above. There is reason to believe, however, that the results of Mr. Upton's work, as embodied in this volume, afford conclusive evidence that his choice was a particularly happy one. It may be frankly stated that he entered upon

[v]

his task with no conscious thought of writing a book, nor was he planning at any future time to follow the historian's profession. He had already decided to seek a career in the law, but it was his earnest desire to utilize the unusual opportunity which was presented to him in order to broaden his understanding of social phenomena and problems. He might have set about to accomplish his purpose in any one of a number of ways. But a natural leaning toward history, his interest in his native state, and his belief that the period of the American Revolution offered an exceptional opportunity to study the interplay of social, economic, and political forces at a time of crisis, led to the selection of the field which has been indicated.

His choice appears to have been further justified for the following reasons. Since the history of New Hampshire during the Revolution has not been previously explored in any comprehensive fashion, it has been possible for the author to make a modest, but very definite contribution to our knowledge of one of the most significant periods of American history. His work has necessitated the discarding of certain of the broad and occasionally superficial generalizations which have sometimes characterized the history of the Revolution and has involved an intensive study of events and trends of the period in all their complexity. While the volume is concerned with a small area and with a brief span of years, its scope is in another sense as broad as anyone could wish. What the author has attempted is nothing less than an analysis, in cross section so to speak, of a given society at a time when its institutions and its whole outlook on life were changing rapidly, under the emotional and physical stress of war and revolution. It is being increasingly recognized that the American War of Independence as a whole cannot be fully understood until the revolutions which occurred in the individual states have been carefully studied.

Thus we find in the following pages a vivid description of the conflict of interests and viewpoints which helped to form public opinion in New Hampshire during the Revolution. This has in turn necessitated a preliminary survey of the land and the people of the province on the eve of the struggle. We are enabled to follow the rise of a new political and social order, evolving through a process of trial and error. We read of problems of industry and finance, almost bewildering in their complexity and surprisingly modern in some of their implications. It is interesting to learn, for example, that representatives of New Hampshire attended regional and interstate conferences designed to promote economic welfare, though it is scarcely surprising to learn that these conferences were attended by scant success. Taxation, currency, and inflation, all come into the picture. We

Foreword

read of those who sought to improve the occasion by privateering and similar patriotic—and profitable—pursuits. The treatment meted out to the Loyalists brings home to one the fact that the Revolution was a civil conflict, as well as a war for independence, and one is aware throughout of the interplay of the forces of patriotism and sacrifice, mingled with self-interest and prejudice. And yet, from all this strife and confusion, one sees a new order emerging, which gives promise of greater opportunity and freedom. Objectivity and a sense of reality are the qualities most conspicuously revealed in this book, while occasional allusions to present day problems bear witness that the broader significance of events which occurred a century and a half ago has not been lost sight of.

The author would be the last person to assume that he had exhausted the subject of New Hampshire and its relation to the American Revolution. While there were available to him the resources of an excellent college library which specializes in New Hampshire history and extensive collections of original material in the state archives at Concord, it is realized that there is much material elsewhere which has not been examined. Notwithstanding this fact, it is believed that the scope of the material which has been used justifies the conviction that the narrative of events is accurate and the interpretations and conclusions sound. Few persons will be more fully aware than the writer of this foreword of the enthusiasm and effort which went into the writing of the book, and he believes that it effectively demonstrates the possibilities inherent in the institution of the Senior Fellowship. Certainly the producing of this volume has been a genuinely stimulating and valuable educational experience for its author. It also seems reasonable to hope that the result of his labors will not be without interest and value to the wider public to which it is now offered.

WAYNE EDSON STEVENS

Department of History
Dartmouth College

Author's Preface

THIS *volume embodies the tangible results of a project carried out under the terms of a Senior Fellowship at Dartmouth College during the academic year 1934-1935. It will at once be apparent that any definitive piece of historical research on a subject of such scope could scarcely be carried out during so brief a period. One of the motives which influenced my choice of this particular field of study was a belief that there should be a closer community of interests between the state of New Hampshire and Dartmouth College. Another consideration was my interest in the history of the state and a desire to make some contribution in this field which should neither emphasize genealogy nor be colored by hero-worship, and which should attempt to present a body of facts as objectively as possible. A final incentive was the absence of any historical work which stressed the social and economic aspects of the American Revolution in New Hampshire.*

While the major emphasis has been placed upon local events and changes, I have endeavored to include by way of background as much of the American and international setting as seemed to be essential for an understanding of the situation in New Hampshire, subject naturally to limitations of space as well as of opportunities for research. I have also attempted to combine with a recital of the essential facts an essay in interpretation. The first few chapters are almost wholly narrative in form, and they embody an account of the events leading to the revolt against British authority. The later chapters describe some of the political, economic, and social changes which took place in New Hampshire during the Revolutionary period, while embodying a number of conclusions as to their significance. Relatively little space has been devoted to military events. I feel that I have benefited greatly from certain approaches to the history of the period suggested by the works of such recognized authorities as the late Professors Claude H. Van Tyne and Frederick J. Turner, and of Dr. Charles A. Beard, Dr. J. Franklin Jameson, Professor Charles M. Andrews, and Mr. James Truslow Adams.

I take pleasure in recording my appreciation for the many courtesies received in the preparation of this volume. First I wish to express my indebtedness to Professor Wayne E. Stevens, of the Department of History of Dartmouth College, without whose assistance this work would have been largely impossible. Professor Stevens's wide experience, constructive criticism, and exacting standards of scholarship were a continual source of encouragement. I also wish to thank Professors Frank Maloy Anderson and W. Randall Waterman, of Dartmouth College, for reading and criticizing the manuscript. The labor involved in the study of certain of the intricacies of the economic trends and international relationships of the period has been greatly lightened by the valuable counsel of Dr. Lester V. Chandler, of Princeton University, and Professor William A. Robinson, of Dartmouth College. I am, moreover, greatly indebted to my classmate and roommate, Mr. Philip N. Guyol, for helpful criticism and encouragement during the course of this work and for suggestions looking toward the possibility of publication. For assistance rendered during the progress of research, I also owe a sincere debt of gratitude to the Dartmouth College Library, to the New Hampshire State Library, to Major Otis G. Hammond and the New Hampshire Historical Society, to Senator Charles M. Dale and Mr. Arthur I. Harriman of Portsmouth, New Hampshire, to Mrs. Herbert D. Swift of Elkins, and to Deputy State Treasurer F. Gordon Kimball. I would likewise express my indebtedness to Mr. A. I. Dickerson and his associates of the board of editors of the Dartmouth College Publications, for the responsibility assumed by them in connection with the publication of this study; to Miss Mildred Saunders, who made the index; and to Mrs. Wayne E. Stevens, who assisted in the reading of the proof. Finally, I cannot sufficiently express my gratitude to President Ernest M. Hopkins and the members of the Board of Trustees of Dartmouth College, whose award of a Senior Fellowship made this whole enterprise possible.

RICHARD F. UPTON

Concord, New Hampshire
8 September 1935

Contents

	Foreword	PAGE	V
	Author's Preface		IX
I.	Prelude to Conflict		1
II.	The Downfall of Royal Government		17
III.	Revolutionary Organization		32
IV.	Clash of Political Opinion		46
V.	Independence and Confederation		63
VI.	New Hampshire in the Continental Congress		76
VII.	The Army and Its Administration		88
VIII.	Privateering and the Continental Navy		106
IX.	The Suppression of the Loyalists		118
X.	Revolutionary Finance in New Hampshire		132
XI.	Industry and the Revolution		148
XII.	The Revolution and Land Tenure		163
XIII.	The Evolution of State Government		175
XIV.	Secession Movement in the West		188
XV.	New Hampshire and the Peace Settlement		199
XVI.	Advance in Liberal Ideas		207
	Notes		219
	Bibliography		251
	Index		267

Illustrations

Map of New Hampshire, 1761   End Papers

    This was surveyed by Joseph Blanchard and Samuel Langdon and published at Portsmouth in 1761 under the title—"Accurate map of his majesty's province of New Hampshire in New England."

Resolution of the New Hampshire General Assembly on Independence, June 15, 1776.   Frontispiece

    From the manuscript journal of the House of Representatives.

Governor Wentworth's Proclamation of Rebellion, December 26, 1774.   27

Non-Importation, Non-Consumption Covenant Adopted by Concord, August, 1774.   57

    This illustration omits a separate page of signatures.

Proclamation by the First State Government, March 19, 1776.   91

    From manuscript journal of the House of Representatives.

Bond of the Privateer HAZARD Owned by John Langdon of Portsmouth.   129

Notice by Committee of Safety of Londonderry to Apprehend Adam Stuart, a Loyalist.   169

Resolution of the Continental Congress Recommending That New Hampshire Establish a Form of Government, November 3, 1775.   191

The originals of these documents are in the archives of the New Hampshire Historical Society.

CHAPTER I

From this recital you'll see the Genius of the people—and that Candor
& reason are more necessary than Troops and Ships to govern them by—
much depends upon acting with Spirit upon the Occasion.
                    Governor JOHN WENTWORTH *in* 1768.[1]

Prelude to Conflict

WHEN John Wentworth became royal governor of the Province of New Hampshire in 1767, he found a thriving agrarian and mercantile community of some ninety-eight towns containing about fifty-two thousand people, but nevertheless a very sparsely settled country.[2] With a total area of approximately nine thousand square miles the density of population was only 5.5 per square mile.

Coming directly from his travels in the midst of elegant English officialdom and aristocratic southern society, one would perhaps assume Wentworth to have been vastly disappointed with his small provincial jurisdiction.[3] Yet Portsmouth, his new home, and the seat of royal government, could not have been altogether unattractive. A buzzing colonial metropolis containing a population of approximately forty-five hundred souls, it was the abode of a wealthy ship-building and commercial oligarchy which for generations had supplied the greater part of the royal officials and dominated the social and political life of the province.[4] This domination by a seacoast oligarchy, in fact, was responsible for a great deal of the bitter sectionalism which prevailed within the colony. The social characteristics of the settlers, geographical factors, and difficulties of communication only helped further to accentuate this division into three general sections.[5]

The first section roughly coincided with the seacoastal plain, eighteen miles in length, and the Great Bay tidewater region. This area comprised almost half the population and paid nearly two-thirds of the total province taxes.[6] The leading town, of course, was the provincial capital, Portsmouth, which was the only legal port of entry and possessed one of the finest harbors on the New England coast. The chief industries were shipbuilding, commerce, fishing, and agriculture. Because of their relative prosperity and close contact with royal officials, the people of this section seem to have been somewhat conservative in viewpoint down to the actual outbreak of the Revolution.[7]

The second section embraced roughly the area of the Merrimack Valley and contiguous territory.[8] As many of the towns in this valley had been granted by Massachusetts Bay and settled by Massachusetts men, it was not unnatural that their inhabitants should look to Boston for political guidance. They seem to have been completely imbued with a Puritan disrespect for English institutions and the vested interests of the seacoast oligarchy. Among the leading towns were Londonderry with 2,389 inhabitants, a center of Scotch-Irish Presbyterianism, and Concord with 752 inhabitants, an outpost of radical republicanism.[9] While the river valleys were the scene of considerable lumbering operations and the manufacture of linen dominated the Scotch-Irish settlements, the chief industry of this section was agriculture. Good land was scarce and communication difficult. The resulting tendency was toward small farms and local self-sufficiency, with limited external intercourse. The hardy population were, in truth, the backbone of the growing discontent with royal rule. To them money was a scarce article; they laid the blame for their economic straits upon a conservative mercantile class which seemed to abound with wealth. When they made the inevitable demands for paper money issues, the royal governor always vetoed their proposals, all of which only served to increase their contempt for the imperial idea.[10]

The third section was the frontier, coinciding with the Connecticut River valley, the scene of many a French and Indian raid in the past. This region was settled in great part by pioneering men from Connecticut who had pushed up the river to newer lands. The names of Lyme, Enfield, Lebanon, and Canaan—some of the towns they founded—

were borrowed directly from their home province. Ordinarily accustomed to an extremely democratic government, these political radicals resented the fact that they were given little or no part in the government of their adopted province. Far from the arm of the law, His Majesty's name inspired no great emotion in their hearts. Their real interests centered in the river valley rather than in the section of the "down easterners." The chief industries of the region were agriculture and lumbering. Through the river, which was western New England's chief artery of trade, the inhabitants participated in commerce with the outside world.[11]

One might wonder what sort of government was relied upon to control these heterogeneous elements. Perhaps the dominant characteristic of New Hampshire's royal government was its administrative centralization.[12] Since the province was not endowed with a charter, being in fact the only New England province without that small essential, the royal officials had no embarrassing organic constitutional system to contend with in their efforts to enforce the law. The result was a comparatively efficient organization run by and in the interests of a propertied oligarchy which filled most of the responsible administrative positions.

This centralized system of government revolved about the royal governor, who was appointed in England. He was the executive representative of the King and captain general of the provincial militia, sworn to uphold the King's laws. By and with the consent of his council, which he usually dominated, the governor appointed and removed all judges, minor judicial officials, militia officers, and his own administrative assistants. Upon his recommendation to the home government the members of the council and the provincial secretary were appointed. The assembly, which was the only elective body, he might call, prorogue or dissolve at will. All laws had to pass both assembly and council, money bills originating in the lower house, but the governor possessed an absolute veto as did the English administration across the sea.

The dreaded commercial regulations fell under the supervision of the collector of customs and a naval officer whose tasks were rendered relatively easy by the small coast line under their jurisdiction. An arrest was the equivalent of conviction, for trials were before an admiralty judge without jury, and the prosecution was relentlessly conducted by an efficient King's advocate, usually one of the best lawyers in the province.

It was therefore with a full realization of his extensive power and responsibility that John Wentworth assumed the office of governor at Portsmouth on June 13, 1767. Could he have foreseen the future, perhaps he would not have written, "I am extremely happy in the Universal Esteem of all this Province who emulate each other in obliging me and endeavouring to make my Administration honorable easy and as profitable as they Can."[13]

Yet the new Governor had qualifications which would have caused a favorable reception in New Hampshire in any event. Son of a wealthy Portsmouth merchant and a graduate of Harvard College, he was possessed of a pleasing personality, a graceful, even temper, and a keen understanding of mass psychology. He was a liberal in politics, being a relative of the famous Whig, Lord Rockingham, and as a colonial agent for New Hampshire, he had aided in bringing about the repeal of the Stamp Act. Under normal conditions it would have seemed logical for him to look forward to a long life of administrative success, popular esteem, and social security.

John Wentworth's first year as governor was a particularly auspicious one as far as imperial relations were concerned, for an era of good feeling had set in with the repeal of the Stamp Act in 1766. No one appeared to heed the Declaratory Act, attached as a rider to the repeal measure, which had declared the authority of Parliament to bind the colonies by law in all cases whatsoever. True, New Hampshire had openly refused to take part in the Stamp Act Congress at New York, but local feeling had run high nevertheless. A Portsmouth mob had forced the stamp collector to resign his commission and had burned several members of Grenville's ministry in effigy. That this popular outburst drew support from many people of substance is evidenced by their slogan, "Liberty, Property and no Stamps!"—a truly laissez-faire doctrine.[14]

Pseudo-economic philosophers in the colonies had raised a clever point at the time of the Stamp Act agitation. The colonies, they claimed, did not object to Parliamentary taxation, which had as its primary purpose the "external" regulation of trade and in which the raising of revenue was incidental. But they did object to "internal" taxation for purposes of revenue only; this was "Taxation without Representation," nothing less than "Tyranny." To the bewildered

English member of Parliament this was drawing the line a bit finely. What the average Englishman could not understand was that American opinion was opposed to any Parliamentary taxation which could be effectively enforced and the revenue from which could be used to further colonial policies determined in England rather than in America. Prior to 1763 a considerable degree of political and economic liberty had grown up in the colonies. Accentuated by the American environment and the influence of the frontier, personal freedom and democracy had become more extensive in the colonies than in England. Grenville's Stamp Act was a step toward removing the colonies' self-rule and freedom and vesting the control in England.[15]

So far as English politics were concerned, the repeal of the Stamp Act had merely postponed the issue.[16] The acquisition of a great North American domain by the Treaty of Paris in 1763 had presented problems of development, defense, and administration, which could not be consigned to the background. Colonial self-rule was looked upon as too disorderly, too decentralized, and too inefficient a method. A more orderly and conservative expansionist policy, a well-trained and strategically located army, and a more efficient and centralized colonial administration—these measures seemed necessary to the English statesman with a long-range view of continental empire. But the costs of such an imperial establishment would be huge; the British national debt was high. When in 1767 Charles Townshend, Chancellor of the Exchequer, announced in Parliament that colonial defense for the ensuing year would cost four hundred thousand pounds, the cry was again sounded to make the colonies contribute toward their own support. This was precisely the plan of Townshend's budget. In a long speech introducing his budget, he said, "I laugh at the absurd distinction between internal and external taxes."[17] Lord Chatham asserted that Parliament had the right to pass a law which would prevent the making of even so much as a pair of shoes in America.[18] Even the liberal Lord Rockingham observed, with regard to the Parliamentary right to raise revenue in the colonies, "I trust in policy it will not be attempted; but as to the right, it undoubtedly is held to be so."[19]

In the fall of 1767 the Townshend revenue measures became law. These taxes were "external" to please the colonists.[20] They provided for import duties to be laid in colonial ports upon certain kinds of lead, glass, and paper, and upon tea, the whole estimated return being forty thousand pounds annually. In addition the customs service was strengthened by the establishment of admiralty courts, writs of assistance, and a board of commissioners resident in America. With the new revenue Townshend proposed to pay the salaries of the royal administration in America and thus set it free from colonial legislative control. Nathaniel Whitaker in London wrote to Dr. Eleazar Wheelock in Hanover, "May God avert the Storm but I verily fear the Tories here will never rest till they cause America to revolt."[21] So efficient did the new commercial regulations prove that "Townshend might be said to have reënacted all the navigation and trade laws which, from 1660 on, had been endured, chiefly because they had not been obeyed."[22] The "external" taxes, once considered so harmless, now began to touch the purse.

Opposition was not long in crystallizing in the colonies. John Dickinson of Pennsylvania began his famous series of "Letters from a Farmer," some of which later appeared in the *New Hampshire Gazette*, a Portsmouth newspaper.[23] At a town meeting in 1768 Portsmouth instructed her representatives in the New Hampshire Assembly to petition His Majesty that "he would redress their grievances, and protect them in their constitutional rights."[24] On September 30, 1768, an article signed "Americanus" appeared in the *Gazette*, stating, "I affirm, it is in our own Power, (if we will unite) to defeat the operation of the present Act for imposing Duties, for the express purpose of raising a Revenue . . . . that a general Abstinence from the use of TEAS, would alone do it. . . . ."[25] Even Governor Wentworth deplored the irritating methods employed by the Act. Said he, " . . . . I would risque my eternal Salvation—That with Moderation prudence & temper—The Act wou'd have surely taken place— with very little Difficulty."[26]

It was Massachusetts, through the initiative of that master agitator, Samuel Adams, which took the first open step. On February 11, 1768, the Massachusetts House of Representatives sent a circular letter to the lower legislative houses in all the colonies. This letter asserted that taxation without representation was contrary to the constitutional rights of Englishmen; that independence of the royal officials from colonial legislative control "hath . . . . a tendency to subvert the principles of Equity & endanger the Happiness & Security of the Subject." There followed a denunciation of parasitical bureaucracy "from whence it may happen that officers of the Crown may be multiplyd to such a degree as to become dangerous to the Liberty of the people. . . . . " In conclusion it was urged that all the colonies unite in action against the Townshend Acts.[27]

In England the Earl of Hillsborough, Secretary of State for the Colonies, fumed and stormed. In his own circular letter to the colonial governors he denounced the measure and flatly demanded that each colony ignore it.[28] But the Massachusetts House refused to rescind its act by a vote of 92 to 17. The result was that in October, 1768, the first British troops landed in Boston.[29]

All during these happenings in Massachusetts there were various repercussions in New Hampshire. On February 19, 1768, Speaker Peter Gilman laid before the Assembly the Massachusetts Circular Letter.[30] Wentworth appears to have brought great pressure to bear upon the Assembly to decline to take any action. At any rate, in New Hampshire's answer which was written by Speaker Gilman, a close friend of the Governor, the Assembly delayed its final decision and evasively prayed for reconciliation.[31] On June 1, however, it was voted to petition the King, and a select committee was thereupon appointed to compose the document. In this petition the Assembly observed that it had always been willing to support the royal establishment with revenues voted by itself. It added that "we beg leave to Represent to your Majesty the hardships and impropriety that our Property should be granted by the House of Commons of Great Brittain, in which we are not nor can be Represented, who bear no part of the burden of the taxes they are pleas'd to grant to be levied on us and who by their local situation and want of Seasonable intimate knowledge of the circumstances of this Country are unlikely to fix upon the most Expedient and Equitable method of Levying taxes here."[32] Thus while New Hampshire refused to enter into inter-colonial combinations, she had no qualms about making a separate plea for relief. Yet the sending of the petition to England was apparently delayed for nearly two years through the influence of the Speaker.[33]

On August 24, 1768, the Assembly received the famous Virginia Resolves, "an alarm bell to the disaffected," the product of Patrick Henry's eloquence in the House of Burgesses. It was thereupon resolved that the Assembly "heartily concurred" in the sentiment of the Virginia House.[34] In their answer the Assembly stated, "They are very sensible, that the Duties Imposed by the late Acts of Parliament, on some of the most necessary articles of Commerce, for the sole and express purpose of Raising a Revenue, are Equivalent to the most Direct Internal taxation; and that in this Respect a power is claimed and Exercised by the Legislative Authority of Great Britain, to take what sums of money they please from the Collonies, without any Grants made by the People, who are not, and cannot be Represented in the British Parliament." They abhorred the suspension of the New York Assembly and trusted that they should never be put to "the Dreadful Alternative, either to take the Sword, or submit to give up all English Liberties."[35]

All this seditious colonial intercourse only further infuriated the English ministry. The possibility of convicting colonial leaders of sedition or agitation before friendly juries in Colonial courts was remote. So in December, 1768, Parliament revived an old statute of the days of Henry VIII and the Star Chamber, which provided for transportation of agitators to England for trial on charges of treasonl Nothing could have been better calculated to produce a popular outburst.[36] Soon, in 1769, another batch of Virginia resolves was in intercolonial circulation. These resolves together with a similar set from Maryland were received by the New Hampshire Assembly in early 1770. Transportation of suspects to England for trial was declared to be "highly Derogatory of the Rights of Brittish subjects, as thereby the inestimable priviledge of being tryed by a Jury from the Vicinage as well as the liberty of summoning and producing Witnesses on such tryal will be taken away from the party accused."[37] Needless to say, these sentiments were wholly approved by the Assembly.

In the meantime, the colonies had resorted to more stringent methods of opposing what they considered iniquitous legislation. It was resolved to start a boycott against English goods. This move was backed in the main by powerful merchant groups who had no trouble enlisting support among the lower and more radical classes. In August, 1768, a non-importation league was begun along the Massachusetts coast. New York came into the agreement on August 27, and by March 10, 1769, even conservative Philadelphia had fallen in line. As a result imports brought into New England from Britain declined 50 per cent from 430,806 pounds' value to 223,694 pounds in one year alone.[38]

In New Hampshire pressure was brought to bear upon the prosperous Portsmouth merchants to join the boycott, but without success. They were far from the scenes of radical disorder—the large cities. Many of them were royal officials. Some no doubt saw a chance for private gain in abstaining.[39] The matter of non-importation in New Hampshire might never have been brought to an issue had it not been for the Boston Massacre on March 5, 1770. The reaction north of Boston was electric in its swiftness. The *New Hampshire Gazette* ran an issue with black-lined borders of mourning and pictured coffins with skull and cross-bones for each of the dead.[40] In a subsequent issue a letter signed "Consideration" exhorted the people in these words: "O AMERICANS! this BLOOD calls loud for VENGEANCE! . . . . Let it be the DETERMINED RESOLUTION of every Man, that a standing Army shall *never* be permitted in AMERICA, without the free consent of the House of Commons, in the province where they reside."[41] Governor Wentworth wrote to the Earl of Hillsborough, "The Cry of Blood, re-echo'd from One to Another, seems to infuriate them." "Upon this Event the Assembly were prevail'd on to forward their petition [to the King], which wou'd otherwise have slept forever; All the people will not be perswaded but that the Commissioners of the Customs and the Revenue Acts are exerted to absorb the property, and destroy the Lives of the people."[42] On March 19, New Ipswich joined the Boston non-importation agreements; Exeter followed suit.

In Portsmouth an entirely different situation presented itself. A number of Boston merchants led by a wealthy Scotchman, James McMasters, had refused to enter the Boston agreement and had transferred their businesses to Portsmouth, where no non-importation covenant existed. The irate Bostonians determined that if Portsmouth accepted these men, Portsmouth should suffer boycott too. This threat led to a town meeting on April 11 when the inhabitants of Portsmouth resolved to have nothing to do with the newcomers and to isolate them. To the Massachusetts leaders this action was satisfactory.[43]

In May, 1770, Lord North effected the repeal of the Townshend Acts except for the tax on teas. The efficient customs service, nevertheless, remained. In America the boycotts did not collapse immediately, so when in May Boston learned that Portsmouth had begun importing more extensively than ever, retaliatory measures were started. On June 18, Boston initiated a boycott against the Portsmouth group, followed by the towns on the Connecticut River. As this measure failed to move Portsmouth, direct action was the only alternative. Governor Wentworth wrote to the Earl of Hillsborough, "One of the Boston zealotts was immediately dispatched hither, by all means to procure the people to engage with him."[44] The town met on July 12 and adjourned to July 24. At the latter meeting the matter of a boycott was dismissed by a majority of 10 to 1. The Boston agent, it seems, "decampt precipitately for Boston under threats of tar and feathers."

Perhaps a more basic but less obvious reason for New Hampshire's lack of interest in inter-colonial measures was the fact that the province at this time was absorbed in internal reform. Hitherto there had been no county divisions in New Hampshire. All courts of law were located at Portsmouth. Persons having business relating to the probate of wills or registration of deeds might well have to travel all the way from Hanover or Lyme to the seacoast. In many cases, costs of traveling to and from court made the collection of small debts out of the question.[45] Then too, the location of the courts in Portsmouth allowed most of the judicial posts, the "patronage plums" of the day, to be held by the coastal aristocracy. To a rapidly growing and more democratic interior these conditions were intolerable. Soon after Wentworth's accession, demand arose in the Assembly for county division. To the Council, which was controlled by the wealthy conservatives, this was a radical measure "attended with very great expence and a very heavy and unnecessary burthen on the people."[46] They feared that county division might be the beginning of the rise of an agrarian, interior class which might eventually outweigh the mercantile interests of the tidewater region. For two years the Council and Assembly bickered over the number of counties and the prerogative of establishing the courts. Finally, in 1769, through the interposition of the Governor, a compromise was effected. The province was divided into five counties—three to be organized at once and the other two to await a larger population. The act received royal approval in 1771, and by 1773 all five counties were functioning. The Governor named them—Rockingham, after his relative, the liberal Whig leader,—Hillsborough, after the Secretary of State for the Colonies,—Cheshire, after the well-known English county,—Grafton, after the Duke of Grafton, prime minister,—and Strafford, after the famous earl, member of the Wentworth family.[47]

County division failed to bring about the feared upheaval in political control. The Governor called no new members to the Council from the new counties. The old basis of representation in the Assembly remained unchanged. As for the two westernmost counties, in fact, Cheshire had only three representatives and Grafton none. County division, however, did lead to stricter enforcement of the King's law. Where there had only been one sheriff before, now there were five with courts in each county to enforce their authority. The machinery which the farmers and lumbermen of the interior had counted upon to give them a greater measure of "home rule" became a means of their regulation. Inter-sectional collection of debts was facilitated; contracts were enforced—all of which appeared to benefit the moneyed class and wrong the poor man.

Returning to the continental scene, the end of the year 1770 saw the collapse of the economic boycotts. The merchants severed their alliance with the radicals for the time being; their next alliance was destined to end in revolution. Lieutenant Governor Cadwallader Colden of New York wrote, "All Men of property are so sensible of their danger, from riots and tumults, that they will not rashly be induced to enter into combinations which may promote disorder for the future, but will endeavor to promote due subordination to legal authority."[48] The operation of the trade acts, although strictly enforced, was eased somewhat by the springing up of domestic industry. Governor Wentworth wrote to some merchants in London, "All the Country seems possessed with a Madness of manufacture & economy; in this Province we have enough to do to grow Bread, and do not enter into any schemes—but in ye others, ev'ry hovel wears the face of labour & industry."[49]

Smuggling, too, became profitable; especially so the smuggling of tea, for even though losing a large number of his cargoes the smuggler could still undersell the honest merchant. In the *New Hampshire Gazette* for February 8, 1771, appeared the following advertisement.

Choice Bohea—Tea to be sold by Joshua
Wentworth, at his Store in Portsmouth, by
the 10 lb. to 100 wt. at 5 /9 d. extreem good.[50]

One wonders how much of this was smuggled. Although evidence is difficult to discover, there is no reason to suppose that smuggling did not frequently occur along the New Hampshire coast. Despite the fact that this coast was only eighteen miles in length, it was dotted with inlets and small harbors. Then, too, the broken and sparsely settled Maine coast was an open door for illegal trade to reach Portsmouth.

On October 25, 1771, the brigantine *Resolution* cast anchor in Portsmouth harbor. The captain in declaring his cargo purposely forgot to enter one hundred hogsheads of molasses which were on board and which he hoped to unload secretly at night in direct violation of the Sugar Act of 1764.[51] However, the collector of customs, George Meserve, was not thus easily hoodwinked, and his men soon discovered the error of omission. The ship was immediately seized and put under guard of customs officials pending the prosecution of a libel in the Court of Admiralty. So far so good, but about midnight on October 29 "a Numerous Company of Men in disguise Armed with Clubs," boarded the vessel, confined the officers and spirited away the cargo. Immediately the Governor issued a proclamation offering two hundred dollars as a reward for information leading to convictions. Notwithstanding, no information was ever volunteered; the perpetrators remained unknown.[52]

This episode was typical of the problem which the customs service was facing all along the American coast, and so in 1772 the British redoubled the colonial naval patrol. In June of the same year, a particularly obnoxious British patrol boat, the *Gaspee*, ran aground in Narragansett Bay, Rhode Island. With a group of daredevil ringleaders in the fore, a mob boarded the ship and burned it. Soon after, the English government started an enquiry under a royal commission with the avowed purpose of transporting the marauders to England to stand trial. Opportunely too, Samuel Adams chose this moment to raise a hue and cry over a proposed English plan to pay colonial judges' salaries out of the customs duties. Putting the issue on a much exaggerated basis of "freemen or slaves" Adams worked up such a high degree of hysteria that his resolution for establishing a provincial committee of correspondence passed the Massachusetts House of Representatives without opposition.[53]

In New Hampshire the only immediate action was taken by the Assembly which on February 4, 1773, voted to send a petition, embodying a "representation of the Difficulties the American Colonies Labour Under," to Lord Dartmouth, the new Colonial Secretary.[54] Curiously enough the petition itself failed to mention any grievance and confined itself to wishing Dartmouth a successful term of office. On May 28, 1773, however, the Assembly received a circular letter from the Virginia House of Burgesses, which was of tremendous importance. An enclosure in the letter dated March 19 stated that because "the minds of his Majesty's faithful subjects, in this Colony, have been much disturbed by various rumors and reports of proceedings tending to deprive them of their ancient, legal and constitutional rights:—And whereas the affairs of this colony are frequently connected with those of Great Britain, as well as of the neighboring Colonies, which renders a Communication of sentiments necessary . . . . ", Virginia had seen fit to appoint a standing committee of correspondence.[55] New Hampshire was urged to do likewise. On the same day, May 28, the Assembly committed its first overt act in opposition to the popular Governor by appointing seven of its members to such a "Standing Committee of Correspondence & enquiry."[56] These men were a decided contrast to the Massachusetts Committee which Governor Hutchinson had described as composed of "deacons," "atheists," and "black-hearted fellows whom one would not choose to meet in the dark."[57] Of the seven members all came from the coastal region; two were judges, two lawyers, two merchants and one a physician. Yet even the conservative membership of the Committee and their conservative answer to Virginia, restricting New Hampshire to "Constitutional measures," failed to appease Wentworth. He adjourned the Assembly on May 29 probably hoping thereby to end the Committee's legal existence.[58]

In May, 1773, Lord North's Tea Act passed Parliament. Once more were the commercial classes aroused—this time by a threat of severe competition. By the new act the East India Company, which had a tea surplus of some seventeen million pounds, was given a preferred position, in fact a virtual monopoly of the American tea market. The Company was allowed to reëxport its own tea from England to America, duty free, in its own ships, where, after payment of the three pence per pound colonial duty, the tea might be sold through the Company's own agents. By being relieved of the English tax of one shilling, the Company was enabled to lower its price on tea nine pence per pound. Not only could the honest American merchants who bought tea in London be undersold but also those who smuggled tea from Holland. Thus colonial shipowners and sailors who lived on the tea trade, both legal and illegal, were liable to loss and unemployment.

Once more agitators seized upon the issue at hand. Again they were backed by the mercantile classes. When it came to manufacturing instances of intolerable wrongs, they were as usual wondrously successful. The real issue—drastic competition and the lower price of tea—was carefully ignored. On December 16, 1773, after the Boston consignees had refused to cancel their orders, Samuel Adams aroused mob sentiment to such a high pitch that it culminated in the Boston Tea Party. In one night tea to the value of fifteen thousand pounds was destroyed. Said John Adams, "This is the most magnificent movement of all. There is a dignity, a majesty, a sublimity in this last effort of the patriots, that I greatly admire." But Benjamin Franklin looked upon the tea party as "an act of violent injustice."[59]

Upon the same day as Boston's Tea Party, Portsmouth held a town meeting to deliberate on the Tea Act. The leaders argued that the lower price of tea was a disguised attempt to make the people accept the tax. It was resolved "That it is the natural right of men born and inheriting estates in any part of the British dominions, to have the power of disposing of their own property, either by themselves or their representatives." The Tea Act was branded as "a direct attack upon the liberties of America" and as having "a direct tendency to subvert our Constitution, render our assemblies useless, and the government arbitrary."[60] Finally the meeting planned to prevent the landing of any tea at Portsmouth; and then it dissolved without any mention of monopoly or ruinous competition—the more important issues.[61]

Other towns in New Hampshire which passed similar "tea resolves" at the same time were Dover, Barrington, Exeter, Hampton, Haverhill, and Newcastle—all with the exception of Haverhill in the tidewater region.[62] A resident of Portsmouth wrote to a friend in Boston, "Hope that the Resolves past in our Town-Meeting will convince you that we are at last roused from the lethargic Disposition, that has . . . . reigned so long among us."[63]

In the *New Hampshire Gazette* various attitudes were expressed with reference to the Tea Act. One example was a verse entitled "The Blasted Herb," supposedly written by Meshech Weare, an associate justice of His Majesty's Superior Court, which read,

> *Rouse ev'ry generous thoughtful Mind,*
> *The rising Danger flee;*
> *If you would lasting Freedom find,*
> *Now then abandon TEA.*[64]

[14]

On February 18, 1774, the *Gazette* reported the meeting of the Matrons of Liberty at the house of Mrs. Susanna Spindle where they had resolved, "That the Merchants under a pretence of guarding our Liberties, prevented the Landing of the East India Company's Tea; and at the same Time sell their own at such an extravagant Price, make it evident it is not our Interest; but their own private Gain they are pursuing."[65]

It was not long before the sentiment of the province with respect to tea was put to an actual test. On the night of June 25, 1774, the ship *Grosvenor* under Captain Brown came to anchor in Portsmouth harbor. On board were twenty-seven chests of bohea tea. Wentworth had previously received word of the coming of the tea and having instructed the captain, he took no open measures to protect the cargo. Because of this apparent unconcern on the part of the royal officials, the citizens of Portsmouth suspected nothing. The tea was safely landed and stored in the custom-house. In a short time, however, the secret became known; a town meeting was immediately summoned to meet on June 27. This meeting chose a committee of eleven to negotiate with the consignee, Edward Parry, and a guard of freeholders was stationed at the custom-house to prevent mob violence. On the 28th Parry agreed to export the tea to Halifax provided the town of Portsmouth would pay the expenses of reshipment. The duty was openly paid and the tea carted back to the ship "without noise, tumult, or insult." By June 30 the troublesome cargo was on its way north. Portsmouth resolved not to be caught napping in the future. A standing committee of inspection was appointed, and a boycott against the use of tea was begun.[66]

The general character of the whole incident was an excellent example of Wentworth's tact, skillful management, and popularity. To him should go the credit for preventing a Portsmouth tea party. Yet his troubles on that score were not yet ended.

Perhaps in the fall of 1774 Mr. Parry, the tea agent, thought that the sentiment against importation of tea was subsiding. At any rate, he received a consignment of thirty chests of tea which arrived at Portsmouth in the mast ship *Fox* on September 8. This time the town was alert; the news of the coming of the tea had preceded its arrival. An unruly mob stoned Parry's house at night. The Governor at once summoned the Council and the magistrates of the county for an emergency session. But the town meetings on September 9 and

10 proved to be adequate safety valves for the aroused feelings of the citizenry; violence soon subsided. Again the town effected a compromise with agent Parry to reship the tea, which safely departed for Halifax on September 11. Thus Portsmouth had demonstrated its attitude to be one of orderly resistance with a minimum of mob hysteria. The merchant leaders were happily able to effect their design without having to resort to violence.[67]

Substantial issues were really scarce in conservative New Hampshire. Before 1774 it was an unfruitful ground for agitators of the Boston type. On the other hand, the proceedings in Massachusetts could not help making a serious impression on those New Hampshire leaders with more radical tendencies. Restricting Massachusetts' sentiment to the immediate boundaries of that province was impossible. The dangerous element in the situation was that, although revolutionary sentiment lagged in New Hampshire, the province had the precedent of her southern neighbor to follow should her popular leaders be confronted with a real issue or choose to manufacture or to magnify an imaginary one. Wentworth was fully cognizant of this possibility when he wrote to Lord Dartmouth, "Notwithstanding, I can still have the pleasure to represent to your Lordship that this Province continues more moderate than any to the southward; yet, at the same time, truth requires me to suggest, that the union of the colonies in sentiment is not divided nor lost in New Hampshire, although they have hitherto been prevailed upon to abstain from acts of general violence and outrage, and the laws have their course. How long it will remain so is impossible to foresee; *I confess much good may not reasonably be counted upon, while the unhappy distractions in the Massachusetts bay gain ground and spread with such violence. . . . . .*"[68]

CHAPTER 2

By coolness and an unremitted pursuit of the measures that have been adopted I trust they will come to submit; I have no objection afterwards to their seeing that there is no inclination for the present to lay fresh taxes on them, but I am clear there must always be one tax to keep up the right, and as such I approve of the Tea Duty.

GEORGE III *in* 1774.[1]

The Downfall of Royal Government

NOWHERE except in Boston did opposition to the Tea Act of 1773 reach proportions of physical violence and property damage. Elsewhere the popular leaders were less radical and kept a firm hand on the situation, not wishing to be discredited by their more disorderly cohorts. The importance of the "tea party" in the mind of the average provincial would probably have died down rapidly but for King George's feeling that imperial dignity must be preserved at all costs. Unfortunately too, this feeling in England was not confined to George III and his prime minister, Lord North. Even the friends of the colonies in Parliament admitted that grave wrong had been done. There was, of course, some uncertainty as to a fitting punishment, especially so in the heart of Edmund Burke, who alone knew the real temper of America.

As the ministry's first move, Lord North introduced a bill in Parliament providing for the closure of Boston harbor until restitution for destroyed property should be made to the East India Company. Without a division this bill, known as the Boston Port Act, became law on March 31, 1774. Not content with this measure Parliament passed the Massachusetts Government Act on May 13. This Act, the most oppressive of all, was calculated to remove many features of the government of that province from popular control. Councillors in the future were to be chosen in England. Jurors were to be summoned, not at town meetings as in the past, but by the sheriffs who were to be directly responsible to the governor, as were all judges. And finally the town meeting, that "nest of sedition," was placed directly under the governor's supervision. For the better enforcement of the two foregoing acts, two additional acts were passed. One—"an act for the impartial administration of justice"—provided that royal officials who allegedly used undue severity in suppressing riots, should be tried in some other colony or in England in instances of local prejudice. The other—the Quartering Act—provided for quartering of troops in localities of disorder.[2]

Simultaneously and more or less by accident was passed the Quebec Act, which was not a punitive measure but a result of the cherished plans of Lord Shelburne to relieve Canada from the iniquities of the Proclamation of 1763.[3] This legislation established French civil law and the Catholic religion in the province of Quebec. Much more in conflict with colonial interests, the Act extended the boundaries of the new province south to the Ohio River, thus thwarting the western land claims of Massachusetts, Connecticut, and Virginia. This law therefore was classed at once with the other four as an oppressive measure. On May 17, 1774, General Gage, Massachusetts' new military governor, arrived in Boston to inaugurate the régime of the "Five Intolerable Acts."

Before news of the passage of the punitive acts reached America, a new assembly had been called in New Hampshire, which met on April 7, 1774. Wentworth observed in his initial legislative message that, "The experience of Prosperity resulting to the Province from former Harmony & Diligence is the strongest recommendation for the continuance of those Principles."[4] In truth the province was prosperous. The provincial bills of credit of the French and Indian Wars had just been funded; taxes were light; and the treasury had a surplus of 5870 pounds. Every circumstance pointed toward a peaceful session. The Governor wrote to Lord Dartmouth, "I took great pains to prevail on them not to enter into any extra Provincial measures. . . . ."[5] On May 13, however, the proverbial bombshell exploded when the *New Hampshire Gazette* printed news of the passage of the Boston Port Act following the announcement with the text of the Act in its issue of a week later.[6]

The first reactions were ominous. The Committee of Correspondence of Portsmouth wrote to the Committee of Boston, "We think the late Act of Parliament, to shut up the port of Boston, of the most extraordinary nature, and fatal tendency."[7] On May 27 the Assembly refused to provide for more than five men and an officer to garrison Fort William and Mary which guarded Portsmouth harbor. This action was taken despite Wentworth's vehement protests of inadequacy. On the very same day it was moved in the Assembly to appoint a new provincial committee of correspondence—a measure against which the Governor had been zealously guarding. After a fiery debate the motion was carried by a majority of only two. The following day, May 28, this motion was reconsidered and upheld by a majority of one only. By this narrow margin a committee of seven, including the speaker as chairman, was appointed to serve. This Committee boasted some of the best names in the province; six of the members were justices of the peace holding royal commissions. Classified according to occupation, two were lawyers, two merchants, two physicians, and one a large land owner.[8]

Wentworth immediately adjourned the Assembly and kept it under short adjournments hoping to obtain a repeal of the vote appointing the Committee. But on June 8, 1774, he learned that the speaker had received letters urging the election of a general American congress, whereupon he dissolved the Assembly. By dissolution Wentworth hoped to end the activities of the energetic Committee of Correspondence which had no constitutional existence except during sessions of the Assembly. The Committee, however, was not to be thus easily thwarted. Upon receiving a circular letter from Virginia, inviting New Hampshire to participate in a Continental Congress, it was decided to summon an extra-legal meeting of the Assembly. On July 6 a number of the members assembled in Portsmouth but made the mistake of meeting in the Assembly chamber, which was government property. Seizing upon this technicality as a pretext, the Governor attended by Sheriff Parker of Rockingham County invaded the gathering. He read a short proclamation informing them that their gathering was illegal and urged them to disperse. Undaunted, the representatives removed to a nearby tavern. There, undisturbed, plans were evolved for a provincial congress to meet at Exeter on July 21 to elect delegates to the Continental Congress. This provincial congress convened as arranged with the result that New Hampshire was represented at Philadelphia in September.[9]

As mid-summer of 1774 passed in New Hampshire, news of the other Parliamentary acts against Boston began to filter into the province. The *New Hampshire Gazette* printed the texts of the Massachusetts Government Act, the Quartering Act and the Quebec Act.[10] In New Hampshire the Government Act did not seem to arouse much protest. The province was not a chartered colony and was accustomed to centralized rule by a royal governor. But the Port Act and the Quartering Act struck nearer home. Who could tell when Portsmouth harbor might be blockaded or Fort William and Mary garrisoned by a regiment of "red-coats"? Perhaps it was the Quebec Act which aroused the most violent outcry. John Sullivan of Durham classed this measure as "the most dangerous to American Liberties among the whole train" and depicted Catholicism as a cursed religion "so Dangerous to the State & favorable to Despotisms."[11] To the Reverend Jeremy Belknap of Dover, the Church of Rome was "the mother of harlots and abominations."[12] As a good Congregationalist he denounced the Act. Not the least fear aroused in New Hampshire was that in the event of rebellion, border raids from Canada would assume the aspect of fanatical, religious crusades attended with barbarous cruelties. John Phillips of Exeter wrote to Dr. Eleazar Wheelock in Hanover, "I . . . . wish to hear, very soon, how he [Lord Dartmouth] now stands affected toward a Col. so very much *exposed* by ye Quebec Act . . . . Oh Liberty! Oh my Country! and Oh Dartmouth particularly! may'st thou be preserved in this Day of the Lord's anger. . . . . "[13]

When the full extent of the punitive measures became known, a considerable amount of sympathy for Boston was aroused in New Hampshire. This feeling was cleverly nursed along by the Boston radicals, who even went so far as to send one of themselves, their town clerk, William Cooper, to Portsmouth to agitate for relief for their blockaded population. Cooper was in Portsmouth for a week in the latter part of August, but found the popular leaders cautious.[14] At a town meeting on September 12, attended by only fifty-six voters, it was resolved "not to grant the town monies for a donation to Boston; but that a voluntary subscription be opened for that purpose."[15] For some obscure reason, however, the town rescinded this vote at a subsequent meeting on October 10, 1774; and although only fifty-two voters were present, it was resolved to grant Boston two hundred pounds for poor-relief. As this amount was four times greater than Portsmouth's annual province tax, one can well judge the seriousness of her purpose. Her example was soon followed by inland Exeter which granted one hundred pounds for Boston. Other New Hampshire towns to give aid were Chester, Candia, Durham, Newmarket, Londonderry, Temple, and Concord (which sent dried peas). In all only nine towns contributed despite the urging of the provincial congress which had met on July 21.[16] The smallness of this number, however, could be attributed mainly to poverty and difficulty of communication, rather than to apathy.

Indeed, the fall of the year 1774 marked the end of a dilatory policy on the part of the popular leaders in New Hampshire. They were resolved to seize upon the first convenient instance of an "intolerable wrong." Nor had they underestimated the temper of the people. English policy since the Tea Party had not aroused passionate excesses; but resistance was taking the form of a hostile mental attitude ingrained in the spirit of the population. This attitude was emotional, not rational, which made it more dangerous. Local grievances were looked upon as part of a general British plot to enslave the colonists.

Unhappily Governor Wentworth soon provided the "Sons of Liberty" with an excuse for an outburst of feeling—an incident which would have passed unnoticed in preceding years.[17] In October, 1774, General Gage had determined to build new military barracks in Boston, but because of popular sentiment he could hire no Boston carpenters. In this dilemma he wrote to Wentworth asking for aid. The New Hampshire governor, realizing that if he were to have any success he must act secretly, worked through an agent, Nicholas Austin of Middleton, and succeeded in hiring fifteen carpenters for an unnamed project. Surely enough, at the end of October these unsuspecting carpenters found themselves in Boston building barracks. However, the Portsmouth Committee received news of the affair. This Committee was made up of several popular leaders, who resolved to use this incident against the Governor. In a series of resolves framed by John and Woodbury Langdon and Supply Clap, three Portsmouth merchants, Wentworth was branded as "an enemy to the community" and his conduct decried as "cruel and unmanly." In Rochester agent Nicholas Austin was summoned before the Committee of Correspondence which made him confess on his knees and make the following promise: "I do affirm, that for the future, I never will be aiding or assisting in anywise whatever, in act or deed, contrary to the Constitution of the country. . . . . "[18] There was no definitive constitution; perhaps the Committee rightly meant—"contrary to public opinion." At any rate the whole incident of the hiring of the carpenters was widely publicized all over the province and appeared in the *New Hampshire Gazette*.[19] The opposition succeeded in undermining much of the popular confidence which Wentworth had hitherto held.

On October 19, 1774, there was issued a royal order in council prohibiting the export of powder and arms to America. At the same time, Lord Dartmouth secretly wrote to the colonial governors, "It is His Majesty's Command that you do take the most effectual measures for arresting, detaining and securing any Gunpowder, or any sort of arms or ammunition, which may be attempted to be imported into the Province. . . . . "[20] As matters stood in the fall of 1774, this was a wise precaution but it had unfortunate results. Soon after Dartmouth's letter had reached Rhode Island, which had a popular government, the governor of that province made its news public, and the Assembly voted to seize the royal ammunition depot. Meanwhile news of the arms embargo was relayed to the Boston zealots. These men, at once remembering the arsenal at Fort William and Mary in Portsmouth harbor, dispatched Paul Revere to warn the Portsmouth leaders. On the afternoon of December 13, 1774, Revere galloped into Portsmouth delivering his dispatches at the house of Samuel Cutts, a prominent merchant, and chairman of the local Committee of Ways and Means. This Committee was immediately convened and stirred to feverish action by the false rumor that troops were on their way from Boston to guard the local arsenal. Wentworth suspected illegal designs and warned Captain Cochran and his five privates to be on guard against a possible attack on the fort.

At noon on December 14 a drum was beaten about the streets of Portsmouth, and soon a large mob had collected at the center of the town near the townhouse. Wentworth immediately sent Chief Justice Theodore Atkinson to warn the gathering to disperse but to no avail. Led by Captain Thomas Pickering, a daring sea captain, and Major John Langdon, a local merchant, the mob marched off toward the fort. Reënforced by men from the towns of Newcastle and Rye, they numbered about four hundred as compared with the six men guarding the fort. A conflict between two such forces could hardly be called a battle, but it had dangerous possibilities in case of bloodshed. Therefore when the mob charged the fort at about three o'clock in the afternoon, it was altogether to the credit of the men on guard that no serious resistance was shown and that only a few guns were discharged without injury to anyone. Captain Cochran and his five men were confined, and then the mob triumphantly gave three huzzas as they hauled down the King's colors. Immediately the powder magazine was broken open, and one hundred barrels of powder were carted off to a place of safer keeping.

On the morning of the very next day, December 15, another mob invaded Portsmouth led by Major John Sullivan of Durham, who had been a delegate to the Continental Congress. Upon confronting the governor, Sullivan declared his innocence of any evil design; and learning that no troops were coming from Boston, he agreed to disperse his men. Wentworth urged the return of the powder hinting that His Majesty might consider this act an alleviation of the offense. This plan seemed to suit the mob; they voted to disperse. Yet for some unknown reason they failed to do so. That very night, led by Sullivan, they invaded the fort and brought away sixteen cannon, about sixty muskets and other military stores. This seized property remained on the outskirts of Portsmouth all the next day guarded by Colonel Nathaniel Folsom and a party of men from Exeter. In the evening, with a favorable tide, the munitions were placed on gondolas and floated up Great Bay to the inland region. There the booty was distributed among the several towns.[21]

During this insurrection the Governor was powerless. He could muster to his support only a few of his immediate friends. The revenue officers remained in hiding; the militia refused to answer the drum. In a quandary Wentworth wrote to Admiral Graves in Boston asking that a man-of-war be stationed in Portsmouth harbor.[22] On December 17 the *Canceaux* under Lieutenant Mowat cast anchor in the harbor followed two days later by the frigate *Scarborough* under Captain Barkley. Probably only the presence of this armament prevented further looting of the fort and its forty-five heavy cannon.[23]

The winter of 1774-1775 also saw disorder beginning in the country. In Hillsborough and Cheshire counties, which had been restless for some time, government became a farce. The people obeyed the law as much as they chose and no more. Only if he could convict the ringleaders of the attack on the fort, did Wentworth see some possibility of restoring order. The temper of the people was aptly expressed in a letter from a New Hampshire "Watchman" to the inhabitants of the continent, which exhorted as follows: "And I must here beg leave to recommend to the consideration of the people on this Continent, whether, when we are by an arbitrary decree prohibited the having Arms and Ammunition by importation, we have not, by the law of self-preservation, a right to seize upon those within our power, in order to defend the liberties which *God* and nature have given to us. . . . ."[24]

On December 26, 1774, Wentworth issued the usual proclamation of rebellion, ordering the magistrates to use every effort to imprison the offenders and asking for voluntary information. The ringleaders were well known to the Governor but he felt powerless to act. Finally, on January 21, 1775, he wrote to General Gage in Boston asking for two regiments to be stationed at Portsmouth. Wrote he, "The People do not support the Magistrates, who thence are unable to do their duty, And if any Person should be taken up, He wou'd be either immediately rescued or the Jail would be broke open directly, as experience proves the Militia, will not Act."[25] With the aid of troops Wentworth hoped to convict the leaders of the late uprising and restore royal dignity in New Hampshire. For a time it seemed likely that Gage would comply with his request. Captain Gamble journeyed up from Boston to view sites for prospective barracks, but upon his return, Gage decided definitely against the venture.

Notwithstanding, the Governor resolved to take what punitive measures were in his power. Several of the leaders of the fort robbery held royal commissions. As soon as he could find loyal citizens to take their places, Wentworth deprived these men of their commissions. Among those so dealt with were Major John Langdon, Major John Sullivan and Colonel Nathaniel Folsom, who lost their commissions in the militia. Colonel Josiah Bartlett of Kingston not only lost his commission in the militia but his commission as justice of the peace as well. Needless to say these dismissals aroused popular fury against the Governor.[26] Fearing for his personal safety he formed an association of about sixty men—the King's friends in Portsmouth—as a mutual protection society in case of mob violence. Yet the town of Portsmouth voted "that we, the inhabitants of this town, will use our utmost endeavours to prevent any insult being offered to his person or dignity, And that we will take every method in our power, to assist and support him in the due and legal exercise of his authority."[27]

On February 28, 1775, Wentworth issued writs for a new election of the Assembly, but finding many popular agitators elected he postponed the date of meeting to May 4. This Assembly, doomed to be the last one, convened against a particularly ominous background. The first Continental Congress had met in the fall of 1774, and a second one was scheduled to meet on May 10, 1775. In New Hampshire three provincial congresses had already held meetings. On April 19 had occurred the clashes at Lexington and Concord, which had aroused great turmoil in the southern border towns in New Hampshire. In the new Assembly were three new members who had been chosen on royal election writs served on three additional towns in Grafton County, which constituencies the Governor had seen fit to establish without consulting the Assembly itself. The new members were Colonel John Fenton for Plymouth, Israel Morey for Orford, and Jacob Greene for Lyme. They were destined to be the storm center of this last session.

Wentworth opened the Assembly on May 5 with a speech urging "Wisdom, Candour & Moderation" in deliberation.[28] The House immediately appointed a committee to consider the status of the three new members. On May 6 a short adjournment was requested of the Governor that the members might consult their constituents on "several weighty matters." Although the "weighty matters" probably referred to the fourth Provincial Congress to which many members of the Assembly were delegates and which was to convene on May 17, Wentworth was reluctantly persuaded to adjourn the Assembly till June 12.[29]

The body reconvened at that time, and on June 13 voted to exclude the three members from Plymouth, Lyme, and Orford. Since the members from Lyme and Orford had refused to sit, it was apparent that the exclusion measure was directed against the member from Plymouth, Colonel John Fenton. Fenton was disliked because he had moved that the Assembly accept Lord North's conciliatory proposal.[30] This proposal, which had passed the House of Commons on February 27, 1775, provided that whenever any colony had voted an adequate budget for its government, all Parliamentary taxes should be repealed as they applied to that colony, except the acts of trade, the revenue from which would be credited to the colony's treasury in the future. Before his ejection Fenton made a vehement speech criticizing the Assembly's action. Despairing of the immediate adoption of Lord North's proposal, Wentworth adjourned the Assembly until July 11, hoping that the situation would become calmer in the meantime.[31]

On the afternoon of June 13 Colonel Fenton called at the house of the Governor. At this time, because of his vehement speech in the Assembly and because he had previously urged his constituents to refrain from revolutionary activity, he was an extremely unpopular person. Indeed, the Congress at Exeter wished to try him as a Tory. Consequently, while he was visiting Wentworth, a large mob gathered outside the residence. Soon a cannon appeared which was aimed at the house and immediate destruction promised unless Fenton was forthcoming. Fenton quickly surrendered to the mob and was marched off to Exeter. But the Governor foresaw the alarming possibilities which might follow this affront to his dignity. That very night he and his family took refuge in Fort William and Mary under the protection of the guns of the man-of-war *Scarborough*.[32]

The Assembly met again on July 11 but lacked a quorum until July 14, when it announced itself ready to do business. The Governor at once sent down a message demanding that the House rescind its vote excluding the three new members. To this message, the House made the following reply: "As the Councill are appointed for this Province by the Crown we think it not only a cruel but an arbitrary stretch of Prerogative for your Excellency to issue writs to such Towns as you think proper to send Representatives without the concurrence of the other Branches of the Legislature therein, for by that means the Representatives as well as the Councill would in effect be chosen by the Crown."[33]

In demanding a voice in the granting of new seats, the Assembly was in reality calling attention to New Hampshire's already antique system of representation, which was considered a grievance in many localities.[34] It was true that never before the Assembly of 1775 had Grafton County been represented. Yet the governor in designating Plymouth with 382 inhabitants, Orford with 222 inhabitants, and Lyme with 252 inhabitants as the new seats, had pointedly ignored Hanover with 434, Haverhill with 365, and Lebanon with 347 inhabitants—all in the same county. New Hampshire had increased in population by some thirty thousand since 1767, and the number of towns

WHEREAS several Bodies of Men did, in the Day Time of the 14th, and in the Night of the 15th of this Inftant December, in the moft daring and rebellious Manner inveft, attack, and forcibly enter into His Majefty's Caftle William and Mary in this Province, and overpowering and confining the Captain and Garrifon, did, befides committing many treafonable Infults and Outrages, break open the Magazine of faid Caftle and plunder it of above One hundred Barrels of Gunpowder, with upwards of fixty Stand of fmall Arms, and did alfo force from the Ramparts of faid Caftle and carry off fixteen Pieces of Cannon, and other military Stores, in open Hoftility and direct Oppugnation of His Majefty's Government, and in the moft atrocious Contempt of his Crown and Dignity ;----

I Do, by Advice and Confent of His Majefty's Council, iffue this Proclamation, ordering and requiring, in his Majefty's Name, all Magiftrates and other Officers, whether Civil or Military, as they regard their Duty to the KING and the Tenor of the Oaths they have folemnly taken and fubfcribed, to exert themfelves in detecting and fecuring in fome of his Majefty's Goals in this province the faid Offenders, in Order to their being brought to condign punifhment ; And from Motives of Duty to the King and Regard to the Welfare of the good People of this Province : I do in the moft earneft and folemn Manner, exhort and injoin you, his Majefty's liege Subjects of this Government, to beware of fuffering yourfelves to be feduced by the falfe Arts or Menaces of abandoned Men, to abet, protect, or fcreen from Juftice any of the faid high handed Offenders, or to withhold or fecrete his Majefty's Munition forcibly taken from his Caftle ; but that each and every of you will ufe your utmoft Endeavours to detect and difcover the Ferpetrators of thefe Crimes to the civil Magiftrate, and affift in fecuring and bringing them to Juftice, and in recovering the King's Munition; This Injunction it is my bounden Duty to lay ftrictly upon you, and to require your Obedience thereto, as you value individually your Faith and Allegiance to his Majefty, as you wifh to preferve that Reputation to the Province in general ; and as you would avert the dreadful but moft certain Confequences of a contrary Conduct to yourfelves and Pofterity.

GIVEN at the Council-Chamber in Portfmouth, the 26th Day of December, in the 15th Year of the Reign of our Sovereign Lord GEORGE the Third, by the Grace of GOD, of Great-Britain, France and Ireland, KING, Defender of the Faith, &c. and in the Year of our Lord CHRIST, 1774.

By His EXCELLENCY's Command,
with Advice of Council.   **J. WENTWORTH.**

Theodore Atkinson, Sec^y.

GOD SAVE THE KING.

Governor Wentworth's Proclamation of Rebellion, December 26, 1774.

had increased from ninety-eight to one hundred and fifty-five, of which only thirty-six were represented in the Assembly. The small inequalities existent in Grafton County's representation were likewise emphasized in other parts of the state. Provided the three new towns were given seats in the legislature, there were still in other counties some forty-five larger towns unrepresented. Among these were Hopkinton with 1085 inhabitants, Concord with 1052, Brentwood with 1100, and Epping with 1569; these towns had no representation at all. Yet Hampton, an ancient seacoast town with only 862 inhabitants boasted two representatives in the Assembly—perhaps a "rotten borough" and certainly overrated as compared with Londonderry with 2590 inhabitants, which had only one representative.

The prerogative of issuing election writs to new towns was one that the royal governors of New Hampshire had exercised sparingly. The seacoast was adequately represented, as the towns in that region were the oldest. But in the inland region and on the frontier there was no pretense of representation proportional to population. It was suspected that the governors often issued writs to certain towns because they knew that delegates who were the King's friends would be elected.[35] Petitions from towns to the governors for representation were common. As a typical example Hanover's petition of 1774 deserves inclusion here.

> *Humbly sheweth That as your Petitioners—Freeholders of the aforesaid Town of Hanover in the Large and Fertile County of Grafton, are not represented in General Assembly either as a Town or County and regarding that invaluable priviledge as inestimable and at the same time inseperable from Taxation, we humbly pray that your Excellency would grant to us those priviledges inherant in the British Constitution by sending a precept to enable us to return a representative to General Assembly whose Duty it will be to watch over and Serve the interest of his Constituents.*[36]

From the foregoing description it will be seen that the Assembly had much right on its side in the dispute, and it resolved unanimously not to rescind its vote excluding the three new members.[37] Wentworth thereupon adjourned the Assembly from day to day until finally on July 18, 1775, he adjourned it until September 28 remarking,". . . . I am sorry to observe that it appears to me from the Determination not to Rescind the vote for Excluding the three members for Plymouth, Lyme & Orford, that the House did not meet with a Disposition to proceed upon the affairs of the Province."[38]

On March 30, 1775, Lord North's ministry had effected the passage in Parliament of the New England Restraining Act as a punishment for the various revolutionary activities in the New England provinces. This Act restricted all of New England's trade to the British Isles and West Indies, and forbade those provinces to use the Grand Bank fisheries. The enforcement of the Act was placed under the royal navy and customs service. It was the presence of H. M. S. *Scarborough* in Portsmouth harbor to enforce this Act which brought about the final rupture between the revolutionary party and the royal government in New Hampshire and drove the latter out of existence.

It will be recalled that naval armament had been present in Portsmouth harbor ever since the sacking of the fort. Indeed, it was only the presence of the *Scarborough* with one hundred marines, which had preserved the least semblance of royal authority. Late in May, 1775, the inhabitants of Portsmouth were aroused to learn that Captain Barkley of the *Scarborough* had established a blockade of Portsmouth harbor and was seizing provision ships, sending them under convoy to Boston for the use of General Gage and his troops. Despite the intercession of Wentworth the captain refused to modify his activity. To make matters worse he started to impress seamen. This practice created an uproar in the town. A group of the more disorderly class set up a battery of eight cannon on Castle Island and started firing at random on the *Scarborough*. This violence was immediately disavowed on the part of Portsmouth's better citizens at a town meeting. At this juncture Wentworth again intervened and a temporary agreement was effected. Captain Barkley agreed to let fishing boats pass unmolested to the Isles of Shoals and released the impressed seamen; in return the town agreed to sell provisions to the *Scarborough*.[39]

This arrangement worked satisfactorily for several months. The calm was broken only once when the *Scarborough* on June 17 seized the sloop *King Fisher* for attempting to violate the New England Restraining Act.[40] This law had indeed worked a hardship on many of the mercantile and shipping class who had hitherto engaged in no revolutionary activity. Trade had become stagnant; unemployment was rife. Under such conditions peace could not long prevail.[41] In early August another series of arbitrary acts by Captain Barkley caused a new crisis. He seized a fishing sloop which claimed to have been fishing in near-by waters but which Captain Barkley suspected had been fishing on the Grand Banks,—a forbidden action under the Restraining Act. A few days later a deserter from the *Scarborough* escaped. Thinking the people of Portsmouth were shielding this man, the irate captain seized a Portsmouth fisherman as a hostage. Again the town mob grew resentful. When on August 10 the coxswain and a boat crew from the warship came ashore for provisions, they were fired upon and the coxswain captured. Although he was soon released, the Portsmouth Committee decided that matters had reached an impasse and ordered a boycott against the ship on August 13. Captain Barkley endured the situation as long as possible, but soon saw his crew faced with starvation. The only alternative was to return to Boston for supplies.[42]

Since June 13 Governor Wentworth and his family had been living in the fort which lay under the protection of the *Scarborough's* guns. It was a hard life, which the kindly Governor had done little to deserve. Yet he was far from bitter and wrote to a friend, "I will not complain because it wou'd be a poignant censure on a people I love and forgive—For truely I can say with the poet in his Lear 'I am a man much more sinned against than sinning.' This consciousness is a consolation not to be taken away, and excites my utmost powers to over come opposition by continuing to do good, and without a single personal resentment, which I think ought never to influence a public man."[43] On August 18 the Portsmouth Committee cut off all intercourse with the fort except by mail. When Captain Barkley notified the Governor that the *Scarborough* was returning to Boston, he realized that his last element of protection would be withdrawn. So on August 23, 1775, the *Scarborough* set sail for Boston with Wentworth and his family aboard. A short time after their departure an unruly mob demolished the fort.[44]

Upon his arrival in Boston Wentworth hoped for a prompt return to Portsmouth at the head of a naval force. To Admiral Graves such a project was not feasible; and the Governor soberly realized that his authority was at an end. Yet he resolved to take one last step to uphold the royal dignity. The Assembly stood adjourned until September 28. To prevent the humilation of its meeting without his presence was the Governor's plan. Since he could legally prorogue the Assembly only from within the limits of the province, he decided to use

Gosport on the Isles of Shoals as the least dangerous base of operations. Arriving there in a chartered schooner on September 25, Wentworth sent his secretary in a small boat to Portsmouth on the mainland with a proclamation proroguing the Assembly until April 24, 1776. This accomplished, the schooner and its party returned to Boston. Such was the last act of the royal government in New Hampshire.[45]

The revolution in New Hampshire thus far had been in the nature of an arousing of public opinion rather than a violent outbreak. Before the year 1774 there had been no suggestion that the province would revolt. But small local grievances such as Wentworth's frequent dissolutions of the Assembly, his attempts to aid General Gage's building program, his dismissal of the Fort William and Mary ringleaders from public office, the unfair system of representation in the Assembly and the blockade by the warship *Scarborough* had seemed to blend with the general character of British colonial policy. From the time of the Tea Act and the punitive measures against Boston, the people had been swept along in a tide of discontent. Many of the strongest Tories had been lukewarm toward English policy. This unanimity of criticism had enabled revolutionary sentiment to rise quickly to a crisis. When the issue had become clearly defined as lying between submission and revolution, the conservatives perceived too late that they lacked the strength to lead the province back to its former allegiance. Revolutionary disorder had shown a tendency to strengthen and perpetuate itself as it progressed. Had the Royalists pursued a strategic campaign in the year 1774 and had they actively combatted the revolutionary party for control of the large neutral elements in the population, New Hampshire might have remained loyal. However, two conditions defeated them. Lord North's ministry adopted an unwise colonial policy, which was difficult to excuse in the light of reason or sentiment, although legally correct. Massachusetts, the southern neighbor, set a dangerously radical example which New Hampshire finally followed. The friends of royal government realized the gravity of the issue too late to prevent the initial rupture.

[31]

CHAPTER 3

*Moreover, the same eyes that honestly dimmed at the thought of fratri-
cidal war, also peered anxiously into a future where all known landmarks
seemed to be lost and where the shrouded outlines of a strange new order, in
which the power to rule came from below instead of from above, made a
mockery of their inherited instincts and life-long preconceptions.*

JAMES TRUSLOW ADAMS.[1]

Revolutionary Organization

THE American Revolution was characterized by the fact that
it marked a gradual transition from the acceptance of one set
of political institutions to the acceptance of another set. The
royal establishment did not immediately vanish in a whirl-
wind before the first frontal attack. It crumbled by degrees, being
supplanted in authority by the various revolutionary organizations
in an equally gradual and evolutionary manner. From the middle of
the year 1774 to the middle of the year 1775 there were really two
governments in New Hampshire. As time passed there was a transfer
of allegiance from the royal government to the revolutionary organization. When the royal government could no longer command any
degree of obedience nor arouse any spirit of enthusiasm, it fell of its
own weight. Edmund Burke said, "The new institution is infinitely
better obeyed than the ancient government ever was in its most fortunate periods. Obedience is what makes government and not the names
by which it is called."[2]

The revolutionary organization was in reality a temporary or emergency affair. Its historical function was to bridge the gap between the
royal provincial government and the independent state government.

Revolutionary Organization

In its first days it was illegal and unconstitutional, but as soon as it commanded obedience or acquiescence, it became in fact if not in theory the real government. The methods of the revolutionary establishment were those of any purely political organization. Propaganda became an important tool. As a mental process, hysteria supplanted rational thinking. When the organization became powerful, it enforced uniformity in political and economic philosophy. It was intolerant of opposition; its general policy was one of expediency. Its members were governed by zeal for their cause and not by any fixed standards of morality.

The purpose of this chapter is to discuss all of the various revolutionary organizations from the point of view of the political scientist, even at the expense of some repetition. The first instrument of revolutionary organization to find its existence in New Hampshire had been the committee of correspondence. Much difference of opinion has existed as to the origin of this form of revolutionary organization, some awarding the credit to Virginia, others to Massachusetts. A careful analysis of the evidence seems to indicate that a small clique in the Virginia House of Burgesses evolved the idea of committees for inter-provincial correspondence. To Samuel Adams should go the credit for organizing the single province of Massachusetts into correspondence committees on the basis of local units, but the idea of inter-provincial communication cannot be attributed to Adams. Such a conclusion is supported by the writings of Thomas Jefferson.

The Virginia House of Burgesses met in the spring of the year 1773. The immediate subject of discussion was the British court of inquiry in Rhode Island on the *Gaspee* affair and the rumor that the offenders were to be tried in England. Jefferson wrote, "Not thinking our old & leading members up to the point of forwardness & zeal which the times required, Mr. Henry, R. H. Lee, Francis L. Lee, Mr. Carr & myself agreed to meet in the evening in a private room of the Raleigh to consult on the state of things." "We were all sensible that the most urgent of all measures was that of coming to an understanding with all the other colonies to consider the British claims as a common cause to all, & to produce an unity of action: and for this purpose that a commee of correspdce [*sic*] in each colony would be the best instrument for intercommunication: and that their first measure would probably be to propose a meeting of deputies from every colony at some central place, who should be charged with the direction of the

[33]

measures which should be taken by all."[3] On March 12, 1773, this matter came before the whole House of Burgesses, which resolved unanimously to appoint a committee of correspondence and to urge the other colonies to do likewise.

A circular letter to this effect was received by the New Hampshire Assembly on May 28, 1773. On the same day the Assembly appointed seven of its members to a "Standing Committee of Correspondence & enquiry." The duties of the Committee, copied exactly from the Virginia circular, were "to obtain the most early & authentic Intelligence of all such acts & Resolutions of the British Parliament or proceedings of Administration as may relate to or affect the British Colonies in America, & to keep up & maintain a Correspondence & Communication with any sister Colonies respecting those important considerations. . . . . "[4] Upon the establishment of this committee Governor Wentworth adjourned the Assembly and kept it under adjournment for seven months.[5] Such action was the typical method employed by royal governors to combat these pernicious committees. For outside the sessions of the legislature, all legislative committees ceased to have existence from the point of view of constitutional practice.

Local committees of correspondence never seem to have gained a strong foothold in New Hampshire. Portsmouth appointed a committee of correspondence on December 16, 1773, at the time of the resolutions against the importation of tea. In the year 1774 this committee was supplanted first by a committee of inspection and later by a committee of ways and means.[6] All of these committees were revolutionary in character and functioned alike. Other towns to establish committees of correspondence or inspection in 1774 were Exeter, Barrington, Hampton, Newcastle, Haverhill, Rochester, and Dover.[7] The failure of the local committee of correspondence to thrive more extensively can be attributed to poor communications and to New Hampshire's delay in entering the revolutionary movement. When she did enter the field, a new type of revolutionary committee had become more prevalent.

Another Assembly was not convened by Wentworth until April 7, 1774. This Assembly did not immediately choose a new committee of correspondence. In fact the Governor exerted all the pressure in his power to keep the representatives from entering into any revolutionary activities. But news of the passage of the Boston Port Act reached America on May 10, 1774. Three days later the Boston Committee of Correspondence wrote a circular letter to all the colonies urging a boycott against English goods. The result in New Hampshire was the appointment of a new committee of correspondence on May 28. The Assembly had cleverly withheld the supply bill until the passage of the committee resolution, thus thwarting the desire of the Governor to adjourn them.[8] But with the enacting of the supply bill Wentworth adjourned the Assembly and kept it under short adjournments until June 8 when he learned that the speaker had received letters of invitation to a general American congress. Thereupon he sent down the following message: "As I look upon the measures entered upon by the House of Assembly to be inconsistent with his Majesty's service & the good of this Government, it is my Duty as far as in me lies to prevent any Detriment that might arise from such Proceedings, I Do therefore hereby Dissolve the General Assembly of this Province. . . . . "[9] Wentworth did not call the Assembly again until May 4, 1775, nearly a year later. Because of this practice of adjourning or dissolving the legislative body whenever revolutionary activity occurred, he gained much unpopularity.[10]

The movement toward a general American congress seems to have originated in Providence, Rhode Island, where the suggestion was made on May 17, 1774. The measure was next proposed by New York in reply to the Boston circular of May 13. Sometime late in May the dissolved Virginia House of Burgesses instructed its Committee of Correspondence to write the sister colonies inviting them to participate in a general congress. To Massachusetts was extended the privilege of naming the time and place for the meeting. On June 17, the Massachusetts House of Representatives resolved upon convening the congress at Philadelphia on September 1, 1774.[11]

To consult upon the foregoing matters the New Hampshire Committee of Correspondence called an extra-legal session of the dissolved Assembly. The ex-assemblymen met at Portsmouth on July 6, choosing the Assembly chamber as their place of meeting. Governor Wentworth (as has been previously related) invaded this illegal gathering and warned it to disperse.[12] The meeting thereupon adjourned to a nearby tavern and transacted its business in private. A mandate was dispatched to all the towns in the province "warning" them to elect delegates to a provincial congress to be held at Exeter on July 21 for the purpose of choosing representatives to a continental congress. It was also decided to raise three hundred pounds to defray the expenses of the delegates, each town paying a certain sum in proportion to its province tax. In conclusion it was recommended to the towns that July 14 be observed as a day of fasting and prayer. Wentworth wrote to Lord Dartmouth, "It is yet uncertain how far these requisitions will be complied with, but I am apt to believe the spirit of enthusiasm, which generally prevails through the Colonies, will create an obedience that reason or religion would fail to procure."[13]

In accordance with the schedule New Hampshire's first Provincial Congress met at Exeter on July 21, 1774.[14] The eighty-five members present chose John Wentworth, a cousin of the Governor, Speaker of the Assembly, and a judge of one of His Majesty's Probate Courts, to be president of the meeting. Dr. Josiah Bartlett of Kingston and John Pickering, a lawyer of Portsmouth, were the initial choices for delegates to the Continental Congress.[15] However, Pickering, a conservative, declined to serve, and as Bartlett's house had just burned down, he too declined. Thereupon the Congress selected Major John Sullivan, a prosperous lawyer of Durham, and Colonel Nathaniel Folsom, a merchant of Exeter. The delegates were instructed "to devise consult and adopt such Measures as may have the most likely Tendency to extricate the Colonies from their present Difficulties, to secure and perpetuate their Rights, Liberties and Privileges, and to restore that Peace, Harmony and mutual Confidence, which once happily subsisted between the Parent Country and her Colonies."[16] It was voted unanimously that the delegates recommend the relief of Boston to their respective towns. The meeting was adjourned at the end of the day. Judging by the character of the prominent personnel and the tenor of the instructions to the delegates, this Congress was a conservative body with no thought of the measures eventually adopted in the Continental Congress.

Soon after the adjournment of the Provincial Congress, New Hampshire's Committee of Correspondence decided to follow the lead of Boston and organize a non-importation and non-consumption agreement against English goods. During August, 1774, a standard form or covenant was circulated among the New Hampshire towns. Wentworth wrote to Lord Dartmouth, "Some few towns generally subscribed, many others totally rejected it."[17] Concord was the only town to leave documentary evidence of having adopted the covenant. Keene refused to act on the measure pending the meeting of the Continental Congress. Probably most of the towns wished to delay action on this covenant and to observe the policy agreed upon by the delegates at Philadelphia.[18]

In the fall of 1774 a new type of revolutionary organization, common to Massachusetts, came into existence in New Hampshire. In October, Cheshire County held a congress at Walpole.[19] No record of its proceedings has ever been found. In November, Hillsborough County also convened a congress at Amherst. Second and third Hillsborough County Congresses met in April and May, 1775.[20] The county congresses seem to have confined their business to adoption of resolutions, organization of the county internally, detection of Tories, and in general to an imitation of Massachusetts! The second Hillsborough County Congress resolved, "We would Recommend to all Persons of this Community not to engage in any Routs Roits [*sic*] or licentious attacks on the persons or property of any Person or property whatsoever as being subversive of all good order & Government."[21] The third Congress of the same county boldly announced as one of the purposes of its meeting:—"To go into some measure for the better security of the internal Polity of this County to prevent declining into a State of Nature."[22]

In the meantime, the first Continental Congress met in Philadelphia on September 5, 1774, and remained in session until October 26. The most important single measure adopted was the Continental Association, signed by all the delegates. This Association provided for a nonimportation and non-consumption agreement against all English goods to begin on December 1, 1774, and a non-exportation agreement to become effective on September 10, 1775, unless the oppressive English acts had been repealed before that date. Domestic manufactures were encouraged and the strictest economy urged. All merchants who raised prices of their goods to take advantage of the temporary scarcity or otherwise violated the Association were to be boycotted. In conclusion each town was urged to select a committee to enforce the agreement.[23]

The Congress very early in its proceedings had shown a tendency toward radical revolutionary sentiment. On September 18 the inflammatory Suffolk Resolves had been approved. Soon news began to filter back into New England as to the probable outcome of the proceedings. In some New Hampshire towns, at least, a degree of surprise was manifested at this radical tendency. In Hillsborough

County, Francestown, followed by New Boston and Hollis, drew up a series of resolutions as a protest against radicalism.[24] They resolved, "That we will at all times be ready to assist the Civil Magistrates in the due execution of their offices at the risk of our lives; and will at all times show our disapprobation of all unlawful proceedings of unjust men congregating together, as they pretend to maintain their liberties and even trample under foot the very law of liberty, and wholly destroy that law our whole land firmly wish, and desire to maintain."[25]

The Continental Association was to go into partial effect on December 1, 1774. Accordingly on December 2 the New Hampshire Committee of Correspondence sent a warrant to all the towns urging adoption of the Association and appointment of a committee to enforce it.[26] A Portsmouth town meeting voted unanimously, "That they did cordially accede to the just state of the rights and grievances of the British colonies, and of the measures adopted and recommended by the American Continental Congress. . . . . "[27] As for the Continental Association they voted that they "would punctually and religiously execute the same as far as in them lies."[28] A committee of twenty-five, known as a committee of inspection or safety, was appointed to enforce the agreement. On December 26 Exeter also voted unanimously to adopt the Association and appointed a committee of inspection to enforce the same.[29] In fact there is no record to show that any New Hampshire town rejected the Association.

The enforcement of the Association depended largely upon the degree of popular support it received and upon the vigilance of the Portsmouth Committee, since Portsmouth was the only port of entry. Governor Wentworth wrote to Lord Dartmouth concerning the measures adopted, "So great is the present delusion, that most people receive them as matters of obedience, not of considerate examination, whereon they may exercise their own judgment."[30] Publication of the offenders' names and actions in the *New Hampshire Gazette*, thus exposing them fully to the pressure of public opinion, was the chief means of dealing with violators.

The Portsmouth Committee seems to have been very efficient. Before news of the Association reached Portsmouth Captain William Pearne, a merchant, had decided to dispatch a brig to Madeira for a cargo of wines. Upon receiving news of the Association, which forbade such trade, Pearne was persuaded to send the ship to the West Indies instead. The Committee also prevented Captain Chivers from exporting fifty sheep to the West Indies; and he was forced to sell them at a loss. When sixty pounds of dutied tea were found in the store of a Portsmouth trader, that guilty person was forced to burn the same before a large crowd on January 18, 1775.[31] On February 10 the Portsmouth Committee demanded that all gambling and gaming establishments discontinue operations at once. Notice was also given that—"The Committee do likewise recommend it to the Merchants and Traders in this Town, who are dealing in European Goods, that they do not take any advantage of the times, by raising the price of Goods, lest they be found violating the Grand American Association. . . . ."[32]

Outside of Portsmouth in the inland region great difficulties were encountered in enforcing the Association. The principal source of trouble was the efficient salesmanship of traveling Scotchmen and hawkers and peddlers who were "tempting women, girls and boys with their unnecessary fineries."[33] The towns of Exeter, Epsom, Kingston, New Market, and Brentwood passed resolutions against these itinerant traders. Exeter resolved, "It is the opinion of many, that if this vote, with the law of the Province, should prove ineffectual to prevent the intrusion of such persons, an experiment ought to be made of Tar and Feathers."[34]

In early January, 1775, the New Hampshire Committee of Correspondence called a second provincial congress. This Congress of one hundred and forty-four members convened at Exeter on January 25. Judge Wentworth, Speaker of the Assembly, was once again chosen president. The Congress unanimously approved the acts of the Continental Congress. For delegates to the second Continental Congress the members reëlected John Sullivan of Durham and chose as his colleague John Langdon, a merchant of Portsmouth. A new committee of correspondence of nine men was appointed. The makeup of this Committee revealed four merchants, two physicians, two judges of His Majesty's courts, and one lawyer. As their concluding action the Provincial Congress prepared an address to the province. This address recommended maintenance of law and order, the sanctity of private property, strict adherence to the Continental Association, rigid economy, attention to domestic manufactures, and regular exercise of the militia companies to guard against invasion "by his Majesty's enemies."[35]

This second Congress marked a deliberate assumption of governmental authority by an extra-legal body. Not content with taxing the towns to defray the expenses of delegates to the Continental Congress, the organization had dared to regulate the everyday conduct of the towns in its revolutionary address. Governor Wentworth saw the rise of this new power with some misgivings. He wrote to a friend in Dover, ". . . . To attempt an extension of a specific limitation into an uncontrolled dictatorial power, however absurd and dangerous the precedent, a majority were ready to sacrifice their reason and constituents to their fears and to their popularity. . . . . I wish the parties would leave ground for an amnesty; but they strive to augment the reverse. Peace, my dear friend, has by unwise men been driven out. They shut the door against its return."[36]

Military organization seems to have begun spontaneously in New Hampshire in the winter of 1774-1775. The first and most obvious move was to obtain powder and arms. Although the militia law required each town to maintain a stock of munitions, the enforcement of the law had been lax. The first intimation of military activity occurred in the proceedings of the town of Dublin. On November 28, 1774, the town "granted twelve pounds to provide a town-stock of ammunition."[37] The attack on Fort William and Mary on December 14 and 15, as has been related, yielded one hundred barrels of powder, some sixty stand of small arms, and several cannon for the revolutionary party. On December 15 Dr. John Giddinge of Exeter wrote to Dr. Josiah Bartlett of Kingston, "This town is at this time happily furnished with Seventy-two barrils of Powder—part of which think might well be deposited with the Patriotick Sons of Liberty in Kingstown."[38]

The earliest military company, of which there is record, was that of Portsmouth. This body, known as the Portsmouth Volunteers, organized itself on December 20, 1774, elected its officers and resolved to drill twice weekly.[39] Governor Wentworth in alarm wrote to Lord Dartmouth, ". . . . The People here . . . . are arming and exercising Men, as if for immediate War."[40] Sometime in March, 1775, eighty-two "reputable inhabitants" of Durham formed the Durham Company under the leadership of ex-Major John Sullivan of the provincial militia.[41] Their articles of enlistment were modelled after the Portsmouth organization. On April 6, 1775, the Hillsborough County Congress resolved, "Whereas it is Necessary for the Defence of any People that they Perfect themselves in the military art and whereas it is said from the good dissiplin of regular Troops that one Regiment would put to flight ten that are not Dissiplined, we earnestly recommend to this County to form themselves into companys and make choice of such men as they shall think Best Qualified for teaching the military art to meet once a week. . . . . "[42]   On April 13 Chester raised a company of fifty men "to go against any enemy that shall presume to invade us."[43]

It should be remembered that all of the foregoing military activity preceded the Battle of Lexington, which was fought on April 19. From the meagre records extant it seems apparent that most of the towns in the southern part of New Hampshire started organizing and drilling military companies in March and April, 1775. In most cases these towns merely called out their own provincial militia companies. Thus if the royal government complained, the towns could assert that these "extra-curricular" drills were for the greater glory of His Majesty, George III.

When the news of the fighting at Lexington and Concord penetrated New Hampshire on April 20, most of the southern towns called meetings and dispatched their motley troops for Boston and vicinity. The provincial Committee of Correspondence speedily convened an emergency session of the Provincial Congress. This session, known as the third Provincial Congress, met at Exeter on April 21, 1775, "to consult on what measures shall be thought most expedient to be taken at this alarming crisis."[44] Because of the haste with which the Congress was summoned the towns were poorly represented—only sixty-eight delegates from thirty-four towns being present. The members again chose Judge Wentworth as president and pledged themselves to secrecy in their transactions. As an initial measure Colonel Nathaniel Folsom of Exeter was appointed to command the scattered New Hampshire forces already at Boston. On April 25 James Sullivan, a brother of the Durham hero, arrived in Exeter from Boston. As Massachusetts' agent he came to "lobby" in favor of raising a regular body of New Hampshire troops. After some debate the Congress resolved to postpone action on the matter, as not enough delegates were present to determine the true sentiment of the province. On April 26, however, it was resolved unanimously that each town should accumulate military stores and organize its own company of "Minute Men." The Congress dissolved without further action of importance.

The fourth Provincial Congress met at Exeter on May 17, 1775, with one hundred and thirty-three members present.[45] Dr. Matthew Thornton of Londonderry was elected president. Another physician, Dr. Ebenezer Thompson of Durham, was the choice for provincial secretary. Nicholas Gilman, a merchant of Exeter, was elected treasurer. From the beginning of the proceedings the Congress ignored the royal government at Portsmouth and assumed the real authority itself. A provincial post-office was established on May 18. Two days later the Congress resolved to raise two thousand men in three regiments for six months' service. For the support of this force a provincial tax of three thousand pounds was voted. On May 26 was constituted a provincial committee of safety as the congressional executive body. Increasing in daring, the Congress on the same day empowered their Committee on Supplies to borrow ten thousand pounds on the credit of the revolutionary government. On June 3 it was decided to raise a company of rangers to guard the Connecticut Valley frontiers. To meet the mounting expenses incurred the Congress adopted every expedient. It was resolved on June 8 to seize the funds in the royal treasury, and a committee was appointed to carry out the measure. A short time later this committee visited the royal treasurer, George Jaffrey of Portsmouth, and obtained 1516 pounds in cash. To Jaffrey the Congress voted its thanks for his "ready compliance," although he was probably forced to deliver the funds. On June 9, as a climax to its assumption of power, the revolutionary Congress voted to issue paper currency to the amount of 10,050 pounds in anticipation of future taxes.

By June 28 royal authority had practically collapsed; the courts no longer functioned; and the King's sheriffs were powerless. With anarchy in the offing the Congress voted that each town should appoint a committee of safety to enforce law and order. It was also resolved that the provincial records should be transferred from Portsmouth to Exeter. The royal secretary, Chief Justice Theodore Atkinson of Portsmouth, soon received a visit from a revolutionary "flying squadron," and his records were transported to Exeter to be placed in the hands of Secretary Thompson of the new government. On July 8, 1775, Judge Meshech Weare of Hampton Falls, President *pro tempore* of the Congress, wrote, "The Colony is at Present wholly governed by this Congress & the Committee[s] of the respective Towns."[46] Languishing in Fort William and Mary at Portsmouth, Governor Wentworth appreciated the truth of this statement. Wentworth, as has been previously related, finally left the province on August 23 never to return. On the same day the Provincial Congress, now the nominal as well as the actual government, reorganized the provincial militia into twelve regiments under the command of Major General Nathaniel Folsom. With the departure of the British frigate *Scarborough* the Congress assumed active regulation of trade.

In this fashion the fourth Provincial Congress governed the state throughout the summer and fall of 1775. It was in session the greater part of this time. Although most of the executive work was done by the Committee of Safety, the important decisions had to be ratified in the tedious and cumbersome sessions of the whole Congress. The last important measure to be enacted provided for the reapportionment of representation.[47] This new plan of representation, which passed on November 14, 1775, after lengthy debates, was based on a census sponsored by the Congress and consequently was more accurately proportional to the population than any preceding plan. On November 15 the fourth Congress was dissolved.

The fifth Provincial Congress was elected on the basis of the new plan of representation and met at Exeter on December 21, 1775. In accordance with the advice of the Continental Congress, it voted to resolve itself into a house of representatives on December 28. By January 5, 1776, an elementary state constitution had been drafted and approved. The Provincial Congress thereupon passed out of existence as an organ of government. One form of revolutionary organization continued to function, however. This was the Committee of Safety. This Committee had been established by the Congress on May 26, 1775, to fill an obvious gap in government—the lack of a responsible executive and the need of a compact administrative body to execute general policy efficiently or to act secretly and speedily in emergencies.[48]

The powers and duties conferred upon the Committee of Safety at one time or another were wide and extensive, practically dictatorial in fact. Under the heading of "general authority" the members were empowered in the recess of legislative sessions "to take under their Consideration all Matters in which the Welfare of the Province, in the Security of their Rights, shall be concerned, except the Appointment of the Field-Officers & to take Utmost Care that the Public sustain no Damage."[49] By virtue of this delegation of authority the Committee supervised the execution of the policy of the legislative body. It acted as an executive coördinator of the state's military administration. It exercised extensive powers in respect to the regulation of trade. It supervised disbursements from the state treasury for goods and services. It acted as a type of political tribunal for the detection and trial of such crimes as dishonesty in government, counterfeiting, and Loyalism. It represented the state government in business to be transacted with the Continental authorities. Perhaps the Committee's most important power was its authority over the network of local committees of safety, which it might command to enforce its edicts.

The members of the Committee of Safety were elected by the legislative body—first, by the Provincial Congress, and later by the Council and House of Representatives. They served until their terms expired or until they were replaced. Including a presiding chairman the usual number of members ranged from eight to twelve. The turnover of committee personnel must have been rapid, since the average term of office during the war was only one year and nine months. As for the geographical distribution of membership, of the forty-three men who served at one time or another on the Committee, twenty-six were from Rockingham County, eight from Hillsborough, five from Strafford, three from Cheshire, and only one from Grafton County. It is small wonder that the western counties claimed that the revolution had meant no radical change to them. The powerful Committee of Safety was at all times controlled by a small clique of leaders in seacoastal Rockingham County, which section had also dominated the province under royal government.

Despite this unequal geographical distribution, there can be no question but that the Committee at some time claimed the membership of nearly every one of the more able men in the revolutionary party. Perhaps the outstanding member of the Committee was its chairman, Meshech Weare of Hampton Falls, who was also President of the Council and Chief Justice of the Superior Court. Weare served continuously as chairman from 1776 to 1784, and his moderating influence played a major part in the consummation of New Hampshire's revolution. Other prominent members were Dr. Matthew Thornton of Londonderry, Dr. Josiah Bartlett of Kingston, William Whipple, a merchant of Portsmouth, Nathaniel Folsom, a merchant of Exeter, Dr. Ebenezer Thompson of Durham, Phillips White, a merchant of South Hampton, Pierce Long, Samuel Cutts,

George Gains, all merchants of Portsmouth, Israel Morey, a land-owner of Orford, Jonathan Moulton, a landowner and merchant of Hampton, Wyseman Claggett, a lawyer of Litchfield, John Dudley, a farmer of Raymond, Timothy Walker, Jr., of Concord, Nicholas Gilman, John Taylor Gilman, both merchants and landowners of Exeter, Dr. Nathaniel Peabody of Atkinson, and John McClary, a farmer of Epsom. Notable exceptions among the revolutionary party who never served on the committee were John Langdon, John Sullivan, and Samuel Livermore. An occupational analysis shows eight merchants, four physicians, two landowners, two lawyers, and two farmers. These men were New Hampshire's real revolutionary government—the political power behind the scenes.

The Committee of Safety was the only form of revolutionary organization which functioned for the duration of the Revolution. Under the régime of the revolutionary Congress it acted as an executive, and when the first constitution of 1776 also failed to provide for an executive, the Committee was continued as an active organization. Because of the prestige of its members, its power was generally unchallenged. From 1775 to 1777 it sat during the recesses of the legislature. But from 1778 to 1784 it was in continuous session. Toward the end of the war its duties became mainly concerned with the minor administrative details of claim adjustments and demobilization. When the permanent state constitution went into effect in June, 1784, the Committee passed out of existence.

On the whole the Committee interpreted its powers broadly and never shrank from assuming doubtful jurisdiction. Government by such a committee was not unlike a rudimentary cabinet government. The members were all leaders in the revolutionary party, elected by and responsible to the legislative body. They acted as an administrative organization, executing the general policies laid down by the legislature. While there is no evidence that the Committee as a body formulated the state's legislative program, the political influence of the Committee's members ensured that no law would pass without its approval. Though it was an extra-constitutional body, the Committee of Safety must be considered to have been the *de facto* ruling power. A prominent New Hampshire Tory summarized its general character by admitting that "New Hampshire had never a more energetic government, nor a more honest executive."[50]

[45]

CHAPTER 4

When civil madness first from man to man
In these devoted climes like wildfire ran,
There were who gave the moderating hint,
In conversation some, and some in print;
Wisely they spake—and what was their reward?—
The tar, the rail, the prison, and the cord!
Ev'n now there are, who bright in Reason's dress
Watch the polluted Continental press;
Confront the lies that Congress sends abroad,
Expose the sophistry, detect the fraud.

JONATHAN ODELL.[1]

Clash of Political Opinion

As the tide of revolutionary activity swelled and swept relentlessly onward, the fundamental issue became more clearly defined and more sharply outlined against the background of the political arena. Nevertheless political opinion had been painfully slow in crystallizing. At the conclusion of the Seven Years' War in 1763 the economic, political, and social issues between the mother country and the colonies had first begun to assume continental importance. Yet in these early days of sporadic protest against British policy there was not evident as yet anything, with the exception of the Stamp Act agitation, which might be regarded as unified colonial sentiment. Self-interest more than underlying principles ruled the opposition to Great Britain. Thus the make-up of the opposition was heterogeneous, since few measures affected all people alike. Until 1773 there could be no one class cited as consistently and

[46]

unequivocally against British policy, either in New Hampshire or elsewhere.

In 1765 the feeling in the colonies against the Stamp Act had been practically unanimous, except among the most extreme conservatives. This was a measure which had affected the daily lives of nearly everyone. The reaction which had sprung up against the Act was that of a natural, spontaneous self-defense. How then can one explain the fact that many who opposed the Stamp Act in 1765 were Tories in 1775?[2] The answer lies in the fact that in 1765 the majority of the colonists had failed to see the significance which lay behind their opposition to or support of a particular colonial policy. Except for a few far-seeing politicians, the majority had been oblivious of any broader issue, any broader interest than the immediate one of political, economic, or social security for itself. Had John Dickinson correctly foreseen the ultimate implications of his "Letters from a Farmer," he probably would never have written them.

As the temper of the discussion rose slowly to a critical stage, however, the colonies were forced more and more to consider what effect their attitude toward certain British policies might have on the ultimate development of the empire and on the economic and social *status quo* in America. The Stamp Act considered as a separate measure was certainly an iniquitous regulation and tax in the eyes of the majority of the colonists. But the principle behind the Act—the right of Parliament to raise revenue by colonial taxation—was vital to the maintenance of a strong imperial establishment. The same general principle was involved in the Townshend Acts and the Tea Act. Yet important special interests in the colonies had been injured by each of these acts. These special interests had reacted against these measures in accordance with the primitive instinct of self-defense. But they and other groups and forces in the colonies failed, until relatively late in the period of preliminary discussion, to consider the broader principles of imperial policy at stake. They failed to realize that behind their particular differences with Great Britain, arising out of the Townshend Acts and the Tea Act, lay a more fundamental difference—a difference between two philosophies of economics and government. The immediate social, economic, and political issues raised by successive British imperial programs were clear enough inasmuch as they involved certain individuals and classes. But the real, underlying issue—the general trend and ultimate outcome of relations between the colonies and Britain—was not appreciated and dragged into the open until relatively close to the time of actual revolution. Nor did political opinion within the colonies actually find a really consistent line of cleavage until this underlying issue of imperial relations became evident. Only then did people perceive that the existing social structure in the colonies, which had been built up under British rule, was dependent for its preservation on the continuance of that rule, unhampered. With the survival of a strongly centralized empire under Parliamentary control at stake and with the survival of the political, economic, and social *status quo* in the colonies, which was a by-product of that centralized empire, equally at stake, the different classes of colonial society likely to be affected either adversely or favorably by a change, naturally divided in opinion along these lines.

Those colonists who remained favorable to centralized British control and the maintenance of the colonial *status quo* were known as Conservatives, Tories, or Loyalists. Those who advocated a change, an overturn, a revolution, were known as Radicals, Whigs, or Revolutionists. These two parties were respectively the right and the left wings of colonial opinion. Naturally, however, there was a great, uninformed central group consisting of those who fundamentally could neither gain nor lose by the Revolution. This element held the balance of power. As their feeling varied, so did the course of the Revolution. Whichever party, the Loyalists or the Revolutionists, could by various means command the obedience or even the acquiescence of this element, even though such means included the creation of popular illusions, by false promises, by demagogy or otherwise, that party was certain to hold the upper hand. The fact that the Revolutionists organized sooner and more effectively than the Loyalists enabled them to gain control of this central group and to lead it into a position from which it was impossible to recede.

What caused a man to be a Loyalist in 1774? Perhaps he was imbued with reverence and enthusiasm for the imperial ideal. Perhaps he opposed British policy but was unwilling to fight against it or to risk disrupting the empire. Perhaps he feared that the colonies would inevitably lose in any struggle with Britain and be burdened with a still heavier yoke. Again he might have been politically, economically, or socially powerful under the existing royal government. Any change in the character of British control over the colonies might well weaken his position, or lessen his power. New political rulers would come to the fore in any new régime. By gaining the political power the new-comers would also inevitably control the social and economic structure. Consequently the Loyalist was a man who wanted the *status quo* continued. He was fundamentally satisfied with existing conditions, or if he was dissatisfied, he favored remedy by evolution rather than by revolution.

What caused a man to be a Revolutionist in 1774? Perhaps as James Truslow Adams has suggested, the individual Revolutionist had "but the passionate desire to live his life, to express his personality, to utilize his powers, unhampered by any rule imposed from above, of government, of class, or of economic privilege."[3] His protest was a demand on the British government for more complete freedom in his daily activities. Political laissez-faire to the Revolutionist meant more democracy—a chance for more groups in society to participate in government, to gain social prestige, and to break the existing monopoly of political influence. Economic laissez-faire meant an end to privileged economic groups, a dissolution of large concentrations of colonial wealth, and a new freedom for colonial individual initiative to compete unrestrainedly in any field. It finally became apparent to the Revolutionists that the philosophy underlying British imperial government after 1763 was entirely incompatible with the foregoing individualistic aims. Hence their only remedy was revolution. This was made increasingly apparent by the passage of the "Five Intolerable Acts", whose enactment showed that Britain was determined to maintain at all costs its imperial system with all its centralization of control, bureaucracy, economic privilege, rule of the gentry, and arbitrary restraint on colonial activity.

The exact moment, when a man had to face the issue and choose his course as between loyalty or revolution cannot be determined. Except within very general limits there was no particular time when political opinion divided, because the issue did not become apparent or important to everyone at once. As revolutionary activity gathered momentum in 1774 and 1775, an opposition thereto formed spontaneously. Probably the extreme conservatives were definitely aligned in opposition to the radicals at the first symptoms of revolution. Then as the Revolutionists adopted more and more radical measures, greater numbers of men found themselves forced into the Loyalist ranks. Friends and even families were divided. In New Hampshire, Governor Wentworth lost his good friend and Attorney General, Samuel Livermore. John Stark of Dunbarton saw his brother, William, joining the British army. Many men chose to remain neutral, perhaps for reasons of conscience, perhaps because of lack of interest, perhaps for selfish reasons. No doubt many pretended to align themselves with the Revolutionists to escape loss of property or personal violence. No doubt many were unjustly persecuted into becoming Loyalists.

A great many studies of colonial society have been made which attempt to devise general formulae indicating why an inhabitant of the colonies was a Revolutionist or a Loyalist. These theories as to the division of political opinion may be roughly classified under four main headings—(1) division on the basis of geographical location, (2) division on the basis of occupation, (3) division on the basis of social or economic status, (4) division on the basis of religion. The main lesson which a student of history learns from these various theories is that no one of them can be trusted in its entirety. Each one may seem to apply wonderfully well to one section of the colonies and yet be totally useless for another section. History is not quite the exact science that many theorists would make it. Only by perversion or omission of historical evidence can general conclusions as to the division of political opinion be evolved which will apply to all sections. This is because the people of the Revolutionary period inevitably saw continental issues as colored by local issues and conditions, which differed in each colony. The purpose of this chapter, therefore, is to examine each of the four theories mentioned above as it applies to Revolutionary New Hampshire. Any general conclusions may be considered as valid for New Hampshire but are not to be regarded as applicable to other colonies by mere analogy.[4]

The most valuable historical evidence available in order to determine the political status of persons in New Hampshire consists of the Association Test and the Proscription Act.[5] In March, 1776, the Continental Congress recommended to the states that their respective inhabitants be tested as to their sentiment for or against the Revolution. In New Hampshire a standard covenant known as the Association Test was drawn up by the Committee of Safety and on April 12 dispatched to the towns. This test read as follows: "We, the Subscribers, do hereby solemnly engage, and promise, that we will, to the utmost of our Power, at the Risque of our Lives and Fortunes, with Arms, oppose the Hostile Proceedings of the British Fleets and Armies against the United American Colonies." To all white males over twenty-one years of age, lunatics and idiots excepted, the test was submitted for signature or rejection.

Unfortunately the returns of the Association Test have not been completely preserved. Out of 155 towns and a population of 82,000, existing returns cover 77 towns and a little over 50,000 people or about 62 per cent of the population. Yet these returns probably give a fair cross-section of sentiment in the state. The Proscription Act of 1778 stated the names, occupations and locations of 76 prominent Loyalists who were banished from the state. This evidence is valuable because it furnishes a picture of a representative Loyalist group from New Hampshire.[6]

Upon the basis of the foregoing evidence the division of political opinion in New Hampshire may be examined first from the standpoint of geographical location, using the five counties as units. For Rockingham County the returns of the Association Test showed 297 non-signers, and the Proscription Act showed 44 Loyalists to have been from the same county. This seacoast county undoubtedly claimed the largest number of Loyalists and the returns of the Association Test for this county were the most nearly complete, 36 towns out of 38 being represented. But at the same time Rockingham County claimed the largest number of signers of the test—there being 4655 subscribers. The Loyalist element was only 6 per cent of the total to whom the test was submitted. It was natural for Rockingham to contain the greater part of the Loyalists since it was by far the most populous county.

Strafford, the other seacoast county, showed returns of the test from only 7 out of its 19 towns. Hence it is unsafe to draw any far-reaching conclusion from the evidence. There were, excluding Quakers and other conscientious objectors, 697 signers in the county and 55 non-signers or a 7.3 per cent Loyalist element. This was a larger percentage of Loyalists than Rockingham County claimed, but three of the county's largest towns, Dover, Somersworth, and Madbury were not included in the returns.

In Hillsborough County the returns of the Association Test were complete for 16 towns out of 32. There were 1375 signers in the county. The 60 non-signers were therefore only 4 per cent of the to-tal—an unusually small percentage of Loyalists. Then too, the Pro-scription Act allocated only 15 Loyalists to Hillsborough County. Among these few Loyalists quite a number were of Scotch-Irish stock, which racial element dominated the county. Nevertheless an overwhelming preponderance of the Scotch-Irish were for the Revolution. Hillsborough County was perhaps the most radical of all the counties, being situated in the middle of the state and being largely a small-farming district. This characteristic may account for the lack of a strong conservative element.

On the frontier the southern county, Cheshire, gave surprising indications of conservatism. With returns complete from 20 towns out of 33 the test had 1408 signers and 106 dissenters or a 7 per cent Loyalist population. The Proscription Act also gave Cheshire County 17 Loyalists. For a frontier county Cheshire proved to be a surprising reversal of the theory that the west was the home of wild-eyed radicalism. This county was second only to Rockingham in number of Loyalists and had the second highest proportion of Loyalist population among all the counties. Yet when one looks for an explanation, one has only to consider the land grant policies of New Hampshire's royal governors and the strong Episcopalian element to perceive the answer.

Cheshire's showing, however, appears very exceptional when one considers conditions in Grafton County, her northern frontier neighbor and the largest county in territorial extent. Although the returns of the Test were complete from only 5 towns out of 34, the evidence exhibited therein must have been fairly typical of the rest of the county, since all of Grafton's towns were small and more or less in the same social and economic condition. The returns from the Test showed no Loyalists at all, nor did the Proscription Act. Furthermore, the general picture of the county which the correspondence of the period furnishes indicates that its revolutionary sentiment was practically unanimous.[7] Grafton County, then, was a typical frontier county as regards the issue of loyalty or revolution. Viewing New Hampshire as a whole, the seacoast as the most populous district and the seat of royal government contained the greater proportion of the Loyalists. The central part of the colony, as the small-farming district, contained the smallest number of Loyalists. The frontier was predominantly Revolutionist except for the Claremont Episcopalians and holders of large royal land grants.

It has been said that a person's political views are inevitably colored by the character of his occupation. That occupational background was among the paramount factors in determining a person's political status at the outset of the American Revolution cannot be denied.

Then, as well as now, one's occupation was closely allied with his economic and social interests and his philosophy of government.

Perhaps one of the most complex groups to analyze from the standpoint of occupational influence with respect to the issue of loyalty or revolution was that of the royal officials of New Hampshire. Were they predominantly Loyalist or Revolutionist? An examination of the roster of royal officials of the period just before the Revolution shows a total of one hundred in New Hampshire, including county officials, judicial officials, and militia field officers.[8] Out of this total forty-one were definitely Loyalists, three of doubtful status and fifty-six definitely Revolutionists. With the exception of the Attorney General, most of the executive officers remained faithful to the King; and thus we find Governor Wentworth, the Secretary of the province, the Treasurer of the province, and ten out of the eleven Councillors in the Loyalist party. That these men should remain loyal was only natural, since most of them were personal friends or relatives of Wentworth, picked by him because of a known predisposition toward conservatism. New Hampshire's four customs officials were also unanimous in Loyalist sentiment. They were directly responsible to the British government for the efficient conduct of their offices. Of the colony's six admiralty officers, three were Loyalists and three Revolutionists, those directly connected with the centralized customs service at Boston remaining faithful to the King, and those appointed merely to exercise provincial admiralty jurisdiction breaking away from royal control. The colonial judiciary divided unusually heavily in favor of the Revolutionist party. Nineteen judges cast their lot with the Revolutionists while only five, including the chief justice of the Superior Court, became Loyalists. Of the five clerks of court three were Loyalists and two Revolutionists. Among the county officials six were loyal and fourteen joined the Revolution. The militia field officers divided twelve to seven in favor of the Revolution. Outside of the executive group, then, most of New Hampshire's royal officials were in opposition to British colonial policy. It must be remembered, however, that outside of the executive positions, most of the royal offices were only part-time jobs with little remuneration.

Another interesting class in New Hampshire's colonial society, closely allied with royal officialdom was that which included the Esquire, country gentleman, landowner, or justice of the peace. Most of these men were past middle age, conservative, prosperous, and of proved ability. The Proscription Act of 1778, which banished seventy-six Loyalists, showed thirty of that number to have been in this class. Unquestionably this element was the backbone of the New Hampshire Loyalists. Although some of them found their way finally into the Revolutionist party, they were a moderating influence, not radical.

Among the commercial class, including merchants, shipbuilders, and financial enterprizers, political sentiment was fairly evenly divided on the seacoast but overwhelmingly Revolutionist in the interior. A perusal of the list of Portsmouth's non-signers of the Association Test shows a large number to have been rich merchants, not especially prominent men politically, but closely connected with the Wentworth "junto." In the interior, however, the commercial class was almost totally in the Revolutionist ranks. Of the thirteen merchants or traders proscribed in 1778 only one came from outside the seacoast county of Rockingham. The Revolutionists drew many of their most influential leaders from the commercial class. Among them were John Langdon, Continental Agent and Speaker of the House of Representatives, William Whipple, many times delegate to the Continental Congress, Nicholas and John Taylor Gilman and Nathaniel Folsom, three leaders in Exeter, Phillips White, delegate to the Continental Congress, and George Atkinson, Samuel Cutts, George Gains, Joshua Wentworth, prominent Portsmouth leaders. The commercial class as a whole was Revolutionist except for a group of the more wealthy merchants in Portsmouth and vicinity.

New Hampshire's professional men were divided in sentiment on the Revolution. Their natural conservatism caused many of them to hesitate at disorderly and unprecedented action. William Plumer, a contemporary observer, in his biography of Joshua Atherton, wrote that the majority of the New Hampshire lawyers were opposed to the Revolution.[9] Certainly Atherton, Samuel Hale, and Edward Goldstone Lutwyche were three lawyers who furnished virulent opposition to the Revolutionists. Two other leaders of the bar, John Pickering and Samuel Livermore, delayed for some time before casting their lot with the Revolution. On the other hand, John Sullivan, delegate to the Continental Congress and Major General in the Continental army, Wyseman Claggett, Attorney General, Meshech Weare, chairman of the Committee of Safety and President of the Council, and John Wentworth, cousin of the royal governor, many times president of the Provincial Congress, were prominent Revolutionary lawyers. Among the physicians the Proscription Act of 1778 showed four in the Loyalist ranks. Yet several physicians occupied high positions among the Revolutionists. Leading physicians to hold responsible posts were John Giddinge, an early agitator in the provincial congresses, Josiah Bartlett, several times delegate to the Continental Congress and member of the Committee of Safety, Ebenezer Thompson, first Secretary of State, Matthew Thornton, President of the Provincial Congress, Joshua Brackett, judge of the Maritime Court, Nathaniel Peabody, delegate to the Continental Congress, Henry Dearborn, Lieutenant Colonel in the Continental army, and Hall Jackson and Ammi Ruhamah Cutter—both military surgeons. On the whole New Hampshire's professional men were not exceedingly wealthy. They represented the upper half of the middle class—just outside the fringe of political power. They had much to gain by a political overturn, and many of them quickly seized the most lucrative positions under the Revolutionary government.

Perhaps the largest single class in New Hampshire colonial society was that of the yeoman or farmer. There were, of course, wide extremes in the economic status of this class—some being very poor, others fairly well-to-do. The evidence seems to indicate that the few more wealthy farmers, prominent under the royal government, tended to enter the Loyalist party. The Proscription Act of 1778 showed nineteen of the banished Loyalists to have been farmers. The Association Test indicated roughly a much larger number. The great majority of the farmers were poor, however, and barely eked a living out of the land; they were proud, independent, and politically radical. Hence they opposed British restrictions on the issuance of paper money. The royal order in council issued in 1773, which forbade the granting of further crown lands within the province, was an additional grievance.[10] To the farmers the Revolution offered a prospect of welcome change.

In the larger towns on the seacoast the middle of the eighteenth century saw a new social class making its appearance. This class was that of the laborer, mechanic, artisan, and tradesman, springing up as a by-product of early colonial industry. At the time of the Revolution this class was in economic straits because of the business depression following the Seven Years' War. It was this element which in towns like Exeter and Portsmouth formed the backbone of the "Sons of Liberty" and participated in most of the rioting. On June 2, 1775, the chairman of the Portsmouth Committee of Safety wrote to the Provincial Congress, "The Stagnation of Trade and the Returns of our shipping, increases the number of our People, who for want of employment, do too readily fall into disorders, and when numbers are once collected, it is very difficult to persuade them to disperse, untill they exceed the bounds of Reason."[11] Nevertheless there were a few in this lower class in whom the King's name still inspired a degree of reverence. The Proscription Act of 1778 showed five seamen, one printer, one rope-maker, and one post-rider to have been Loyalists. Yet economically, socially, and politically this class had everything to gain by a revolution and nothing to lose. They were overwhelmingly revolutionary in sympathy.

Professor Claude H. Van Tyne has written, "After the Revolution passed the bounds of peaceful resistance it was (except in Virginia) distinctly a movement of the lower and middle classes. A new set of leaders came forward, hitherto unknown, less educated, and eager for change. The very public documents became more illiterate. To the aristocratic and cultured class it seemed that the unlettered monster was unchained, and while they waited for British power to restore the old order, they withdrew for the most part from what seemed an undignified contest."[12] If by "the aristocratic and cultured" class Professor Van Tyne means the wealthy and privileged group, his generalization would probably be true concerning New Hampshire. However, the Loyalist party in New Hampshire could hardly have claimed to possess a monopoly of culture since very few men in New Hampshire boasted more than an elementary education. Governor Wentworth was a Harvard graduate, but so was Meshech Weare, chairman of the Committee of Safety. Probably the best educated class in the colony was the Congregational clergy, and they were almost all in the Revolutionist party.

Among the Loyalists, there were a few outstanding leaders such as Wentworth, Colonel John Fenton, "gentleman," of Plymouth, Colonel Stephen Holland, "gentleman," of Londonderry, Theodore Atkinson, Chief Justice and Secretary of the province, respected and honored by all and reputed to be the wealthiest man in New Hampshire, Joshua Atherton, a lawyer of Amherst, one of the most brilliant men in the colony, and Daniel Rindge, merchant of Portsmouth. Yet these men could all be matched among the Revolutionists and in greater numbers. The majority of the state's ablest men were Revolutionist,

WE the Subscribers, Inhabitants of the Town of *Concord* having taken into our serious Consideration, the precarious State of the LIBERTIES of NORTH-AMERICA, and more especially the present distressed Condition of our Sister Colony of the Massachusetts-Bay, embarrassed as it is by several Acts of the British Parliament, tending to the entire Subversion of their natural and Charter Rights; among which is the *Act for blocking up the Harbour of* BOSTON: And being fully sensible of our indispensible Duty to lay hold on every Means in our Power to preserve and recover the much injured Constitution of our Country; and conscious at the same Time of no Alternative between the Horrors of Slavery, or the Carnage and Desolation of a civil War, but a Suspension of all commercial Intercourse with the Island of Great-Britain, DO, in the Presence of GOD, solemnly and in good Faith, covenant and engage with each other:

1. That from henceforth we will suspend all commercial Intercourse with the said Island of Great-Britain, until the Parliament shall cease to enact Laws imposing Taxes upon the Colonies, without their Consent, or until the pretended Right of Taxing is dropped.   And

2. That there may be less Temptation to others to continue in the said now dangerous Commerce; and in order to promote Industry, Oeconomy, Arts and Manufactures among ourselves, which are of the last Importance to the Welfare and Well-being of a Community; we do, in like Manner, solemnly covenant, that we will not buy, purchase or consume, or suffer any Person, by, for, or under us, to purchase, nor will we use in our Families in any Manner whatever, any Goods, Wares or Merchandise which shall arrive in America from Great-Britain aforesaid, from and after the last Day of August next ensuing (except only such Articles as shall be judged absolutely necessary by the Majority of the Signers hereof)--and as much as in us lies, to prevent our being-interrupted and defeated in this only peaceable Measure entered into for the Recovery and Preservation of our Rights, and the Rights of our Brethren in our Sister Colonies, We agree to break off all Trade and Commerce, with all Persons, who preferring their private Interest to the Salvation of their now almost perishing Country, who shall still continue to import Goods from Great-Britain, or shall purchase of those who import after the said last Day of August, until the aforesaid pretended Right of Taxing the Colonies shall be given up or dropped.

3. As a Refusal to come into any Agreement which promises Deliverance of our Country from the Calamities it now feels, and which, like a Torrent, are rushing upon it with increasing Violence, must, in our Opinion, evidence a Disposition enimical to, or criminally negligent of the common Safety :--It is agreed, that all such ought to be considered, and shall by us be esteemed, as Encouragers of contumacious Importers.

Lastly, We hereby further engage, that we will use every Method in our Power, to encourage and promote the Production of Manufactures among ourselves, that this Covenant and Engagement may be as little detrimental to ourselves and Fellow Countrymen as possible.

Non-Importation, Non-Consumption Covenant Adopted by Concord, August, 1774. This illustration omits a separate page of signatures.

although all but a few could be considered of high ability only by comparison with their neighbors. Most of this able majority consisted of upper middle-class men, who were not wealthy, who were not of high social position, and whom Wentworth had not invited to join his little clique of political associates. The rich men in the province were almost all of Loyalist leanings. A list of Portsmouth taxpayers for the year 1770 showed that four men, who were later prominent Loyalists, paid the highest taxes in the town on the basis of property-holdings and income.[13] The middle class, because it was excluded from political power and social prestige by the wealthy minority, though it was not lacking in ability, was predominantly Revolutionist. The poorer classes and debtors were Revolutionist, because the psychology of the poor and the debtors has usually been characterized by an attitude of discontent with the *status quo*.

Religion no less than occupation or economic status played an important part in influencing the political views of the colonial inhabitants of the Revolutionary period. The influence of religion was important for two reasons. First, men of that time were fairly religious and attached great importance to the views of their clergymen. Secondly, outside of the press the pulpit was the main source of political propaganda. The clergy of New Hampshire were probably the best educated element in the society of the province.[14] No single group was in a better position than they to mold and to lead public opinion. It was not surprising that on the issue of loyalty or revolution many persons followed the tendency of their particular faith as taught by the local minister.

Among the most interesting religious groups in New Hampshire to express an opinion on the Revolution were the Quakers and other conscientious objectors. The Association Test showed 131 persons who did not sign for reasons of conscience or religion, preferring not to take sides. Of this number 73 were Quakers. In all there were probably about 200 Quakers in the colony located principally in Weare, Dover, Rochester, Brentwood, and Kensington. The greater part of them expressed their opposition to the general principle of war when the Test was submitted. For a time they were suspected of Loyalism. On November 8, 1777, the House of Representatives ordered a legislative investigation of the records of the Quaker Societies throughout the state.[15] No evidence of a Loyalist tendency seems to have been found.

On the whole the religious scruples of the Quakers were tolerated and respected.

Of the 58 persons who did not sign the Test for reasons of conscience and who were not Quakers, many gave odd excuses. In the town of Richmond the twelve non-signers gave the following reason for their attitude.

> *We do not Believe that it is the Will of God to take away the Lives of our fellow crators, not that We Come out Against the Congress or the American Liberties, but When Ever We are Convinct to the Contory We are Redy to join our Amarican Brieathen to Defend by Arms Against the Hostile Attempts of the British fleets and Armies.*[16]

In Gilmantown there were twenty-one non-signers who begged to be excused on the ground of "Religious principles" although they were willing to bear their just proportion of the taxes to support the war.[17]

A religious group which was torn by dissension during the Revolution was the Episcopal Church or the Church of England.[18] This denomination had three definite centers in New Hampshire—Claremont, Holderness, and Portsmouth, and in addition about 1100 widely distributed rural communicants. The Society for the Propagation of the Gospel in Foreign Parts, an Episcopal organization in Great Britain, supplied the organized parishes of Claremont and Portsmouth with rectors and sent a traveling missionary for the rural sections. In Portsmouth the Episcopal organization was known as Queen's Chapel. To it belonged almost all of the royal officials and a part of the wealthier merchants as well as substantial numbers of the middle and lower classes. Curiously the Portsmouth parish had no official rector during the Revolution. On the issue of loyalty or revolution the parish seems to have been sharply divided. With the fall of the royal government and the flight of many Loyalists that part of the congregation favorable to the Revolution gained control. They instituted a modified service obliterating all mention of the King and of England.

In sharp contrast to Portsmouth's Episcopalians was the devoutly Loyalist Claremont Church, headed by the Reverend Rana Cossit. Despite relentless persecution and heavy fines Cossit took just pride in never "omitting even the prayer for the King" all during the war period. His communicants were suspected, abused and treated with violence—in some places driven from their homes. Yet their resistance only became more dogged, and their leader seems to have kept up their morale. Claremont's stand would indicate a wide division of feeling among the Episcopalians in the province. Such a condition was probably due in no small part to the absence of an official clergyman in Portsmouth and the aggressively Loyalist leadership of the Reverend Cossit in Claremont.

Among religious faiths the Congregational was probably the mainspring of Revolutionary New Hampshire. In 1776 eighty-four of the one hundred and eighteen churches in the province were Congregational.[19] In fact the Congregational Church was the established church; only persons belonging to exempted parishes could escape paying tithes to it. The leading Congregational ministers in New Hampshire were the Reverend Jeremy Belknap of Dover, Dr. Samuel Haven of Portsmouth, the Reverend Abiel Foster of Canterbury, and the Reverend Timothy Walker of Concord. All of these men were pro-Revolutionary, though they tended to exercise a conservative influence. The Congregational parishes throughout the province followed their lead. Then too, the great majority of the Revolutionist leaders were Congregationalists.[20] Why was the Congregational Church so overwhelmingly for the Revolution? First, the faith was founded on the principle of religious democracy which logically developed into political democracy. Secondly, the Congregational clergy resented and feared the efforts of Governor Wentworth to spread the Episcopal faith, which might some day threaten their established position.[21]

Closely allied with the Congregationalists was the Presbyterian Church, an institution introduced by the large Scotch-Irish element in central New Hampshire's population.[22] Of the province's fifteen Presbyterian ministers only four refused to accede to the Association Test. Among the fifteen who were Revolutionists, Dr. Eleazar Wheelock of Hanover and the Reverend David MacGregore of the largest parish, Londonderry, were the leaders. Dr. Wheelock was forced to remain neutral for a long period because he was dependent upon Governor Wentworth for political favors and upon British friends for funds for his Indian school.[23] Yet once the Revolution was under way, he was unquestionably a patriot. He, too, had had reason to fear the Episcopal ogre in the person of Wentworth. Probably indicative of true Presbyterian sentiment was the action taken by the New England synod at its Londonderry meeting in September, 1776. It was voted that "any suspected to be inimical to the liberties of the independent states of America . . . . and who refuses to declare his allegiance to the same" should not have "a seat in this judicature."[24] The Presbyterians were on the whole inclined toward the Revolutionist party but they were frequently conservative in action because of close ties with the British Isles.

A relatively new faith in New Hampshire at the time of the Revolution was represented by the Baptist Church.[25] In 1776 this denomination had only eleven parishes in the province with but five clergymen to minister to them. Of the five Baptist ministers three signed the Association Test and two opposed it. Yet one of this opposition was the Reverend Samuel Shepard, Rockingham County's traveling missionary and the Baptist leader of the province. Furthermore, in ten of the towns where Baptists predominated considerable numbers refused the Test. The opposition of the Baptists was unusual. Baptists have usually been depicted as radical supporters of the Revolution. In searching for a possible reason for their exceptional attitude, one is impressed by the fact that the Baptists were a new faith fighting to gain exemption from the Congregational tithes. Probably they were lukewarm towards the new revolutionary régime because its leaders were almost all Congregationalists and could logically be expected to entrench their church even more firmly in any new political setup.

The final problem which arises from the preceding analysis of New Hampshire's Revolutionists and Loyalists relates to the probable number of each party in the entire state. The Association Test was submitted to a total of 9348 white males over 21 years of age. The number of signers was 8567. Excluding those who failed to subscribe for reasons of conscience or religion, there were 646 who refused for no other reason seemingly than opposition to the Revolution. This number constituted about 7 per cent of the whole. Applying this percentage to the total 16,000 men in New Hampshire of the required age, there were at the outside around 1100 adult male Loyalists in the state. Assuming that each one of these 1100 Loyalists exercised a determining influence on his family, their number probably totaled between 4500 and 5500.[26] Subtracted from the state's total population of 82,000, this left some 77,000 persons who were not Loyalists. Nor were they necessarily all Revolutionists. It is probable that in the beginning, the Revolutionist leaders did not far outnumber their Loyalist opponents. As in all political campaigns each party had its rock-bottom number of supporters. A large fluctuating central group controlled the balance of power. These centrists for reasons of similar culture and environment were probably more likely to follow the Revolutionists in crises although they possessed no rabid enthusiasm for the cause. Nevertheless, the Revolutionists ensured their control and leadership. Once they had seized the political power they made the opposition party illegal. Its activities were suppressed, and its attempts to spread counter-revolutionary propaganda were censored. It was deprived of all civil rights. The division of political opinion marked the beginning of an internal revolution within the colonies, which was fully as important as was the revolt against Great Britain.

CHAPTER 5

We most devoutly implore His Divine Goodness to protect us happily through this great conflict, to dispose our adversaries to reconciliation on reasonable terms, and thereby to relieve the empire from the calamities of civil war.

General GEORGE WASHINGTON, July 2, 1775.

Independence and Confederation

THROUGHOUT the whole first year of the war against Great Britain the majority of the disaffected colonists insisted that they had no idea of separation or independence. In New Hampshire the idea of independence was a relatively late phenomenon. On April 24, 1775, the Reverend Paine Wingate of Hampton Falls wrote to a friend, "I would not urge to measures that were cowardly or servile but cannot but hope that some plan might be devised, even in the present circumstances, for an honorable pacification if some hot and furious men who were never fit for council should hold their tongues or loose their influence."[1] In May, 1775, John Pickering, a conservative lawyer of Portsmouth, wrote to John Langdon, "If the Colonies would propose to contribute liberally towards the national expense, and recommend it to the several Assemblies to petition his Majesty for removal of the Grievances, Restoration of their violated Rights . . . . I'm well convinced that a happy Reconciliation wou'd soon be established. . . . ."[2]

Unquestionably the first warfare at Lexington and Concord on April 19 caused a vast stir of feelings. The importance of the whole affair to the radicals was to circulate the impression that the British troops were the aggressors. New Hampshire's third Provincial Congress convened at Exeter a few days after the battle to consider the expediency of any action. They immediately received a bloodthirsty epistle from the Massachusetts Committee personally delivered by its envoy, James Sullivan. This letter informed the New Hampshire congressmen that, ". . . . General Gage has suddenly commenc'd open Hostilities, by a large body of the troops under his command, secretly detached in the Night of the 18th Instant, which on the morning ensuing had actually begun the slaughter of the innocent Inhabitants in the very heart of the Country, before any intentions of that kind were suspected; & altho' the rouzed Virtue of our brethren in the Neighborhood soon compelled them to a precipitate retreat, they mark'd their savage rout with Depredations, ruins and butcheries hardly to be match'd by the armies of any civilized Nations on the Globe."[3] But the members of the Provincial Congress were not too gullible and refused to be stampeded into raising troops. Envoy Sullivan wrote to Joseph Warren in Boston, "There seems some opposition here to the assistance we have expected from this quarter. . . . ."[4] At any rate the third Provincial Congress took no action, for it was felt that not enough delegates were present to determine the true sentiment of the province.

Hundreds of men in companies from the southern New Hampshire towns flocked into Massachusetts at the first reports of fighting. These towns had been drilling men for several weeks before the time of the Battle of Lexington. Consequently they were at a high pitch of excitement, needing only the slightest incentive to begin warlike proceedings. Governor Wentworth wrote to General Gage concerning the battle, "This unfortunate transaction immediately excited great commotions in this province, and many discovered a disposition to assist the people of your government, which they have been greatly induced to by repeated accounts that the troops had actually fired first on the inhabitants, and committed great barbarities on them."[5] When the news of fighting reached northern New Hampshire, it had been equally distorted; so much so that Dr. Eleazar Wheelock of Hanover wrote to a friend, "The Colonies have ever been propence to peace and Reconciliation till these late horrid Murders & Savage Butcheries So inhumanly committed under pretence of ordering Rebells to Obedience."[6]

With such wild rumors circulating throughout the province it was no wonder that the fourth Provincial Congress assembled on May 17,

1775, with radical action in mind. Since New Hampshire already had an unofficial army of irregulars in Boston and vicinity, the Congress quickly decided to raise more troops on an official basis. A resolution to this effect was passed on May 20 with the following preamble: "Whereas by the late Acts of the British Parliament & conduct of the Ministers in pursuance thereof it appears very evident that a plan is laid, & now pursuing to subjugate this & the other American Colonies to the most abject Slavery, And the late Hostilities committed by the British Troops in our Sister Colony of the Massachusetts Bay leaves us no doubt in determining that no other way is left us to preserve our most darling Rights and Inestimable Privileges, but by immediately defending them by arms. . . . ."[7] On June 2, 1775, the Congress justified its move in an address to the province. The address stated, "Painful, beyond expression, have been those scenes of Blood and Devastation which the barbarous cruelty of British troops have placed before our eyes. Duty to God, to ourselves, to Posterity—enforced by the cries of slaughtered Innocents, have urged us to take up Arms in our Defence."[8] Such propaganda was mightily effective, particularly since the opposition could not reply.

On June 17, 1775, was fought the Battle of Bunker Hill. This battle immediately caused renewed enthusiasm among the radicals in New Hampshire. On a large scale, raw colonial troops had courageously fought the British regulars. Governor Wentworth wrote to a friend, "I observed, the Affair at Bunker's Hill made an useful impression for two days, in which time it was industriously propagated to be so greatly in favor of their own side, that they resumed fresh, and I think increased spirits."[9]

These early military successes inspired the radicals all through the colonies with a "chesty" cocksureness. The Continental Congress even approved of an invasion of Canada although by a majority of only one vote. The progress of what to the radicals seemed successful warfare made them all the more unwilling to temporize. The extremists became more extreme and the moderates more radical.

On the whole, however, the colonists were loath to place themselves in an uncompromising position. Constitutional action still carried weight with many. On July 6, 1775, the Continental Congress published a Declaration of the Causes and Necessity of Taking up Arms. Two days later the Congress prepared the famous Olive Branch Petition to the King. This petition did not reach Britain until September

1, 1775. But George III, because he did not recognize the legal existence of the Congress, would not receive the petition. On the question of whether the petition offered ground for reconciliation, it was resolved in the House of Lords by a vote of more than two to one that it did not. This summary rejection of the petition was undoubtedly a strategic error on the part of the British government. Legally and constitutionally their action was correct. Yet popular petitions carried great weight in the colonies as an ancient, constitutional means of obtaining redress. Arbitrary rejection of such petitions could be viewed in no other light than as a condemnation without hearing and a deliberate snub of public opinion. Hence the total rejection was an inexpedient and unwise policy. It had a very depressing effect on the conservative and moderating influence in the right wing of the radicals. An additional factor contributing to the creation of a hostile attitude was the British action of August 23, 1775. On this date the King proclaimed the colonies in a state of rebellion. A Philadelphia conservative in the Continental Congress wrote that this proclamation made many of the people "desperate" and added, "This is putting the Halter about our Necks, and we may as well die by the Sword as be hang'd like Rebels."[10] Apparently Lord North and the King thought that the uprising was nothing more than the suppression of a passive majority by a virulent minority and that the correct remedy was to subdue this minority. In their characterization of the situation they were partially right, but their remedy only put the radical party in a favorable position to attract more and more members from those colonists who had hitherto been neutral.

On July 1, 1775, the British Lords of the Admiralty instructed the navy in colonial waters to begin such operations on the New England seacoast as should be judged most effectual to suppress the rebellion. Portsmouth, New Hampshire's only seaport, had suspected such designs and resolved to be prepared.[11] In the middle of August two large forts were built at the narrows of the harbor under the direction of the "town engineer." The British navy, meanwhile, proceeded with occasional bombardments along the coast. Stonington and Bristol were fired upon; and on October 18, Falmouth (now Portland, Maine) was bombarded and burned. Four hundred buildings were destroyed and one hundred and sixty families left destitute. Portsmouth expected that it would be the next in line for destruction, and the town became the scene of a great war-time panic. Its Committee of Safety sent a hurried request for aid to General Washington at Boston, [12] who immediately dispatched General Sullivan to the scene. Sullivan arrived on October 23 and in a short time organized a system of defense.[13] Nevertheless the people's fears were not calmed for a long time; false rumors circulated repeatedly. Reconciliation with Great Britain was hardly furthered by such nerve-torturing suspense.

The experience of New Hampshire under several months of government by the Provincial Congress had hardly been satisfactory to many of the radicals. Although the town governments continued to function as under royal control, the county governments and courts had collapsed. Law, contracts, and debts were not strictly recognized nor enforced. The Provincial Congress because of its temporary character and haphazard methods of operation found difficulty in building up confidence in the revolutionary government or borrowing money on public credit. On July 8 chairman Meshech Weare of the Committee of Safety wrote to the Continental Congress, "But we greatly desire some other Regulations as our present situation is attended with many Difficultys; but shall not attempt anything of that kind without Direction."[14] Apparently there was no advice forthcoming from the Congress. On September 1, 1775, President Thornton of the Provincial Congress wrote to New Hampshire's delegates, "And if it should happen that a Plan for the establishing a form of Government in the respective Colonies should come under your consideration—You will have a Particular Regard to this Colony. That our establishment be such as shall secure our essential Rights, as fully as in the other Colonies."[15] In early November New Hampshire's Provincial Congress began work on a plan for redistricting and reapportioning the representation of the towns in the legislature. Such a plan was adopted on November 14. The Congress dissolved on the next day with the understanding that the new provincial congress was to be elected on the basis of this plan. The towns were asked to instruct their delegates either for or against the proposal to resolve the new congress into a House of Representatives and to set up a form of government.

In the meantime the Continental Congress had acted on New Hampshire's request for advice. On November 3 it had resolved, "That it be recommended to the provincial Convention of New Hampshire, to call a full and free representation of the people, and that the representatives, if they think it necessary, establish such a form of government, as in their judgment will best produce the happiness of the people, and most effectually secure peace and good order in the province, during the continuance of the present dispute between G[reat] Britain and the colonies."[16] The fifth Provincial Congress met on December 21, 1775, against the background of this resolution. After deliberating for several weeks a tentative plan of government was ratified by a majority of two to one. On January 5, 1776, the Congress formed itself into a House of Representatives and next proceeded to elect an upper house, designated the Council. Thus New Hampshire was the first colony to set up a state government. Among the reasons for this action, given in the preamble of the Constitution, the following deserve to be included here. "The Sudden & Abrupt Departure of his Excellency *John Wentworth* Esqr our Late Governor, and Several of the Council, Leaving us Destitute of Legislation, and no Executive Courts being open to Punish Criminal Offenders; whereby the Lives and Propertys of the Honest People of this Colony, are Liable to the Machinations & Evil Designs of wicked men; Therefore for the Preservation of Peace and good order, and for the Security of the Lives and Properties of the Inhabitants of this Colony, We Conceive ourselves Reduced to the Necessity of establishing A Form of Government to Continue During the Present Unhappy and Unnatural Contest with Great Britain; Protesting & Declaring that we Never Sought to throw off our Dependance upon Great Britain. . . . ."[17]

Although the greater number of the towns had approved the establishment of an independent government, many became fearful of the results of such action once it had been taken. Portsmouth held a town meeting to remonstrate against the new Constitution.[18] On January 12 twelve members of the House protested against the organization of a state government, "Because it appears assuming for so Small & Inconsiderable a Colony to take the Lead in a Matter of So great Importance . . . . Because our Constituents never Expected us to make a New Form of Government, But only to set the Judicial & Executive wheels in Motion . . . . Because it appears to us too much like Setting up an Independency on the Mother Country."[19] This protest was followed on January 18 by petitions from the towns of Portsmouth, Dover, Newington, Rochester, Stratham, North Hampton, Rye, New Market, Kensington, Greenland, and Brentwood —all of which criticized the new government.[20]

There was indeed a good deal of sentiment in New Hampshire

against anything which even remotely resembled independence. On January 9, 1776, the *New Hampshire Gazette* published an anonymous letter which had resounding repercussions because of its subject matter. The unknown writer observed, ". . . . We began the Controversy, on this Principle, to seek Redress of Grievances: since, we have lost Sight of the Object, and are in Quest of what will terminate most certainly in our Ruin, & Destruction;—I mean Independency upon Great Britain; a Step that the Public are exceedingly averse to; but the Public in general are ignorant of the Design & Tendency of the Conduct of their Representatives. . . . . Soon will they see it [Independency] arise in Order before their Eyes, attended with all its hellish Pageantry, so closely connected with other seeming necessitous Measures; that to oppose one, you must a Multitude of others; so that no prudent Man can withstand it. . . . ." Continuing the writer argued, "Can we gain independency? . . . . A Continent of 1000 Miles Sea Coast defending themselves without one Ship of War against 310 Battle Ships compleatly manned and fitted—A Country that can pay but 30 Thousand Men, at War with a Nation that has paid, and can pay 150 thousand—A Country of three Millions of Inhabitants, fighting with a Nation of 15 Millions— A Country that can raise but 1 Mil. of Money at War with a Nation who can raise 20 Mils. in Specie. A Country without Arms, without Ammunition, without Trade, contending with a Nation that enjoys the whole in the fullest Latitude."[21] Was it any wonder that the article created an uproar in the House of Representatives at Exeter? Publisher Daniel Fowle of the *Gazette* was summoned before a legislative committee of inquiry. When he refused to divulge the name of the letter-writer, his paper was suspended—an example of Revolutionary censorship of the press. The *Gazette* did not appear again for several weeks and then only under a new editor and a new name, as *Freeman's Journal.*[22]

Turning from provincial to continental issues, the opening of the year 1776 marked the appearance of some especially effective propaganda in favor of independence. On January 9 there appeared in Philadelphia the first copies of Tom Paine's pamphlet—COMMON SENSE. Full of violent language, emotional appeal and some fallacious reasoning, the pamphlet was an open argument for independence. The writer advanced the theory of the "natural rights of man" —an empirical doctrine after Locke and Rousseau. He upheld the principle of strict non-interference or laissez-faire by government, the only legitimate function of which was to provide "freedom and security" for the people—an anarchic philosophy. Instead of the divine right of a hereditary monarchy Paine extolled the divine right of the people and of public opinion. COMMON SENSE "carried ready conviction to the man of ordinary 'common sense,' who, impatient of the fine-spun political disquisitions and cautious policies of past years, was eager for a political philosophy of plain, unqualified phrases and for a definite program of action in which he could take aggressive part."[23]

The pamphlet had an immediate influence on Dr. Josiah Bartlett, New Hampshire's delegate in the Continental Congress, who wrote to John Langdon on January 13, "On consideration there will not appear anything so terrible in that idea, [independence] as they might at first apprehend, if Britain should force us to break off all connections with her."[24] The remoteness of New Hampshire, coupled with the tremendous demand for the pamphlet, prevented it from reaching there for several months. On March 4 David MacClure in Portsmouth wrote to Dr. Eleazar Wheelock in Hanover, "I was in hopes to have been able to forward the late famous publication, intitled *common sense*—but none of them have yet come to hand from the Printer."[25] By June the demand for the pamphlet had become so great in New Hampshire that the publisher of *Freeman's Journal* decided to start printing it. On June 22, 1776, and in subsequent issues his paper ran the following advertisement:

> *The Book so much admired, entitled*
> *COMMON SENSE,*
> *may be had at the Printing Office*[26]

Notwithstanding that sentiment in New Hampshire was opposed to independence at the beginning of 1776 the colony was inevitably drifting toward that goal. The new state government was functioning regularly and satisfactorily. Its every act was in effect an assertion of independence. And the people were surprised at the ease with which they were governing themselves. The new government interfered to a minimum degree with popular activity, and people began to prefer it vastly to the former régime.

In the field of national policy the Continental Congress had replied to the British Prohibition of Trade Act of December 22, 1775, by issuing commissions to privateers and opening the American ports to foreign ships on March 1, 1776. The British use of mercenary troops excited feelings of repugnance in all the colonies from New Hampshire to Georgia. Soon the Congress opened negotiations with other European powers. Step by step independence was becoming an actuality even if unacknowledged. On June 7 Richard Henry Lee of Virginia offered the following resolution: "Resolved that these United Colonies are, and of right, ought to be, Free and Independent States. . . . ."[27] Consideration of Lee's motion was postponed until July 1, pending action by the separate colonies. Yet on June 11 a committee, of which Thomas Jefferson was a member, was appointed to draft a declaration of colonial independence.

By an unusual coincidence New Hampshire acted likewise on the same day. News of the intended action of Virginia's delegates had reached New Hampshire before June 7, and sentiment in the two houses of the legislature was fast becoming too radical to postpone the matter. So on June 11 a joint committee of six was selected by the Council and the House to "make a Dra't of a Declaration of this General Assembly for Independence of the United Colonies on, Great Britain."[28] Four days later independence was unanimously voted with the following justification: "That Notwithstanding all the dutiful Petitions and Decent Remonstrances from the American Colonies, and the utmost Exertions of their best Friends in England on their Behalf, The British Ministry, Arbitrary & Vindictive, are yet Determined to Reduce by Fire and Sword our Bleeding Country, to their absolute obedience; and for this Purpose, in Addition to their own forces, have Engaged great Numbers of Foreign Mercenaries, who may now be on their passage here, accompanied by a Formidable Fleet to Ravage and Plunder the Sea-Coast. . . . ."[29]

On July 2 Richard Henry Lee's resolution again came up for consideration in the Continental Congress and was passed. Two days later a draft of the Declaration of Independence was adopted. The delegates signed the Declaration at some time during the succeeding months, although the signatures were not actually complete till 1781. Two of New Hampshire's delegates, Josiah Bartlett and William Whipple, probably signed on August 2, 1776. But Matthew Thornton, the third signer, was not elected to fill the vacancy occasioned by John Langdon's resignation until September 12, and he did not sign until November 4, 1776.

On July 18 the Declaration of Independence was proclaimed in New

Hampshire. In Portsmouth it was received "with lively expressions of joy notwithstanding their former votes."[30] Major General Nathaniel Folsom of the state militia wrote to Josiah Bartlett at Philadelphia, "The Declaration is well receiv'd here . . . . It will (I doubt not) have a happy tendency to unite us in the present glorious Struggle, for by it many of the objections of wavering (tho' perhaps otherwise well disposed) persons are entirely answered. . . . . Who, my dear Friend, among us, two Years ago thought of withstanding the Mighty Monarch of Britain aided by his Almighty (as he calls them & they call themselves) Parliament."[31]

Concomitant with the idea of independence in Lee's resolution of June 7 had been a proposal for a confederation of the colonies. A plan of confederation had been submitted to the Continental Congress by Benjamin Franklin as early as July 21, 1775. On June 12, 1776, the day after the appointment of a committee to draft a declaration of independence, the Congress had selected a committee to draft a form of confederation. Prominent on the committee were John Dickinson and Samuel Adams. Josiah Bartlett was New Hampshire's member. On July 12, 1776, this committee had reported a first draft and on August 20 a second draft.

In New Hampshire sentiment for a confederation had existed early in the Revolution. This sentiment had originated among the mercantile interests on the seacoast, who desired a central government to regulate foreign affairs and trade. On May 18, 1776, William Whipple of Portsmouth wrote to John Langdon, "A Confederation, permanent and lasting, ought, in my opinion, to be the next thing, and I hope it is not far off; if so, then the establishment of foreign agencies, I hope, will fill our ports with ships from all parts of the world."[32] Later in July, Langdon wrote to Josiah Bartlett, "I was happy to find that the Confederation of the Colonies was like to take place soon, as I think it a most Necessary step; —It has always appeared to me to be good policy, hitherto not to interfere with the internal Policies of any Colony but the Matter is now very Different as the whole Continent have taken Government. The Congress will no doubt Act as a legal body and no doubt interfere in any Government that seems to go wrong—"[33] Langdon envisioned a strong central administration.

In the Congress deliberation on a confederation government began in early August, 1776. From the very first, certain sectional, political and economic issues were apparent. It was realized by many that these obstacles were of major importance. William Whipple, a New Hampshire delegate, wrote home from Philadelphia to a friend, "I fear a permanent one [Confederation] will never be settled; tho the most material articles are I think got thro', so as to give great offence to some, but to my Satisfaction."[34] Argument and discussion continued for the balance of 1776 and most of 1777. Finally on November 15, 1777, the Articles of Confederation were adopted and transmitted to the states for approval.

The new government provided for a congress of delegates from all the states, each state having one vote. In the interim of meetings of the congress a committee consisting of one member from each state was to act as the governmental body. A procedure for settling disputes between states was established. With the consent of nine states, the congress had full power over making war and peace, might enter into treaties, regulate privateering, coin or borrow money, ask each state to appropriate funds in proportion to the value of its surveyed land, ask each state to raise troops in proportion to the number of its white inhabitants, and appoint a commander-in-chief of the army. Amendments to the Articles required unanimous consent of the thirteen states.

Delegate Nathaniel Folsom on November 21, 1777, wrote home to New Hampshire, warning of objectionable features in the Eighth Article, which required each state to lay Continental taxes in proportion to the value of its surveyed land. Folsom thought that this article was unjust, since a state's wealth was not always proportional to the value of its lands. Then too, negroes—the main source of wealth in the South—were exempted.[35] The Articles were received in New Hampshire on December 24, 1777. The legislature at once ordered 250 copies printed and distributed. The Articles were then submitted to a plebiscite of the towns at their various town meetings in the winter of 1777-1778.

Fortunately chairman Weare of the Committee of Safety preserved among his papers returns of the plebiscite from thirty-six towns.[36] Out of these thirty-six towns, sixteen approved the Articles in their entirety. Portsmouth voted general approval but did not instruct its representatives. Sixteen towns objected to the apportioning of each state's tax quota on the basis of the value of its surveyed land. It was generally held that this provision would bear heavily on New Hampshire, whose wealth consisted mostly of real estate, and would give those states with a large volume of trade, large stocks of merchandize, personal property, and slaves an unfair exemption and advantage. Thus the town of Marlboro at its meeting on January 6, 1778, voted "that all the articles In the Confederrece Be concured with oute the Eight artecle which wee Loock uppon that Everre Reasidant In the United States Should Bare thair Eaguel Proporshon acording to what Thay Poses Barth In Real and Parsonnal Estate."[37] Seven towns urged that each state's quota of troops should not be apportioned according to the total of white inhabitants only but that the population base should also include negroes. In four towns declaration of war by the congress was regarded as a power of such importance as to demand unanimous approval of the states instead of the consent of merely nine. The town of Wilton made the following objection: "The Ninth Article, the first clause, grants to the United States in Congress assembled, the sole and exclusive Right and power of Determining on Peace and War. . . . . Is it not a power Greater than the King of great Brittain in Council or with the House of Lords ever had. . . . . ? May we not suppose that the Members of that August Body [Continental Congress], conscious of the Rectitude of their own Intentions; have no Room left to Suspect the Integrity of any future Members thereof?"[38] The town of Hawke (now Danville) protested against the binding of all of the states in any matter by the consent of only nine. Such action was construed as "too Perogetive"; the town observed, "We Cannot Consent to So Small a Majority."[39] Two towns suggested that the requirement of unanimity for amendment of the articles should be modified so as to permit amendment by majority vote.

On February 24, 1778, the plebiscite completed, both houses of the New Hampshire legislature met in joint convention to consider the Articles. In committee of the whole the members deliberated throughout the morning and passed the first seven articles without serious dissent. Opponents of the Confederation centered their attack on the Eighth Article which provided for the apportioning of each state's tax quota according to the value of its surveyed land. Unable to reach agreement the members adjourned for several hours. When discussion was resumed in the afternoon, the disputed article was finally passed, whereupon the opposition collapsed. The last five articles were quickly approved.[40] On March 4 it was resolved by the House and Council "That we do agree to said articles of Confederation, perpetual union &c. And do for ourselves & Constituents engage that the same shall be inviolably observed by this State."[41] The last formality was fulfilled in the Continental Congress on July 9, 1778, when one of New Hampshire's delegates, Josiah Bartlett, signed the Articles on behalf of the state.[42] The other delegate, John Wentworth, Jr., was ill at this time and did not sign until a few weeks later.

However, the final chapter had not been written. The Articles required unanimous ratification of the states before taking effect. James Lovell of Massachusetts aptly described the situation when on July 14 he wrote to William Whipple of New Hampshire, "Nine States have signed the Confederation and there is no doubt but, Georgia, Delaware and Jersey will soon sign. Maryland will take airs and plague us, but upon our determination to confederate with 12 will do as she has always before done—come in without grace."[43] Delegate Lovell was an accurate prognosticator. Maryland did not sign the Articles until March 1, 1781.

The new government marked a complete reversal of the centralizing tendencies of the British colonial system. The Articles established no independent executive body. All the states were equal, and the congress was only a "village debating society." There were no national courts to facilitate collection of just interstate debts. The central government had no control over state finance. State laws lacked uniformity in meaning as well as in enforcement. The central government could not regulate trade. What could have been a more direct antithesis of the top-heavy centralized machinery of the old régime?

CHAPTER 6

Whenever anything decisive and important is set on foot, designing men will always find out a Diana, or some other favourite Goddess, in danger, and under her banners, with Great Zeal, Alarm EVEN *the honest and well-meaning among the Citizens, and excite them violently to oppose the measure. . . . . I have known a people whose* GRAND MULTIFORM'D SANHEDRIM *were often-times in the midst of a Fog.*

NATHANIEL PEABODY, 1780.[1]

New Hampshire in the Continental Congress

THE one institution of the American Revolution, in the denunciation of which historians have been almost unanimous, has been the Continental Congress. The Congress was in practically continuous session from 1775 to the end of the war, and upon it has fallen the blame for nearly all of the shortcomings of the American Revolutionists, since it was the only national governing body. The incompetence of the Congress was naturally owing in some degree to the sheer perversity of human nature.[2] Special interests, personal ambition, emphasis upon pure materialism, bickering and delay—all of these factors were obstacles to efficiency. Furthermore the Congress had no well established system of administration to take over from the previous government; it had to develop its own. There was no unified national sentiment in America in 1776. In reality the Congress was constituted as the agency of thirteen equal states, and it had no more power than those states unanimously chose to delegate to it. To make matters worse, the sectional differences which created interstate hostility also found their way into the congressional proceedings. All of these difficulties would have rendered government by the Continental Congress difficult in peace-time. But in the prosecution of a war for which the country was not prepared and during which organization was forced to take the form of hasty improvisation, the Congress was well nigh powerless to work efficiently.

The life of the delegates was little conducive to facilitating able conduct of the public business. Quarters in the city of Philadelphia were poor, and the heat was unbearable at times during the summer months. The delegates were frequently in poor health. Delays in state action and the slowness of travel often caused the members to be late in attending sessions.[3] In 1778 William Whipple, New Hampshire's delegate, wrote to Meshech Weare, "Only nine States have been represented since my arrival 'till within three days. there are now Eleven States barely represented. this tardiness in the States or their Delegates, besides retarding the most important Business makes it exceeding fatiguing to those that do attend."[4] The delegates were never certain when they might be relieved of their offices, since the lengths of their respective terms were dependent upon the whims of their state legislatures. The states were often slow to instruct their delegates upon important measures leaving them in grave doubt as to the course of action expected from them.

The custom of having each state represented on all important committees placed a heavy strain upon the delegates, especially if a state happened to have only one delegate present. In 1777 William Whipple of New Hampshire wrote to Josiah Bartlett, "Col. Thornton intend[s] seting out in a few days. I leave you judge what my situation will then be, as I shall then be obliged to attend some committees that he is now on, besides, the business of the two committees that I am now on, is daily increasing."[5] Delegate Nathaniel Folsom had a similar complaint, and he wrote to Bartlett, "my Duty is Very hard, and if you have any Comepashon left for me, hope you will Joyne Congress Soone, as the buisiness is too much for one to live [under]."[6]

As the war years passed and the paper money depreciated, it became increasingly difficult to persuade able men to serve in the Congress because of the uncertainty of pay and the increasing cost of living. The states were often very niggardly in paying the delegates' salaries. Furthermore, persons living on stipulated salaries inevitably suffered during the period of inflation. To obtain funds the delegates at Philadelphia usually drew drafts upon their respective states payable at ten days' sight. Frequently these drafts were not diligently honored to the full amount or else were not paid in hard money. In the later war years it became the customary procedure to make a draft payable to Robert Morris, the Continental financier, in return for needed money. Morris would then forward the draft to the Continental prize agent in the state upon which it was drawn. The agent merely charged the state for that amount of his expenditures. In 1780 John Sullivan, New Hampshire's delegate, wrote to Meshech Weare, "I wish . . . . to know what Wages I am to expect (in real value) as the duty I owe to myself and Family will no longer permit me to serve the Publick in the highest and most perplexing offices to the ruin of my Fortune . . . ."[7] The following year Sullivan amplified his complaint to Weare when he wrote, "I am willing to Submit to any Inconvenience to Serve my Country but to be an Embassador and a Beggar at the same time would be disgraceful, not to me but to my constituents."[8]

The rules of procedure followed by the Congress were not at all suited to an organization characterized by so much personal and sectional jealousy. Although there were generally only twenty or thirty delegates present out of a membership of fifty-five, they took a surprisingly long time to accomplish a small amount of business. There was no general rule upon limitation of debate. Endless amendments could be offered to the measures under discussion. Foes of different measures adopted all sorts of sharp parliamentary strategy to delay action. The journals of the Congress are filled with motions of the previous question, motions to postpone, to table indefinitely, to reconsider, and motions to adjourn and thus throw the measure under discussion into the category of unfinished business. The Congress was scarcely ever able to finish its order of the day as scheduled. It was frequently necessary to take as many as six roll-calls on preliminary technicalities before voting upon the main question. In 1778 Josiah Bartlett of New Hampshire wrote to William Whipple, "I am sorry to say that sometimes matters of very small importance waste a good deal of precious time, by the long and repeated speeches and chicanery of gentlemen who will not wholly throw off the lawyer even in Congress."[9] In a subsequent letter to John Langdon, Bartlett added, "But the multiplicity of business that is daily crowding on Congress and the time it takes to transact matters in so large an Assembly filled with lawyers and other gentlemen who love to talk as much as they will not allow me to hope that our affairs will be very soon properly arranged. . . . ."[10]

A further obstacle to efficient conduct of the congressional business was the horde of office-seekers and persons demanding raises in salary which swarmed about Philadelphia. In 1780 Nathaniel Peabody of New Hampshire wrote to Meshech Weare deploring "the intollerable burden . . . . in Supporting Legions of Continental Sinecures who appear in Swarms like Locusts, upon the Land of Egypt, and not only draw Numberless rations; but are in every other respect rioting upon the blood and Treasures of the virtuous Citizens (if any Such there be) in these united States."[11] When the Reverend Duché, chaplain of the Congress, protested to Washington in regard to the meagerness of his salary, Nathaniel Folsom of New Hampshire was outraged. He wrote to Josiah Bartlett, "I inclose you a Coppey of a letter from the Revt. mr. Ducha to general Washington that you may See what a Judas wase a Chaplin to congress."[12]

Two schools of governmental theory were represented within the Continental Congress. The one school maintained that the executive and administrative functions of the Continental government could be conducted by standing committees of the Congress. The other maintained that administrative efficiency could only be brought about by the establishment of independent executive departments. Delegate Josiah Bartlett of New Hampshire was a strong opponent of the standing committee system. In 1778 he wrote to John Langdon, "I am sorry to say our Treasury, Marine and Commercial Affairs are in a very bad situation owing to their being conducted by members of Congress who can spare but little of their time to transact them, and are so constantly changing that before they get acquainted with the business they leave Congress and new members totally ignorant of the past transactions are appointed in their stead."[13] The standing committee system prevailed from 1775 to 1780. Usually the committee members were so engrossed in trivial and personal details that they could give but little attention to matters of real emergency character. The policies of the several standing committees lacked the least vestige of unity of purpose. The committees were entirely dependent upon the Congress for their power and could not act independently without specific authorization. The Board of Treasury, for example, could not order payment of accounts against the Continental government.[14] It could merely recommend that the Congress appropriate the required sum of money. The Congress usually saw no necessity for immediate action upon such recommendations and might postpone them, amend or reject them, or refer them to a committee for investigation. Political expediency rather than public service was the byword of congressional administration. It was not until 1781 that the supporters of independent executive departments succeeded in gaining their objective. Before that time the system of standing committees had nearly lost the war.

In another respect the procedure of the Continental Congress was equally detrimental to an effective prosecution of the war. This related to the matter of appointing and promoting general officers and of instructing them as to the proper military measures to be taken in the field. The New Hampshire delegates continually objected to the appointments and promotions made after the Battle of Saratoga, particularly those gained by the Gates and Wilkinson clique. On January 2, 1778, delegate Nathaniel Folsom wrote to Josiah Bartlett, "[I have] Constantly opposed the makeing allmost all the general officers that have been made Since I have been here, it appearing to me they were made more upon the Principle of Intrest or frindship, then Justice and ecquity, and the Consequences that have followed has Confirmed me in that opinion. grate uneasiness in the army has been the Sure and sertaine Consequence . . . ."[15]

When the Congress in 1776 appointed Horatio Gates to the position of major general over the head of Brigadier General John Sullivan of New Hampshire, who was Gates's senior in rank, Sullivan became incensed and signified his intention of resigning. Thomas Jefferson in the Continental Congress wrote to Richard Henry Lee, "General Sullivan . . . . came here to resign on Gates' appointment. His letter of resignation was just in on Friday. It was referred to this morning that a proper rap of the knuckles might be prepared, but on the advice of his friends he asked leave to withdraw it and repair to his duty."[16] At the opening of the year 1777 there occurred a vacancy among the Continental brigadier-generalships due to the retirement of James Reed of New Hampshire. Colonel John Stark of the First New Hampshire Regiment was the senior New Hampshire colonel and according to custom, next in line for the promotion. Nevertheless, the Congress appointed Colonel Enoch Poor of the Second New Hampshire Regiment to the coveted position. Stark accordingly resigned his commission in disgust. During the summer of 1777 he was given command of a brigade of the New Hampshire militia which was raised to meet Burgoyne's invasion. The state instructed Stark to coöperate with the Continental army, if he saw fit to do so. Stark, however, preferred to keep an independent command. General Lincoln wrote to General Schuyler concerning Stark's attitude, "He seems to be exceedingly soured & thinks he hath not had justice done him by Congress. He is determined not to join the Continental army until the Congress give him his rank therein. . . . ."[17] When Stark's attitude became known in the Continental Congress, a great furore was aroused. The Southern states led by Maryland's ever-disgruntled Samuel Chase became "very warm on the occasion, threw out many illiberal reflections on General Stark, and some on the Legislative authority of the State of New Hampshire."[18] On August 19, 1777, the Congress passed a resolution censuring Stark's instructions as "destructive of military subordination, and highly prejudicial to the common cause at this crisis." On August 21 there arrived news of Stark's victory at Bennington, stilling the criticism. Finally on October 4, 1777, the Congress elected Stark to a Continental brigadier-generalship, thus giving him a belated recognition.[19]

Perhaps the greatest bar to congressional harmony was the spirit of sectionalism which overshadowed all of the proceedings. This sectionalism was based partly upon the idea of state sovereignty, in accordance with which all the states were held to be sovereign and equal and the actions of the Congress were thought to bind no state without its consent. On March 7, 1779, William Whipple of New Hampshire wrote to Josiah Bartlett, "I wonder much that a court of Law should be in doubt whether a Resolution of Congress can superceed the Law of a *Sovereign* State however I hope in time N. H. as well as the other States will feel the importance of Sovereignty."[20] But there also existed a sectional attitude which was founded upon fundamental differences in the society and economy of the various states. The New England states tended to vote as a bloc upon various social and economic questions. The Southern states had a similar tendency while the Middle Atlantic states were often divided between the New England and Southern points of view.

It was in the discussion of the Articles of Confederation that these interstate differences developed into sharp antagonisms. Upon the question as to how many votes each state should have in the proposed confederation, it was at first suggested that each state should have one vote for every 50,000 of population. It was also proposed that each state's vote should be proportional to the amount of taxes paid by it. New Hampshire as a small state voted against both of these proposals, which were, of course, supported by the larger states.[21] As the Thirteenth Article was finally adopted each state was to be allowed one vote. This provision was supported by New Hampshire's delegate. On October 14, 1777, Article Nine relating to the apportioning of direct taxes in case of war was under discussion in the Congress.[22] It was moved that the taxes be apportioned among the states according to the value of each state's surveyed real estate. This motion was opposed by New Hampshire and the New England states but supported by the five Southern states as it had no provision for taxing slaves as property. The motion finally passed by a vote of five states to four. At the same time there was brought up the question of how many delegates each state should be allowed in the Confederation Congress.[23] It was proposed that no state be allowed more than seven delegates nor be permitted to send less than two. This proposal was opposed by New Hampshire, Rhode Island, and New Jersey, all small states, because they were unwilling to incur the expense of supporting more than one delegate. Discussion of the western land claims of the larger states under the proposed confederation occupied the attention of the Congress from October 15 to October 30, 1777. New Hampshire and other small states, having no western land aspirations, consistently vetoed all schemes for a confederation which would confirm the western land claims to the various claimant states.[24] Thus the small states took a nationalistic attitude on this question, but not from an unselfish motive.

An issue rooted in the very depths of the theory of state sovereignty was the question of delegating to the Continental Congress the power to levy tariffs. In early 1781 the Continental Congress recommended to the states that they empower the Congress to levy a five per cent duty upon all imports for purposes of raising revenue. To be effective the unanimous delegation of this power to the Congress by the states was necessary. New Hampshire readily assented to the recommendation and on April 6, 1781, passed the necessary legislation.[25] Less fortunate was the congressional proposal in other states. On January 9, 1783, delegate John Taylor Gilman of New Hampshire wrote to Josiah Bartlett, "The State of Rhode Island (you are Undoubtedly informed) have Unanimously Rejected the plan of an Impost, Virginia have Repealed their act and at present I See no prospect of Congress having any Funds on which to Secure their Creditors. . . . . The Conduct of some States Seems to be Such as tho' they Expected each State would be obliged to Settle with their own Citizens. For my own part I hope the Confederation will be Strengthened and that we Shall Continue United for a long time to Come, but if other States make Use of Such Policy, will it not be necessary for N. H. to do so too."[26]

New Hampshire and the New England bloc were none too favorable to the French and other foreign officers who demanded high rank in the Continental army.[27] The Southern states on the other hand welcomed the advent of these noble soldiers of fortune. This issue illustrated a conflict between New England democracy and Southern aristocracy, and a similar issue arose in the controversy over officers' pay.[28] The New England states were constantly opposed to a system of half-pay for life for officers. This savored too much of a pensioned aristocracy. The Southern states, on the other hand, favored a half-pay pension for the very reason that their northern opponents disapproved of it. A compromise plan was agreed upon by the Congress at the end of the war whereby the officers were to receive a bonus of full pay for five years. New Hampshire and Rhode Island opposed this plan to the bitter end, although it passed on March 22, 1783.

During the early part of 1780 the Congress was deliberating over a system of supply requisitions to be levied upon the states. A schedule whereby each state was to be given a certain amount of specie credit for each kind of supplies furnished was in process of evolution from February 17 to February 25, 1780. The New England states were to supply meat and rum; the Southern states grain and foodstuffs. This period was characterized for the most part by quibbling between the two sections as to how much monetary credit should be allowed for each type of provision, each section fearing that the other might gain undue advantage.[29] In the end the Southern states succeeded in having grain and foodstuffs priced at 200 per cent in advance of the 1774 price level whereas the rum and beef of the New England states were priced at but 50 to 100 per cent in advance of the same price level.

It was perhaps on the issues of currency expansion and national expenditure that the most consistent sectional cleavage was exhibited.[30] New England after 1778 favored stabilization of the currency and economy in national expenditures. The Southern states with their agrarian economy generally favored currency expansion and opposed deflationary policies. It should be recalled that the Southern states were responsible for 92 per cent of the total state currency issued during the Revolution.[31] This in some measure explains the Southern opposition to the 40 to 1 redemption plan which was approved by the Congress on March 18, 1780.

As early as 1779 there began a discussion in the Continental Congress of possible terms of peace with Great Britain.[32] New Hampshire and the New England states from the first demanded that recognition of the American rights to participate in the northeastern fisheries off the coast of Newfoundland and Labrador, should be an indispensable prerequisite to any peace agreement with Britain. The Southern states were opposed to making this a condition of peace, since they had not the least material interest at stake. New Hampshire and Massachusetts on the other hand, were equally hostile toward making the principle of free navigation of the Mississippi River a necessary condition of peace. To the Southern states with western land claims this New England attitude seemed sacrilegious. Fortunately the Treaty of 1783 contained ample provision for the fishing rights and for free navigation of the Mississippi, thus ensuring its approval by both sections.[33]

Nearly all of the states supplied a high order of talent to the councils of the Continental Congress. While New Hampshire sent no great leaders to Philadelphia, several of its delegates had high ideals of public service and were distinctly above the average in ability. Any attempt to evaluate the services of the state's delegates could not help giving the foremost position to William Whipple of Portsmouth. Whipple was one of the most popular and respected members of the Congress. Especially valuable was his wide experience and knowledge in marine affairs. He was also a warm supporter of the Continental navy. During his two years in the Congress Whipple was active in debate and served upon such important committees as the Marine, Secret Correspondence, Commerce, Claims, and others relating to military affairs and finance. On November 26, 1779, he was elected one of the three Commissioners of the newly established Board of Admiralty. Also exhibiting conspicuous ability in the business of the Continental Congress was New Hampshire's delegate, Dr. Josiah Bartlett of Kingston. Bartlett served during three periods in the Congress. His medical experience was of great aid; in fact he was regarded as the congressional medical expert. Like Whipple he was interested in the construction of a Continental navy. Nathaniel Folsom of Exeter also represented New Hampshire for three terms. He was a member of the Board of Treasury and achieved recognition for his aggressive, singlehanded representation of the state during the deliberations on the Articles of Confederation. Major General John Sullivan of Durham was another able New Hampshire delegate, representing the state both before and after his period of service in the Continental army. He was a close friend of John Adams and an excellent orator. It was Sullivan who wrote the original draft of the Declaration and Resolves of the first Continental Congress in 1774. Upon his retirement from the army his military knowledge was an asset in the congressional debates. He was a sound money advocate and favored the levying of a tariff for revenue by the Continental Congress. Other noteworthy New Hampshire delegates were Nathaniel Peabody of Atkinson, conspicuous in the field of army organization, and Samuel Livermore of Holderness, New Hampshire's legal agent in her dispute with New York over the New Hampshire Grants, now included in Vermont.

Considering the ability of the men in the Continental Congress, it is surprising that its business was so haphazardly conducted. Yet among the members there was no closely knit majority united by a common, specific aim. There was no leader to seize dictatorial powers and enforce his will upon the Congress. In fact the lack of group organization was a triumph of individualism in politics. Republican government was shown in its weakest and most inefficient aspect. Nor did the Congress readily improve in respect to the efficiency of its operations as the war years passed. No one was more conscious of this than a contemporary observer, delegate Nathaniel Peabody of New Hampshire, who wrote in 1779, " . . . . When I take a retrospective view of those truly Patriotic Characters which at first adorned the Councils of these United States and laid a foundation for a Vast Empire, an Asylum for Civil and Religious *Liberty* . . . . and at the same time reflect how the scene is now changed; when I see Banqueting, Pageantry, Luxury, Dissipation and unhappy disputes and divisions . . . . I am filled with solemn surprize. . . . . "[34]

In view of the irrepressible disagreements which plagued the Congress, it is surprising that the delegates were able to accomplish as much as they did. It must be remembered that the Continental Congress did act as the national directing agency, that it supervised the war, that it conducted foreign relations, and consummated the French alliance and the final treaty of peace with England. To argue that the Revolution was won in spite of the Congress is beside the point. Perhaps the most valuable contribution of the Continental Congress in the long run was its service in bringing about better interstate understanding. The Congress was an assembly, an open forum, where the delegates of the thirteen sovereign states met upon a common ground and aired their differences. Inevitably they grew to understand each other better and to appreciate and make allowance for their sectional jealousies. It was in this way that they were enabled to visualize the necessity for a higher sovereignty than that of the states. The Continental Congress was perhaps a true proving ground of American nationality.

New Hampshire's Delegates
1774-1783
and The Date of Their Attendance[*]

JOHN SULLIVAN: *September 5–October 26,* 1774

NATHANIEL FOLSOM: *September 5–October 26,* 1774

JOHN SULLIVAN: *May 10–June 22,* 1775

JOHN LANGDON: *May 10–August 2,*1775; *September 16–November 12,* 1775; *December 23,*1775–*January 2,* 1776 (resigned in May)

JOSIAH BARTLETT: *September 16,* 1775–*March 18*(?), 1776; *May 18–October 26,* 1776

WILLIAM WHIPPLE: *February 29–August 12,* 1776; *October 24,* 1776–*June 18,* 1777

MATTHEW THORNTON: *November 4,* 1776–*May 2,* 1777

GEORGE FROST: *May 16–September 17,* 1777; *December 20*(?), 1777–*April 7*(?), 1778

NATHANIEL FOLSOM: *July 21,* 1777–*January 17*(?), 1778; *March 24–April 1,* 1778

JOSIAH BARTLETT: *May 21–November 3,* 1778

JOHN WENTWORTH, JR.: *May 30–June 18,* 1778 (or later)

WILLIAM WHIPPLE: *November 5,* 1778–*September 24*(?), 1779

GEORGE FROST: *November 25,* 1778–*April 16,* 1779

NATHANIEL PEABODY: *June 22,* 1779–*April 24,* 1780

WOODBURY LANGDON: *September 3-17,* 1779; *September 27–November 20,* 1779

NATHANIEL FOLSOM: *December 30,* 1779–*September 15,* 1780

SAMUEL LIVERMORE: *February 7–February 28,* 1780

JOHN SULLIVAN: *September 11,* 1780–*February 28,* 1781; *March 1–August 10*(?), 1781

SAMUEL LIVERMORE: *May 14–October 11,* 1781; *October 30,* 1781–*April 29,* 1782

JOHN TAYLOR GILMAN: *June 20,* 1782–*March 31,* 1783

PHILLIPS WHITE: *November 4,* 1782–*May 19,* 1783

ABIEL FOSTER: *July 29–November 4,* 1783; *December 13,* 1783–1784

---

*Compiled from Burnett, *Letters,* passim.

CHAPTER 7

To undisciplined militia belong the honors of Concord and Lexington; militia withstood the British at Bunker Hill; by the aid of militia an army of veterans was driven from Boston; and we shall see the unprosperous tide of affairs, in the central states and in the South, turned by the sudden uprising of volunteers.

GEORGE BANCROFT.[1]

I could put no Dependence upon the Militia—such another Set of Scoundrills is not in America—when their all is depending they had Rather see it all go to Ruin than to hazard the least fighting. . . . .

General JOHN STARK.[2]

The Army and Its Administration

THE opening of actual warfare saw New Hampshire faced with a threefold problem of military defense. Her frontier, including the Connecticut River valley, was open to British and Indian raids from Canada and constituted an excellent avenue for a chain of Tory espionage stations. Her seacoast and the harbor of Portsmouth were exposed to naval raids. Although several defending forts had been built, they necessitated large garrisons in continuous attendance to their duty. Lastly, New Hampshire had to maintain its quota in Washington's army.

The very remoteness of the state from centers of administration and government placed it at a disadvantage. Communications north of Boston were poor and very slow at best. It was often impossible for the state's leaders to coöperate effectively in emergencies because of their lack of reliable intelligence. William Whipple wrote to del-

[88]

egate Josiah Bartlett in Philadelphia, "One day we heare there has been an engagement wherein 6,000 are slain on one side 5,000 on the other, the next day our army are totaly routed & then that our army have Killed 13,000 of the Enemy & so on . . . . In this state of suspence we have been for 3 or 4 weeks past without having one piece of intelligence that can be depended on."[3]

To meet the military emergency what potential resources did New Hampshire have at the outset of hostilities? Under the old colonial militia law each male inhabitant between the ages of sixteen and sixty had been expected to provide himself with a musket, bayonet, knapsack, cartridge box, one pound of powder, twenty bullets, and twelve flints. In addition each town had been required to keep in readiness one barrel of powder, two hundred pounds of lead, and three hundred flints for every sixty men as well as to provide individual equipment for the poor.[4] Such an outlay required quite a respectable armament budget. In days when taxation was decidedly not the vogue, it was small wonder that these requirements were loosely observed by the towns. On the other hand, the personnel and morale of the provincial militia had been vastly improved under the administration of Governor John Wentworth. Frequent drills and parades had been held, and equipment had been regularly inspected. Wentworth had divided the militia into twelve regiments and had appointed prominent and popular men as officers. He probably did not suspect that he was unwittingly organizing New Hampshire's revolutionary army![5]

In the spring of 1775 the greater number of the southern New Hampshire towns had been energetically drilling militia companies as a defense against invasion "by his Majesty's enemies."[6] With the beginning of hostilities at Lexington and Concord hundreds of men from these towns flocked into Massachusetts. These irregulars had little or no organization; and most of the companies presented a motley appearance. Officers were in general elected, and consequently discipline was lax. Indeed many of the men returned home when the first alarm had subsided. Only John Stark of Dunbarton possessed sufficient qualities of leadership to maintain a fairly large body of men on active duty. On May 20, 1775, New Hampshire's Provincial Congress officially decided to organize an army of two thousand men in three regiments and to incorporate in this establishment those men already in the field.[7] Stark was thereupon given command of one regiment, and James Reed and Enoch Poor were placed at the head of the second and third regiments respectively. Over this brigade of three militia regiments Major General Nathaniel Folsom was placed in command. Such was New Hampshire's military organization before the establishment of the Continental army.

A unified command was essential to any military success which the colonies might hope to achieve. It soon became apparent that the first skirmishes were only the beginning of what might be a long war and that the first year would probably see several major campaigns. Consequently the Continental Congress proceeded apace in May and June, 1775, to organize a Continental army. George Washington of Virginia was chosen commander-in-chief. Each state was allotted as its quota in the Continental army a number of regiments roughly in proportion to its population. Since New Hampshire's quota was fixed at three regiments, it was a simple matter for the state to shift its three militia regiments, already in the field, from their status as state troops to the Continental roster. These three regiments were maintained continuously until 1781 when their number was reduced to two. With the evacuation of New York by the British in 1783, they were finally disbanded.

The establishment of the Continental army presented the most vexing problem of appointing officers. The general practise was to allow each state to elect all officers in its own regiments up to and including the rank of colonel. All general officers above the rank of colonel were appointed by the Continental Congress. The vesting of elective power in the civilian state authorities resulted in friction with the general officers chosen by the Congress, who thought that they should choose the minor regimental officers. In March, 1776, Brigadier General John Sullivan wrote to the New Hampshire Committee of Safety, "Surely by my having the Choice of Thirty one Set of Officers who have been under My Immediate Inspection I could have a much Better Oppertunity of Selecting Eight good ones than You who were not here and Could not know how they behaved."[8]

Politics naturally played a controlling part in the selection of officers both by the states and by the Congress. There was much jealousy, friction, trading, and jockeying for position. As early as April 23, 1775, Andrew McClary, a member of the New Hampshire forces around Boston, had written home to the Provincial Congress, "Pray Gent: dont let it always be Reported that New Hampshire men were always Brave Soldiers, but never no Commander; the

Proclamation by the First State Government, March 19, 1776. From manuscript journal of the House of Representatives.

dissertion of those men causes much uneasiness among the remaining Troops. . . . ."[9] Nathaniel Folsom, a veteran of the Seven Years' War, who had been made commander of the state militia, was the logical person for the Continental Congress to appoint to the position of brigadier general over New Hampshire's Continental regiments. Yet there was so much bitter feeling between Folsom and Colonel John Stark, who thought that he too deserved the high command, that the Congress compromised by awarding the position to a third person of no military experience—John Sullivan of Durham. Reed, Stark, and Poor were awarded the colonelcies of the state's three regiments by the New Hampshire legislature. In 1776 Sullivan was elevated to the position of major general in the Continental army. It then became necessary to appoint a New Hampshire colonel as brigadier general to fill the vacancy left by Sullivan's promotion. In this instance the rule of seniority was followed, and the senior colonel, James Reed, was elected by the Continental Congress on August 9, 1776. Reed, however, became blind and had to retire from the service before he ever took command. Stark as the senior colonel was next in line for the coveted brigadier-generalship. Here politics entered into the situation, and Colonel Enoch Poor, Stark's junior in rank, was awarded the position on February 21, 1777.[10] Stark became so incensed at the injustice that he resigned. In the fall of 1777, however, he was made a Continental brigadier general as a reward for his brilliant leadership of the militia at Bennington. With Stark, Reed, and Poor passing to higher commands, New Hampshire's three colonelcies were left vacant. The state legislature at different intervals awarded these positions to Joseph Cilley, Nathan Hale, and Alexander Scammell. Hale was captured in July, 1777, and replaced by George Reid. Cilley's regiment was discharged in 1781. Scammell was killed at Yorktown and succeeded by Henry Dearborn.

Such were the men who led New Hampshire's troops.[11] Stark, Cilley, Dearborn, and Scammell were distinguished officers with excellent records. Sullivan and Poor had creditable reputations as generals. To them all should go a major share of the credit for maintaining the morale of the troops in the field. What sort of background did they have to qualify for command? John Sullivan of Durham had been a lawyer and a major in the provincial militia but had had no practical military experience. John Stark of Dunbarton, a farmer, had made a brilliant record in the Seven Years' War as a captain in Rogers' Rangers, a battalion attached to the regular British army. James Reed, tailor, landowner and innkeeper of Fitzwilliam, had also served with repute throughout the Seven Years' War. Enoch Poor, cabinetmaker, trader and shipbuilder of Exeter, had participated in a Nova Scotian expedition in 1755. As for the others—Joseph Cilley, a farmer of Nottingham, Nathan Hale, a farmer of Rindge, George Reid, a yeoman of Londonderry, Alexander Scammell, a school-teacher of Durham and Henry Dearborn, a physician of Nottingham—not one of them had had any military experience prior to the Revolution. They learned by the difficult and costly method of trial and error. Curiously enough, one of those who had had no previous experience, John Sullivan, rose to the highest rank—that of major general. On the other hand, John Stark, a colorful, outspoken character who would cater to no one and who was best qualified of all the New Hampshire men to command, could gain only a belated recognition.

The problem of keeping the Continental army at full strength, once it was in the field, was a most difficult one. The size of the army was entirely dependent upon how faithfully the states kept their quotas filled. Terms of enlistment were constantly expiring since it was customary to enlist men for only short terms. Desertions were quite numerous especially when the cause seemed most hopeless. On January 23, 1777, Washington wrote to chairman Weare of the New Hampshire Committee of Safety, "We have a full army one day and scarce any the next."[12] Again on January 31 he wrote, "Unless some very effectual means are fallen upon to prevent it [desertion], our new army will scarcely be raised, before it will dwindle and waste away. . . . ."[13] The average Continental regiment was supposed to include about 550 men. Yet Baron von Steuben is known to have said, "I have seen a regiment consisting of *thirty men* and a company of *one corporal*."[14]

One of the most curious anomalies of the military administration was the political opposition to the development of an efficient war machine.[15] The Continental Congress with a civilian fear of military autocracy opposed the establishment of a permanent standing army. The Congress proposed instead that each state maintain its quota in the Continental army by a system of temporary enlistments from the state militia. On July 18, 1775, the Congress recommended that each state reorganize its militia system.[16] New Hampshire made a preliminary reorganization in August, 1775, but this was found to be unsatisfactory. A permanent militia system was established by law on September 9, 1776.[17] The entire state had already been divided into twelve regimental districts. Under the provisions of the new law the state legislature was to appoint a colonel and minor field officers to the command of each district. The command of the entire state militia was vested in a major general, also to be appointed by the legislature. Within each regimental district all able-bodied white males between the ages of sixteen and fifty, certain officials and vocations exempted, were to be registered as members of the "training band" and were required to provide themselves with military equipment. Members of the "training band" in each town were to be organized into companies of sixty-eight men. For each such company the separate towns were required to keep in reserve a certain minimum supply of powder and shot. Each company was empowered to elect its own captain and non-commissioned officers. As a militia reserve there was constituted within each regimental district an "alarm list" which was to include, with practically no exemptions, all able-bodied white males between the ages of sixteen and sixty-five, who were not members of the "training band." The members of the "alarm list" were to be divided into companies and were empowered to elect their own officers in the same manner as the "training band."

The "training band" companies were required to be assembled by their captains eight times annually for military drill. The "alarm list" companies were only required to be mustered twice annually. Captains who failed to call out their companies for training as provided by law were liable to be cashiered. Privates who neglected to attend the required drills were liable to a fine of not more than twenty shillings nor less than five shillings. Disobedience or disorderliness by privates on training days was punishable by a fine of from one to ten shillings.

Such in brief was the military nucleus from which the Continental Congress suggested that each state supply the Continental army. The methods adopted by New Hampshire to maintain its full quota in the Continental army varied with the degree of revolutionary enthusiasm. During 1775 and 1776 voluntary enlistments from the militia and the payment of bounties sufficed to keep the state's quota fairly well filled. To encourage enlistment a system of bounties was maintained throughout the war.[18] The towns paid varying amounts, generally around ten pounds per enlistment. In addition the state offered a bounty of ten pounds upon enlistment, eighteen shillings to be paid annually, and twenty shillings to be paid semi-annually. In 1779 service men were exempted from state taxes. Yet there was still further reward for the volunteer. In addition to town and state bounties the Continental Congress offered a bounty of twenty dollars, one hundred acres of land, and a suit of clothes. Even so the raising of troops became difficult, especially as the war lagged and money depreciated. On January 18, 1777, the state legislature enacted its initial draft law.[19] This law provided that whenever voluntary enlistments failed to fill the state's quota the colonels of each militia regimental district were empowered to draft enough men from each town within their district to complete the quota. Many of those drafted still contrived to evade service by hiring substitutes or merely by refusing to march with their levy and paying a nominal fine. In 1779 and 1780 these fines and penalties for evasion of service had to be made so high that evasion was practically impossible, in order that an adequate number of men might be maintained in the field.[20] On January 12, 1781, the legislature passed "An Act for the raising and completing this State's Quota of the Continental Army."[21] This law established an entirely new system of filling the quota. The whole number of men to be raised was divided among the several towns in proportion to their population. Each town neglecting to supply its required number was fined a sum sufficient to hire substitutes. But the new system failed to function satisfactorily. Throughout the last three years of the war New Hampshire's quota was fixed at 1152 men comprising two regiments, yet the state never had more than 744 men in the Continental service at one time during this period.[22]

Not only did the Continental Congress obstruct the establishment of a well-trained army but it also opposed long enlistments. Washington was continually pleading for a greater degree of permanency in the military personnel.[23] Had the 90,000 Americans under arms in 1776 been incorporated into a regular army with enlistments for the duration of the war, the American leader might have decisively defeated the British within a year or less. The Congress, however, never made this concession. The terms of enlistment of New Hampshire men in the Continental army differed greatly.[24] Some enlisted for the duration of the war or three years but nearly always left at the end of three years. In 1777 and 1778 several levies enlisted for eight and nine month periods. In 1780 and 1781 a large proportion of the enlistments were for terms of six months. Thus throughout the war Washington had to depend upon a Continental army whose men enlisted for widely varying periods and whose regiments hardly ever equalled their paper strength. On October 18, 1780, he wrote to chairman Meshech Weare of the New Hampshire Committee of Safety, "I am religiously persuaded, that the duration of the war and the greatest part of the misfortunes and perplexities we have hitherto experienced are chiefly to be attributed to the system of temporary enlistments."[25]

From the time when the state levies were enlisted until the time when they were mustered into the Continental army, they were under state supervision. The assembling of the levies at military centers was supervised by the legislature and in its recess by the Committee of Safety. Each soldier was expected to provide himself with arms and clothing; and if he was too poor to buy them himself, the responsibility fell on his town. Frequently, however, the towns were financially unable to equip their men. The only alternative was for the state government to assume the responsibility. In the early years of the war, purchases of clothing and military stores were made by special legislative committees or by the Committee of Safety. Purchase was generally by contract. There is no evidence to show that contracts were awarded on the basis of competitive bidding. Apparently a suitable contract was arbitrarily agreed upon by the contractor and the committee.[26] Once the contract had been negotiated the committee felt no responsibility to see that delivery was made or that the quality of the goods delivered was high. In many cases, no doubt, the soldiers were sent off to war with useless equipment. On April 7, 1781, the state legislature passed "An Act to prevent fraud in Shoes made for the Army of the United States of America."[27] This law provided for strict inspection of shoes and for punishment for their faulty manufacture. In 1778 New Hampshire established a permanent "Board of Warr" of three persons "to supply the Continental regiments of this state with cloathing & all other Necessaries, and to transact any other business as they shall from time to time be directed."[28] This board supplanted the special committees and their haphazard methods and provided a centralized administration of state military purchases.

The Army and Its Administration

When the state levies were mustered by a deputy from the Continental department of mustermaster general, they were full fledged members of the Continental army, beyond state supervision. The paying of the Continental soldiers was administered by the department of paymaster general. The following were the monthly salaries, expressed in dollars, offered to the several ranks in the Continental army.[29]

MAJOR GENERAL	166
BRIGADIER GENERAL	125
COLONEL	75
LIEUTENANT COLONEL	60
MAJOR	50
CAPTAIN	40
LIEUTENANT	27
ENSIGN	20
SERGEANT	8
CORPORAL	7⅓
PRIVATE	6⅔

Payment was in paper money, and allowance was made for depreciation. However, schedules were not revised fast enough to keep pace with the rate of depreciation. Major General John Sullivan of New Hampshire received $1328 in Continental paper as his salary for the month of November, 1779. This amount had a specie value of only $43.81, roughly $120 less than the stipulated salary.[30] In the lower wage brackets this hardship was even more accentuated. Then too, the small difference between the minor officer's pay and the private's pay aroused resentment. The officers several times organized to gain increases.[31] But the privates possessed no such collective bargaining power. The Continental Congress frequently failed to vote an adequate payroll within reasonable time. In one case at least this laxness caused a mutiny within Brigadier General Enoch Poor's brigade of New Hampshire regiments, which took place at Fishkill, New York on November 2, 1777. The pay was then ten months in arrears. General Israel Putnam wrote to Washington, "I am sorry to inform you that, for want of pay, General Poor's brigade of Continental troops have refused to cross the North River. The troops mutinied, the officers endeavoring to suppress them, and they so determined to go home, that a Captain, in the execution of his duty, ran a soldier through the body, who soon expired, but not before he shot the Captain through, who is since dead."[32]

To the Continental department of clothier general fell the duty of overseeing the clothing supply of the army. At specified times the deputies of the department made returns for the regiments of each state, showing what kinds and quantities of clothing the men needed. These returns were forwarded to the separate states which were asked to supply the necessary articles.[33] The department of clothier general paid for these articles upon delivery by the states and issued them to the soldiers, who reimbursed the department out of their pay. Frequently the Continental Congress imported articles of clothing in job lots for the entire army. In such cases the clothing was distributed by the clothier general. Nevertheless, he could not act without authorization by the Congress which often forgot to allocate the available supplies of clothing.[34]

The failure to clothe the Revolutionary army properly was in some measure excusable, although irresponsible organization contributed to the débacle.[35] Prices of clothing rose tremendously because of the depreciation of the currency and the scarcity of goods created by the British blockade. Some enterprizers who did own supplies of clothing speculated by withholding them from the market. American manufactures were few in number and inferior in quality. There were no standard specifications covering the size and material of goods. Where purchases were made by contract, both the size of the contracts and the haste with which they had to be filled encouraged excessive prices and waste.[36]

The laxity of the nation in feeding the army adequately, however, was due to nothing less than downright inefficiency. There was plenty of food to be had in the states at large, but maladministration and incompetency in the army departments always resulted in a shortage. The department of commissary general of purchases, on which fell the responsibility of purchasing food, the department of quartermaster general, on which fell the duty of transporting supplies and furnishing fuel, forage, and camp equipment, and the department of commissary general of issues, on which fell the duty of issuing food, were somehow unable to coöperate or to function effectively. The following standard ration per man only serves as an illustration of the degree of their failure.[37]

1 *lb.* of bread or flour daily
1 *lb.* beef, ¾ *lb.* pork or 1 *lb.* of salt fish daily
1 *pt.* milk daily
3 *pints* of peas or beans per week
1 *half-pint* of rice or 1 *pint* Indian meal daily
1 *qt.* of spruce beer or cider daily
8 *lbs.* hard soap per 100 men per week

Such a meager ration could easily have been maintained throughout the war. A Continental bakery was established in 1777, yet the men repeatedly suffered from lack of vegetables, beer, rum, and soap. The Continental Congress was niggardly in appropriations and urged the army to draft supplies at fixed prices, but this policy only served to alienate the inhabitants and to make conditions worse. Food supplies were usually purchased through contracts negotiated by the deputy purchasing commissaries, but there existed no adequate central supervision. Persons possessing beef, salt, and other supplies were unwilling to sell them without definite assurance of payment. The private business of the commissaries too often militated against the public interest. Haphazard methods of distribution and indifferent performance of duty caused terrible suffering.[38] Sutlers and camp followers sold trifles to starving soldiers for extortionate prices. In Philadelphia the Board of War, delegated by the Congress to act as executive coördinator of the army administration, was so absorbed in small matters that it could spare no time for larger ones.[39]

Major Henry Dearborn of the Third New Hampshire Regiment near Valley Forge wrote in his journal on December 18, 1777, "This is Thanksgiving Day through the whole continent of America, but God knows we have very little to keep it with this being the third day we have been without flour or bread—and are living on a high uncultivated hill, in huts and tents. Laying on the cold ground, upon the whole I think all we have to be thankful for is that we are alive and not in the grave with many of our friends—we had for Thanksgiving breakfast some exceeding poor beef which has been boiled and now warmed in an old short-handled frying-pan in which we were obliged to eat it having no other platter—I dined and supped at General Sullivan's today and so ended Thanksgiving."[40] The winter at Valley Forge (1777-1778) saw the worst suffering of the war. The soldiers were three times without provisions and once without meat for six days. On December 23, 1777, 2898 men were unfit for duty on account of lack of clothing, but by February 5, 1778, the appalling total had risen to 3989. Washington's effective forces numbered barely 4000 men. And this situation need never have arisen; it was due solely to mismanagement.

The story of the maladministration of the Continental army reflects the story of the evolution of the executive departments of the Continental Congress. The first five years of the war clearly demonstrated that standing committees of the Congress were unable to coördinate and centralize the military administration. The prejudice within the Congress against the establishment of executive departments very nearly lost the war.[41] On January 22, 1781, Washington wrote to Meshech Weare of New Hampshire, "I dare not detail the risks we run from the scantiness of supplies."[42] Again on May 10 he wrote, "Supplies . . . . must be speedily and regularly provided, or our forts cannot be maintained, or the army kept in the field much longer."[43] In 1781 the departments of War and Finance were established, and the various army services were centralized under the control of the Secretary at War. All purchasing was delegated to Robert Morris, the new Superintendent of the Treasury. For the last two years of the war conditions within the army were immeasurably better.

The Continental army, however, included but a small proportion of the men under arms. At least half or more of those who participated in the war were irregulars or state militia acting as auxiliary troops. Thus the Continental regiments were not only originally filled with recruits from the militia, but they were also supplemented by militia regiments in grave military emergencies. The members of the New Hampshire militia had little or no uniform training. They were required to drill only eight times annually. When called out for service the militiamen were subject to the Articles of War drawn up by the New Hampshire legislature.[44] The basis of these Articles was too democratic, and the punishments too moderate to preserve strict discipline. Officers refusing to call out the militia were fined ten pounds. Militia privates neglecting to spread the alarm in time of emergency were fined an amount between ten and forty shillings. If a militiaman refused to march, he was liable to a fine varying from twenty shillings to three pounds. Swearing and cursing in the service carried a fine of one shilling for privates and non-commissioned officers and a fine of four shillings for commissioned officers. Disrespect toward officers, striking officers, desertion, duelling, sleeping or drunkenness while on guard duty, creating false alarms, rioting, robbery, spying for the enemy, selling supplies to the enemy—all of these offenses were punishable at the discretion of the general court-martial. The court-martial was empowered to order the degrading, cashiering, drumming out of camp, whipping not more than thirty-nine lashes, fining, or the imprisonment not more than one month of all militiamen found guilty of the foregoing acts. Only two offenses carried the death penalty—cowardly abandoning one's post in time of danger or urging others to do so, and revealing the password to the enemy. If any private thought himself wronged by an officer, he might appeal to the colonel of his regiment, who was thereupon required to convene a regimental court-martial to inquire into the complaint. These Articles of War were adopted on September 19, 1776, but proved so little conducive to discipline and good order after four years of operation that they were repealed by the state legislature on March 18, 1780. At that time a new militia law was passed placing the militia under the same rules and regulations as the Continental army.[45]

Not only were the militiamen ill-trained and ill-disciplined, but their equipment was generally inferior. They lacked that group solidarity and morale which is only possessed by troops which have been through great hardships and critical campaigns. Naturally they were unreliable forces to post at strategic positions or on the front line. Washington wrote to Meshech Weare, "I solemnly declare, I never was witness to a single instance that can countenance an opinion of militia or raw troops being fit for the real business of fighting. I have found them useful as light parties to skirmish in the woods, but incapable of making or sustaining a serious attack."[46] Brigadier General Stark of New Hampshire was even more denunciatory. He wrote to Weare, "I could put no Dependence upon the Militia—such another Set of Scoundrills is not in America—when their all is depending they had Rather see it all go to Ruin than to hazard the least fighting. . . . ."[47]

Nevertheless, within the state the New Hampshire militia did furnish valuable service. Several companies performed the tedious drudgery of serving as garrisons in the Portsmouth forts. On the Connecticut Valley frontier a ranger service was organized. It continued throughout the war to police the district for Loyalist spies and to guard against possible border raids. Perhaps the most famous leaders of the rangers were Major Benjamin Whitcomb of Westmoreland and Colonel Timothy Bedel of Bath, who took his regiment north on the Canadian expedition of 1776 only to have it disgracefully surrendered at the Cedars on the St. Lawrence River.[48]

The surrender of the British at Yorktown on October 19, 1781, has been generally regarded as marking the end of the Revolution, despite the fact that the British did not evacuate New York until November 25, 1783. Washington had to labor with all his tact and persuasiveness to prevent the people of his day from gaining this same erroneous impression. On January 31, 1782, he wrote to Meshech Weare, "Let me recommend, in the warmest terms, that all the fruits of the successes, which have been obtained the last campaign, may not be thrown away by an inglorious winter of languor and inactivity."[49] One of New Hampshire's Continental regiments was discharged in January, 1781, in line with a policy of gradual retrenchment. In January, 1783, the number of New Hampshire regiments was reduced to one. But the nucleus of the Continental troops, including a remnant of New Hampshire's remaining regiment, was kept in service until December 23, 1783, when these forces were disbanded at West Point.

One of the most embarrassing problems of the closing years of the war was that of officers' pay.[50] Believing that the only alternative to higher pay was the granting of more leaves of absence, General John Stark wrote to General William Heath, "It must be unnecessary to mention the difficulties that officers and soldiers labour under for want of proper supplies, wages &c. when all these difficulties are enumerated you will easily perceive that indulgence becomes almost necessity, and without it, no officer with a large family and common circumstances can continue in Service."[51] Faced with return to civilian life, many of them bankrupt and ruined and their property depreciated, the officers contrasted their position to that of the British officer who received half-pay for life upon retirement. As early as 1779, Continental officers had petitioned the Congress for similar pensions. But they encountered tremendous opposition among the meticulous and officious congressmen, especially the New Englanders. When in the period January to October, 1780, one hundred and sixty officers resigned, the Congress was visibly impressed and approved a pension plan but provided no appropriation for carrying it into effect. After 1781 the Congress apparently had no intention of carrying out this pledge. In 1783 the "Newburg Addresses" and the threatened mutiny of the officers rudely brought the Congress to its senses again. A compromise plan was finally passed providing for payment to the officers of five years' full salary either in cash or securities bearing six per cent interest. Much bitterness was evinced throughout the debates on the subject. The New England delegates charged that a privileged and parasitical aristocracy was being foisted on the nation. Their contention appeared to them to have been justified when, as an aftermath of the aforementioned dispute, the Revolutionary officers in late 1783 formed a society known as the Order of the Cincinnati.

The first meeting of the Cincinnati in New Hampshire was held at Exeter on November 18, 1783.[52] The society's membership was open to all Revolutionary officers with at least three years' service, and was to be kept hereditary in the officers' families, being transmitted from eldest son to eldest son. Of approximately 120 eligible officers in New Hampshire only 27 ever saw fit to join the society. Major General John Sullivan was elected first president. Conspicuous by his absence was Brigadier General John Stark who was opposed to the principle of military organizations. In New Hampshire and elsewhere the formation of the society evoked bitter criticism. This hostility was a part of the popular prejudice against perpetual military establishments and hereditary aristocracies. The members of the Cincinnati never seem to have used their organization for more than social purposes. Nevertheless, the history of veterans' organizations since the day of the Roman Empire has adequately demonstrated that they tend to apply political pressure and to lobby for special concessions. The Cincinnati was the first veterans' organization in America. Despite its innocuous activity, America would have been far better off had such military societies been thoroughly and finally discredited at that time.

But what of the common soldier of the Revolution—what did he receive by way of compensation? On August 26, 1776, the Continental Congress had resolved that all men totally disabled in the service should receive half-pay for life and that those partially disabled should receive such proportionate compensation as seemed adequate.[53] No person, however, was to be allowed a pension unless he produced a certificate signed by his commanding officer or his medical officer, certifying that his disability was received while in the service of the United States. Pensions were awarded by act of the state legislature to each claimant whose case seemed worthy. The state government in turn was reimbursed for its expenditure for pensions by the Continental government. Accordingly on April 12, 1777, the New Hampshire legislature appointed John Taylor Gilman of Exeter as pension agent.[54] His duty was to register all New Hampshire men who had been disabled in the Continental army, and to examine their claims and certificates. Further aid to common soldiers took the form of town grants for the support of the families of men serving as privates in the army. The towns were repaid for their expenditures by the state government. Aid to soldiers' families was stopped on June 20, 1783, with the demobilization of the army.[55] The disability pension system, however, was continued with only slight modifications throughout the Confederation period. The state act of June 23, 1786, modelled upon a congressional resolution of June 7, 1785, provided that all ex-service men producing certificates of disability were entitled to compensation—in the case of commissioned officers, half-pay; in the case of non-commissioned officers and privates, five dollars per month.[56] Officers' widows were awarded the half-pay of their deceased husbands. To the Continental government was charged the total state expenditure for pensions. This act was very strictly administered. The records for 1789 showed the existence in New Hampshire of only 83 pensions for invalids and 15 pensions for widows of officers, although many more qualified persons must have been in need.[57]

Considering the Revolution as a whole, one wonders how the Americans ever won a decisive victory. In 1775 the colonies possessed a total white population of roughly 2,250,000. Out of such a population could be derived a potential army strength of nearly 490,000 males of fighting age. Yet the peak year for military service, 1776, saw barely 90,000 men under arms, counting Continentals, militia, and all types of irregulars. Had even this number been willing to make the sacrifice of a few years' service, the war could have been quickly pushed to a successful conclusion. The American Revolution presents a bewildering picture of indifference. In the first two years thousands thronged to the battle front in great excitement. But the hardships of military life soon cooled their ardor. The strength of the Continental army dropped steadily from 44,920 in 1777 to 26,826 in 1780 and then to 13,476 in 1783.[58] Even this small army was kept in the field only by the heroic efforts of Washington and his few unselfish associates.

New Hampshire was the only state of the original thirteen, which was not invaded by the British forces during the Revolution. Out of its approximately 18,000 men of fighting age the largest number to render military service at any one time was in the year 1777 when Burgoyne's invasion threatened the New Hampshire frontiers. In that year 4483 men, mostly militia, answered the call to the colors. The greater part of the real fighting, however, was done by a small nucleus, varying from 1000 to 2500 men, in the First, Second, and Third New Hampshire regiments of the Continental army.[59] They helped repulse the British at Bunker Hill. They marched with Sullivan's ill-fated Canadian expedition and died like flies from smallpox on the retreat. They composed the right wing at Trenton and participated in the rapid counter-march to "outfox" Cornwallis at Princeton. They followed Arnold in his headlong charge at Saratoga. They shivered and starved at Valley Forge. They counter-attacked savagely at Monmouth. They devastated the country of the Six Nations. They were present at the surrender at Yorktown. They watched the British finally evacuate New York. The First New Hampshire Regiment had served continuously for a period of eight years and eight months,—probably the longest service record of any Revolutionary regiment. Charles A. Beard has fittingly written, "All in all, it had to be said that the cause of American independence was won in the field by the invincible fortitude and unconquerable devotion of a relatively small body of soldiers and officers who kept the faith to the last hour."[60]

CHAPTER 8

The bare statement of the condition in which the United States would be placed, after having surrendered the right to resort to privateers, in event of a war with a belligerent of naval supremacy, will show that this Government could never listen to such a proposition.

President FRANKLIN PIERCE, *Second Annual Message*, 1854.[1]

Privateering and the Continental Navy

THE naval situation at the opening of the Revolution was preponderantly favorable to Great Britain. With the largest navy in the world, with a national economy based increasingly upon the idea of commercial and naval supremacy, she looked upon the sea as her natural domain and ruled it by no other standard than expediency. In 1775 the British navy had embarked upon a campaign of blockade, bombardment, and impressment of seamen along the American coast. Colonial shipping was quickly swept from the seas; the New England fishing industry was utterly destroyed.

Against the British leviathan of the ocean what hope did the American Revolutionists have? They had one hundred and fifty years of experience in the shipbuilding and carrying trade but no naval background except for privateering during the colonial wars. It was quickly realized in Revolutionary councils that the only logical target for American naval enterprize was Britain's most vulnerable point—her far flung, sea-going commerce. It would have been a waste of time for the small colonial vessels to attack British warships of the first line only to be smashed by a splintering gunfire. To prey upon British commerce the first proposals in the Continental Congress contemplated a Continental navy. There were several reasons why such a project was not entirely feasible, not the least among which was the cost of construction. Within the few short years in which the Revolutionary struggle might be decided the number of war vessels which could be constructed would be inconsequential. But even were they constructed, there would be great difficulty in manning them. Most of the experienced American naval men who had a taste for seafaring were already in the British service.[2] Thus a Continental navy could probably never reach formidable proportions.

The Congress eventually determined upon the only practicable alternative—privateering. On November 25, 1775, certain tentative rules on the subject were recommended to the states for enactment into law.[3] It was further resolved that no privateer should cruise against the enemy without the permission of the Congress. All British ships and all vessels carrying contraband to the British were designated as legal prizes. All prizes were to be brought into port for trial before condemnation. For the trial of prize cases the Congress urged the states to establish admiralty courts from whose decision appeal should be allowed to the Congress itself. Advisory rules for the division of prize money were also drawn up. Finally on March 23, 1776, the Congress resolved "that the inhabitants of these colonies be permitted to fit out armed vessels to cruize on the enemies of these United Colonies."[4] This was the final step necessary to bring into existence a "marine militia"—"a volunteer navy."[5] On April 3 blank commissions for privately owned vessels and letters of marque and reprisal, all signed by the President, were forwarded to the states by the Congress. All owners of privateers, before receiving commissions and letters, were required to post bond for the faithful observance of international maritime law—$5,000 for vessels under 100 tons, $10,000 for larger vessels. These bonds were to be payable to the President of the Congress in case of forfeiture and to be held in trust by the states during good behavior of the privateers.

In New Hampshire an early interest had been manifested in privateering, especially in Portsmouth. Many of its old sea dogs remembered handsome profits made from such enterprize in the halcyon days of King George's War. As early as January 24, 1776, the state legislature had authorized Captain Daniel Jackson of the *Enterprise*, a Portsmouth schooner, to prey on British shipping upon depositing a bond of £1,000 with the state for the observance of maritime law.[6]

On July 3, 1776, the state enacted into law the recommendations of the Continental Congress concerning privateering.[7] This law legalized as prizes all ships aiding the British, all British naval vessels, and all British ships of any other character. To the Council was delegated the duty of receiving the privateers' bonds and issuing the commissions as instructed by the Congress. All prizes were to be brought into port and libeled before a maritime court. In New Hampshire the court was established to sit in Portsmouth. Trials were by judge and jury of twelve. Upon the libellee-owner of the seized vessel fell the burden of showing cause why the said vessel and cargo should not be condemned and sold for the benefit of the captors. If the captors were private persons, the entire proceeds of the sales of condemned prizes were to be theirs. On the other hand, if the captor ship was a vessel outfitted at Continental or state expense, the proceeds were to be divided—one-third for the crew, two-thirds for the state or Continental government. In cases where the seizures were of vessels originally owned by Americans, they were to be returned to the original owners, who in turn were to be required to pay the recaptors a salvage fee. From the judgment of the maritime court appeal was allowed to the state superior court. If the captor ship was a Continental vessel, further appeal was allowed to the Continental Congress. In 1779 a state law widened the appeal from the state court to the Continental Congress to include cases where the owners of the condemned vessel were citizens of nations in amity with the United Colonies.[8] Except in these two instances, New Hampshire denied appeals beyond the state superior court. This was contrary to the recommendations of the Congress, which felt that appeals should be allowed to it in all prize cases, since all privateers had posted bond with the Congress to observe maritime law.

Was patriotism or profit the motive for privateering? It must be admitted that by reason of the character of the business, pecuniary gain was probably the main incentive. The glory of the United Colonies occupied a secondary·position. There were operating out of Portsmouth, New Hampshire, probably around one hundred privateers at one time or another after 1776. These were mostly small ships of eight or ten guns. The average crew ranged from thirty to fifty men. At opposite extremes were the lugger *Betsey* with two guns and a crew of ten and the ship *Amphitrite* with twenty-four guns and a crew of one hundred and sixty. A conservative estimate would indicate that New Hampshire had about 3,000 men engaged in privateering. Who cared to starve in Washington's army or be flogged in the Continental navy when such a profitable occupation was open? The crews had definite interest in the seizures, as their remuneration was on a contingent basis. They received a fixed proportion of the profits of each cruise. The owners were often among the state's political leaders. John Langdon of Portsmouth, Speaker of the House of Representatives and Continental Agent for New Hampshire, owned at least seven privateers and became rich from the war. Other prominent men to own privateers were the Nichols brothers of Portsmouth, the Gilmans of Exeter, Captain Robert Parker of Portsmouth, George Gains, Jacob Treadwell, the Sheafe brothers, and Supply Clap, also of Portsmouth. Two firms of merchants—Spence & Sherburne Company of Portsmouth and Ladd, Jewett & Osgood of Exeter—were also in the business. The merchants as a class frequently preferred privateering to foreign trade, as there was less risk, and the profits from sales of cargoes were enormous.[9]

An almost unique privateering organization was that of the owners of the ship *General Sullivan* of Portsmouth.[10] The ten owners drew up rules of proprietorship on November 18, 1777. Each one of them contributed equally to a total capitalization of £10,000. Seven of the proprietors were declared a quorum to do business and vote money. The members of the crew received as pay half of the total prize money for each cruise. They divided this amount into shares out of which the captain received the largest number and the lower officers and crew, a number commensurate with the relative importance of their services. Certificates of these shares circulated, and there was speculation in them based upon the probable success or failure of each cruise. The fact that the members of the crew had a direct interest in the business only served to make them all the more rapacious in their plundering. The *General Sullivan* captured one prize in 1778 which sold for £168,-400 and another in 1780 which brought £350,000.

Indeed, the incentive for profit frequently put privateering on a plane not much higher than piracy. Neutral rights were repeatedly violated despite the conscientious efforts of the Continental Congress. In 1778 William Whipple of Portsmouth wrote to Dr. Josiah Bartlett on the subject of privateering, "Those who are actually engaged in it soon lose every Idea of right & wrong, & for want of an opportunity of gratifying their insatiable avarice with the property of the Enemies of their Country, will, without the least compunction, seize that of her Friends."[11] A flagrant example of this devil-may-care attitude was furnished by a Portsmouth privateer under Captain John Hart, which sailed right into the mouth of the Garonne River in France to capture a British merchantman.[12]

So great was the rage for privateering in New Hampshire that it competed with other more legitimate activities. William Whipple of Portsmouth in a letter to Dr. Josiah Bartlett observed, "Some of the towns in this State have been obliged to give 400 Dolls. Bounty (pr. man) to serve 3 or 4 months at Rhoad Island, exclusive of what's allow'd by the State; this is wholly owing to privateering. The Farmers cannot hire a laborer for less than 50 or 40 Dolls. pr. month, and in the neighbourhood of this town, 3 or 4 Dolls. pr. day, & very difficult to be had at that. This naturally raises the price of Provision—Indian corn is not to be purchased, under 6 Dolls. pr. Bushel. There is at this time 5 Privateers fitting out here, which I suppose will take 400 men. These must be by far the greater part Countrymen, for the Seamen are chiefly gone, & most of them in the Hallifax Goal. Besides all this, you may depend no public ship will ever be manned while there is a privateer fitting out."[13]

Among the more successful New Hampshire privateers were the *McClary*, the *General Sullivan*, the *General Mifflin*, the *Rambler*, and the *Portsmouth*.[14] These vessels cruised along the American coast from Nova Scotia to the West Indies and even carried their activities into the middle Atlantic, the English Channel, and the North Sea. With foxlike prudence they avoided superior strength. They swooped down upon the unarmed, unsuspecting British merchantmen or the supply ships of the British army. Not all privateering, however, resulted in easy plunder. Less fortunate than many was the Portsmouth privateer *Hampden* under the adventurous Captain Thomas Pickering. Pickering took command of the *Hampden*, a vessel of 400 tons and 22 guns, for a single cruise off the coast of England in 1779. On Sunday, March 7 at 10 A. M., Lat. 47° 13′ N., Long. 28° 30′ W., the *Hampden* sighted a sail at two leagues distance and gave chase. The strange ship took flight, and the race lasted until daybreak on Monday, when the *Hampden* crept up on its prey, only to discover it to be an East Indiaman of 800 tons armed with 34 guns. At 7 A. M., Pickering debonairly sailed his smaller vessel into close quarters and opened fire. General action continued at broadside for two hours. But as Captain Pickering was preparing to lead a boarding party he was killed. Finally, with three masts splintered, sails and rigging in shreds and ammunition nearly exhausted, the *Hampden* was forced to draw off, leaving her foe a blood-soaked, smoking hulk. Two months later she limped into Portsmouth harbor with flag at half-mast. The casualties of the engagement had been "Captain Pickering, killed; Mr. Peltier, a Frenchman, killed; Samuel Shortridge, so badly wounded that he died in two hours after; John Bunten, both legs shot away, but lived nine days; John Tanner, master's mate, left arm shot off; Michael Blaisdell, left hand shot off; Peter Derrick, his mouth shot to pieces; and twelve others wounded, but not dangerous."[15]

Death or life-long disfigurement were not the only liabilities of privateering. Thousands of American privateersmen were captured, impressed into the British navy, or imprisoned in foul jails. Life on the sea was no safer than in an African jungle as the experience of Hugh Hunter of Portsmouth well demonstrated.[16] In January, 1775, before hostilities, Hunter shipped for the West Indies and London under Captain Alexander Nate. Upon his arrival in London he was seized and impressed onto a British man-of-war. After fourteen months' service he contrived to desert. Under an assumed name he signed as first mate on board a British brigantine bound from London to Halifax, hoping to get back to Portsmouth. During the transatlantic voyage, however, a storm came up and forced the ship off its course. Near the West Indies it was captured by an American privateer the *Fanna* and taken into Martinique, a French colony, where the crew was discharged. Hunter next offered to navigate the schooner *Betsey* from Martinique to Halifax. Halfway to its destination the *Betsey* was seized by the American privateer *Friends Adventure* out of Portsmouth under Captain Kinsman Peverly. Hunter finally returned home in June, 1778, after three years of perilous knocking about.

Imprisonment was perhaps the fate most dreaded by all privateersmen. The British navy captured no less than 216 American privateers and their crews during the course of the Revolution.[17] In America the British deposited most of the captured seamen either in the dreaded "Halifax Gaol" or at Newport, Rhode Island. Those taken near England generally found themselves inside gloomy, grim Dartmoor Prison. In the close confinement of loathsome cells, especially at unfavorable seasons of the year, hundreds slowly died. They were "not only Exposed to Penury & Want, but to the Ravages of Putrid Fevers, & Infectious Distempers."[18] In 1778 the crews of two Portsmouth privateers—the *Portsmouth* and the *McClary*—were captured and thrown into the Halifax Gaol. Only after many months in their dreary and unhealthy surroundings were they released under the terms of a cartel for the exchange of prisoners, negotiated by New Hampshire with the British naval authorities. Such was the life of a privateersman.

In contrast the Continental navy was never more than a shadow of the vast swarm of privateers. The total number of privateers for all the colonies probably numbered around 2,000 with crews totaling 30,000. But the Continental navy at its peak early in the war included only 21 vessels and a personnel of barely 3,000 men.[19] Before the end of the war most of its ships had been destroyed or sunk by the British.

The construction of three Continental naval vessels was allotted to the Portsmouth shipyards during the Revolution.[20] The first warship to be launched was the *Raleigh* of 32 guns which left its ways on May 21, 1776. It was commissioned in 1777 under Captain Thomas Thompson but was captured in 1778. Later in 1776 was launched the *Ranger* of 18 guns. This small frigate was commissioned under John Paul Jones and was the first warship to carry an American flag. It was destroyed by the British in the harbor of Charleston, South Carolina, in 1780. The largest ship to be constructed by the Continental navy was the *America* of 74 guns which was launched at Portsmouth on November 5, 1782. It was presented to the French navy to compensate for the loss of their first line warship, the *Magnifique*, which had been wrecked on the American coast.

From 1776 to 1779 the Continental navy was administered by the Marine Committee in the Congress assisted by two Navy Boards—one for the Eastern Department including New England and one for the Southern Department.[21] These executive bodies determined upon the general naval policy, supervised the naval officers, and managed the naval finances. In 1779 the Marine Committee was abolished, and its place was taken by a Board of Admiralty of five members, three of whom were to be non-members of Congress. William Whipple of New Hampshire, as an authority on marine affairs, was elected to this board.[22]

For the most part, however, the really significant naval duties were performed by the Continental agents in each state.[23] The Continental agents superintended the construction of all naval vessels. They contracted for the rigging and outfitting of such naval vessels and all privately owned ships desiring Continental naval commissions. They received Continental monies from the Navy Board to pay all demands for services and goods against the Continental navy. They were delegated to import and export supplies for the Continental government and to assemble naval stores. When prizes were brought into port by naval vessels, the agents prosecuted the libel in the maritime court, sold the seized ship and cargo and distributed the prize money—one-third to the captor-crew, two-thirds on the account of the Continental government. Each agent, at regular stated intervals, was required to account to the Marine Committee, later to the Board of Admiralty, for all Continental funds expended and all prize money received. The agents, however, never seemed to know where their private business ended and the public interest began. They had inside information concerning the probable future demand for naval and military stores and were able to speculate accordingly. The power of awarding contracts afforded them a lever for political advancement. In New Hampshire the position of Continental agent was held temporarily in early 1776 by Joshua Wentworth of Portsmouth. Wentworth was succeeded in the latter part of the same year by that very artful politician, John Langdon, who wanted the position badly enough to resign from the Continental Congress as a prerequisite to obtaining it.

A major obstacle to efficient administration of the navy was the competition of the privateers. Private shipowners bought up naval stores in large quantities, outbidding the Continental government. While privateers of ten guns abounded, Continental naval vessels lay idle in their home ports because of the scarcity of armament. Men could not easily be induced to serve in the navy when the wages of privateering were so high. Pay in the Continental navy ranged all the way from sixty dollars per month for a captain down to eight dollars per month for an ordinary seaman.[24] In addition, if a prize happened to be taken by a Continental warship, one-third of the prize money was divided among the crew. On the other hand, the commanding officer of the Portsmouth privateer *General Sullivan* received £36,793 as his share of a single prize in 1780.[25] The share of an ordinary seaman on the same privateer probably amounted to about £2500. It was no wonder that the average man preferred privateering to naval service and that the owner of a privateer could corner the supply of naval stores. The Continental warship *Raleigh* was launched at Portsmouth on May 21, 1776. Yet she was not ready to go to sea until July, 1777, because of lack of rigging, armament, and sufficient personnel for a crew.[26] In fact a full crew was not signed until the New Hampshire legislature had given Captain Thomas Thompson the power to draft men for the service.

The wide extent which maritime operations and the business of privateering attained gave rise to many perplexing questions of admiralty law. As has been previously stated, all prizes had to be taken into port for trial. One of the most complicated cases to arise during the Revolution was that of the ship *Susannah* owned by Elisha Doane, Isaiah Doane, and James Sheppard, all of Boston.[27] In the spring of 1775 the *Susannah* sailed for England with a cargo for Lane, Son & Fraser, an English trading house. By the time the vessel reached London, the Revolution was well under way, and to escape confiscation the vessel's ownership was transferred to Doane's son-in-law, a British subject. The transfer, however, was merely a paper transaction for expediency's sake. The *Susannah* was then registered as plying between the ports of London and Gibraltar. Taking advantage of this false registration, the ship set out in 1777 on a return voyage to America under the British flag. On October 30 while still on the transatlantic voyage it was captured by the privateer *McClary* commanded by Captain Joshua Stackpole and owned by eleven citizens of Portsmouth, New Hampshire. In due time the *Susannah* was brought into Portsmouth harbor. On November 11, 1777, libels were filed in the New Hampshire Maritime Court. The case came to trial on December 16 before Judge Joshua Brackett. The libellants—the owners of the *McClary* by their agent, Joshua Wentworth, and the crew by their agent, George Wentworth—contended that the *Susannah* was a British ship carrying contraband. The libellees, the owners of the *Susannah* by their agent, argued that the ship was an American vessel in disguise, returning of its own volition to its original owners. The jury, however, brought in a verdict for the libellants, whereupon the court ordered the *Susannah* and cargo to be sold. The owners of the condemned vessel immediately filed notice of an appeal to the New Hampshire Superior Court. This appeal was tried before a judge and jury in September, 1778, at Exeter. The jury again found for the libellants. The owners of the *Susannah* then asked for an appeal to the Continental Congress. But the Superior Court refused to grant this request, since the state law allowed no appeals to the Congress unless the captor ship was a Continental vessel. The *Susannah* was sold and the prize money distributed, one-half to the owners of the *McClary* and one-half to the crew.

On October 9, 1778, Elisha Doane, acting for himself and the other two owners of the *Susannah*, petitioned the Continental Congress to review the case, which was then referred to the Continental Commissioners of Appeals. The first question before the Commissioners was whether they had jurisdiction to hear an appeal from the Superior Court of New Hampshire. The *McClary* owners claimed that all states were sovereign, that state law was supreme, and that the New Hampshire law allowed no appeal in this case. The Commissioners, however, decided that since all privateers were responsible to the Congress for observance of maritime law, the Congress had power to hear appeals in all prize cases. This decision on the question of jurisdiction was rendered on June 29, 1779, but the Commissioners delayed hearing the case.

On March 2, 1781, the Articles of Confederation went into effect. Under the provisions of the Articles, there was delegated to the Congress the sole and exclusive power of establishing a court of appeals to hear and determine finally all appeals in prize cases. Since the case of the *Susannah* was still pending before the Commissioners of Appeals, it was merely transferred to the docket of the newly established Court of Appeals. This court heard the case at Philadelphia in September, 1783, and reversed the decision of the New Hampshire Superior Court. It was ordered that the owners and crew of the *McClary* should repay to Doane and his associates an amount equal to the value of the *Susannah* and cargo. Here the matter rested for ten years as the Court of Appeals had no interstate machinery to enforce its orders. New Hampshire refused to give full faith and credit to the decision. In fact, in November, 1783, the state legislature remonstrated sharply against this invasion of states' rights.

A short time later Elisha Doane, the principal owner of the *Susannah*, died. In 1789 the federal courts were organized under the Constitution of 1787. In 1793 Elisha Doane's administrators brought suit in the Federal District Court of New Hampshire against John Penhallow *et al.*, owners of the *McClary*. The plaintiffs demanded that the District Court issue an order enforcing the decision of 1783 of the old Confederation Court of Appeals. The case was transferred to the

Federal Circuit Court at its New Hampshire sitting. On October 24, 1793, the Circuit Court affirmed the decision of the Confederation Court of Appeals and ordered the defendants to pay damages of $38,500.00. The defendants, the owners of the *McClary*, immediately appealed to the Supreme Court of the United States. By this time the cause of the *McClary* owners had become a political issue in New Hampshire. Governor John Taylor Gilman in his inaugural address in June, 1794, recommended that the legislature memorialize Congress upon the unfairness of the Circuit Court's decision.[28] The pending appeal was finally argued before the Supreme Court in 1795, the arguments requiring from February 6 to February 17 for completion. On February 24 the Court rendered its decision upholding the judgment of the Circuit Court. This decision did not examine the facts of the case, but merely determined whether the Confederation Court of Appeals had originally had legal jurisdiction. On this question it was decided that since a privateer sailed under the commission of the Continental Congress, its owners and crew were responsible to the Continental Congress or the constituted authorities for the legality of their captures. It was also decided that the Federal District Court had original jurisdiction in all admiralty cases and hence had full power to enforce the judgment of the Confederation Court of Appeals. The owners and crew of the *McClary* were thereupon required to pay Elisha Doane's administrators $38,500.00 as restitution for the illegal sale of the *Susannah*. Thus ended a chapter in New Hampshire privateering which had far-reaching ramifications.

It may be wondered what was the effect of the extensive American privateering operations on the final outcome of the Revolution. Dr. Josiah Bartlett of Kingston, New Hampshire, perhaps described their effect accurately in a letter to William Whipple in 1778, in which he said, ". . . . I think experience has shown that privateers have done more toward distressing the trade of our enemies, and furnishing these States with necessaries, than Continental Ships of the same force; and that is in my opinion the greatest advantage we can at present expect from our Navy; for at this early period We can not expect to have a Navy to cope with the British."[29] From 1776 to 1778 American privateers captured 733 British vessels to the value of £1,800,633. For the entire war the records of Lloyds' showed 3087 British merchantmen captured and only about one-fourth of that number retaken or ransomed.[30] The British West India trade declined

66 per cent in value, and its insurance rates rose to 23 per cent. Even the English Channel was considered unsafe, as the 10 per cent insurance rate for British vessels plying between Dover and Calais testified. With France, Spain, and Holland entering the war and the Baltic powers forming an Armed Neutrality, Britain was faced with almost universal opposition. A decisive victory against the Revolutionists thus became impossible. Would Britain temporize or recognize American independence? Francis R. Stark in his treatise THE ABOLITION OF PRIVATEERING AND THE DECLARATION OF PARIS writes, "And here is precisely where the effect of the privateers was felt; for with that mighty force striking unceasingly at its one vital part, its trade, the English nation simply could not afford to temporize."[31]

CHAPTER 9

A zealous father of sedition
Took up the good man on Suspicion;
Forced him without a grain of pity,
Before th' inflexible committee.
Committee men are dreadful things
More haughty far than Europe's kings;
The latter mostly rule by laws,
The first are governed by a Cause.

JACOB BAILEY.[1]

The Suppression of the Loyalists

T HE suppression of the Loyalists by the American Revolutionists was one of the most ironical occurrences of the eighteenth century. The proponents of the liberal political system which fostered free thinking, free speech, free press, and other English constitutional ideals were for the time being overthrown by the colonial outgrowth of their liberalism. It is true that the Revolutionists were at first only seeking a return to the degree of personal freedom which Britain had permitted to prevail in the colonies before the imposition of the imperial system in 1763. Yet, "the freest of peoples were the first to revolt."[2] Despite the objectionable political and economic restrictions imposed after 1763 by the unwise and inexpedient British imperial system, more social justice, more democracy, and more economic welfare existed in the American colonies than in any other contemporary colonial system in the world. In fact the American colonies of the eighteenth century were accorded as much if not more self-rule than the United States has usually seen

[118]

fit to extend to its colonial possessions. Professor Claude H. Van Tyne has written, "The British Empire was doomed to be broken asunder, but it was brought to that disaster by the insistent demand of Englishmen in America for the full enjoyment of those liberties which England had fostered beyond any other country of the world."[3]

Presumably one great revolutionary ideal was political liberty. Nevertheless, the suppression of the Loyalists was as complete a negation of that ideal as could have existed. Apparently the methods of revolutionary political parties in dealing with opposition have not changed since the beginning of history. In 1777 William Whipple of Portsmouth wrote to Dr. Josiah Bartlett of Kingston, "I can conceive of no reason for an abatement in the spirits of the People unless it is that those miscreants who are aiming at the distruction of theire Country, are not treated with that just severity which their crimes deserve. What purpose will it answer to fill the Goals! . . . . If they are under Ground or out of the Country they will soon be for got. The necessity of the case will surely justify the most severe & decisive measures. . . . ."[4] What could have been more frankly Machiavellian?

There can be no doubt that some Loyalists took such an extreme position as to arouse an almost justifiable hatred on the part of the Revolutionists. One of the most conservative of them, in an anonymous letter to the *New Hampshire Gazette*, wrote, "We shall have fine Times indeed when every Shoemaker and Plough-Jogger fits up for a Statesman, and pretends to find Fault, not only with the Ministry, but even the Acts of the British Parliament! Who made the Populace judges of what is constitutional . . . . ? In truth, it is necessary that the common People should be taxed as high as they can well bear, that they may be kept in better Order. . . . ."[5] The sentiment of this writer was typical of the bitter class hatred engendered among the Loyalists by the Revolution. On October 29, 1775, General John Sullivan at Portsmouth wrote in complaint to Washington, "That infernal crew of Tories, who have laughed at the Congress . . . . walk the streets here with impunity; and will, with a sneer, tell the people in the streets that all our liberty-polls will soon be converted into gallows."[6]

In the early days of revolutionary activity in New Hampshire boycotts and mob violence were the most popular methods of dealing with the Loyalists. On March 4, 1777, a boycott was declared against four prominent Loyalists of Concord "untill they give satisfaction to the Public."[7] Those who broke the boycott were also to be declared public enemies. The experience of Joshua Atherton of Amherst with mob tyranny was typical of the situation often to be faced by Loyalists. The incident was vividly described by Matthew Patten of Bedford in his diary.

> [*Sept. 20, 1774*] . . . . *I went to Amherst and about 300 men assembled and chose a Commitie who went to Mr. Atherton and he came to the people to the Court house and He Signed a Declaration and Read it to the people who accepted it he Invited them to go to Mr. Hildreths and Drink what they pleased the people Dispersed about Midnight without doing any Out Ragious act.* . . . .[8]

The one means to which most Loyalists were forced to resort to escape mob violence, tar and feathers, or demolition of property, was to sign a recantation. These recantations followed a more or less standard form, the following being a typical specimen.

> *Whereas, I the subscriber, have, for a long series of time, both done and said many things that I am sensible has proved of great disadvantage to this Town, and the Continent in general; and am now determined by my future conduct to convince the publick that I will risk my life and interest in defense of the constitutional privileges of this Continent, and humbly ask the forgiveness of my friends and the Country in general for my past Conduct.*[9]

Throughout the war Loyalist scares disturbed the peace of New Hampshire. As soon as hostile feeling had died down, the political authorities would hysterically announce that an alleged British plot had just been nipped in the bud. Enthusiasm would again be whipped to the bursting point, causing a renewed period of Loyalist persecution. Every man was suspicious of his neighbor. Loose talk, gossip, and all sorts of exaggeration were the most popular types of news. Men seen meeting in groups or buying large quantities of provisions were likely to be immediately investigated. On January 20, 1775, an anonymous letter appeared in the *New Hampshire Gazette* protesting against the general and supine acceptance of such herd psychology. The unknown observer wrote:

The Suppression of the Loyalists

*At a Time when the Reins of Government are evidently slack-
ened, when the sacred Name of Liberty is so villainously pros-
tituted to the most licentious Purposes; when nothing more is
wanting to pull down the ungovernable Rage of a furious Mob
on the Head of an honest and worthy Citizen, than for some
malicious disappointed Wretch falsely to represent him as an
Enemy to the Constitutional Rights of his Country . . . .
whether these Reports and Insinuations come dressed in the sly
garb of a Horse Jockey, the hypocritical Cant of a Saint, or the
still more detested authority of a Trading Justice, they are
equally despicable and unworthy of Notice.*[10]

While New Hampshire was undergoing the transition from royal
government through revolutionary organization to state government,
the campaign against the Loyalists was in the hands of the local committees of safety. Occasionally important cases were reserved for the
provincial Committee of Safety. The investigations were purely political, not judicial in character. The investigators had the crusader's
anxiety to discredit the Loyalists by any means, fair or foul. On June
12, 1775, Joseph Kimball of Henniker was put under a "third degree"
by the local Committee, because he was reputed to have made favorable comment about the royal governor, John Wentworth.[11] He was
acquitted upon his apology for having made such an erroneous statement. On July 13, 1775, the Hillsborough County Committee of Safety
convicted the royal sheriff, Benjamin Whiting of Hollis, of Loyalism.[12]
The principal evidence was that he had called John Sullivan, the Durham hero, a "damn'd perjured villain" and a "damn'd rebel, and deserved to be hanged" because of his leadership in the attack on Fort
William and Mary.

With the establishment of the state government in January, 1776,
the campaign of the Revolutionists against the Loyalists took on a
more organized aspect. On March 14, 1776, the Continental Congress
resolved to recommend to all Committees of Safety that they "cause
all persons to be disarmed within their respective colonies, who are
notoriously disaffected to the cause of America."[13] To single out those
who were opposed to the Revolution, it was suggested that an oath
or test should be submitted to all citizens for signature or rejection.
Accordingly on April 12, 1776, the New Hampshire Committee of
Safety dispatched an Association Test to all the towns. Subscribers

to the test promised to support the Revolution to the utmost of their power, even by arms if necessary. The returns of the test were complete by the fall of 1776, and those who had refused to sign (conscientious objectors excepted) were at once labelled as Loyalists.

In September, 1776, Colonel Asa Porter of Haverhill was tried in Exeter before the House of Representatives on the charge of conspiring to organize a British and Indian raid on the upper Coös country.[14] The trial resembled in some ways a grand inquisition. Porter put up a clever defense and pleaded for trial in the regular courts before a jury. He objected to the jurisdiction of the House "Because it is the legislative Body, and it doth not consist with the liberties of the People that the same Body which hath the Power of making Laws, should also have the Power of executing the Laws, or determining the causes of Individuals."[15] Nevertheless, he was found guilty and sentenced to indefinite confinement. It is a curious commentary on the methods of the Revolutionists that they, who claimed to be so meticulous concerning constitutional liberties, should rarely have allowed Loyalists to be tried in courts of law.

One of the most disgraceful performances of the entire Revolution in New Hampshire was the treatment of the Claremont Episcopalians. In this instance religious intolerance fanned the flames of patriotism, and the whole affair only demonstrated to what depths of bigotry and prejudice human nature could descend. At the outbreak of the Revolution the Claremont Church had been suspected of Loyalism and probably with good reason. Its rector, the Reverend Ranna Cossit, had fought the Association Test and had openly declared, "I mean to be on the side of the administration, and I had as leave any person should call me a damned Tory as not, and take it as an affront if people don't call me a Tory, for I verily believe the British troops will overcome by the greatness of their power and the justice of their cause."[16] Unfortunately their Loyalist tendencies were not the only cause of the popular hatred of the Claremont group. Many of the church leaders in the Connecticut Valley feared the influence of the Episcopal denomination—particularly Dr. Eleazar Wheelock, the Hanover Presbyterian and founder of Dartmouth College.[17] According to the account of Colonel John Peters, a member of the Claremont Church, Dr. Wheelock was one of the leaders in the attack on the congregation.[18] The members were confined to close jails after having been beaten and drawn through water and mud. On April 10, 1776, they were tried en masse at Charlestown and convicted. Some were imprisoned and others restricted to the limits of their town.

During the last three months of 1776 two hundred and thirty-one Loyalists from Dutchess and Albany Counties, New York, were sent into New Hampshire for supervision, since the New York jails were overflowing. Most of them had been arbitrarily condemned without trial. They came on foot in small parties under guard. The New Hampshire authorities were naturally reluctant to assume the expensive burden of caring for these people. They were treated leniently and distributed among the towns of Dover, Exeter, Amherst, and Portsmouth. Many of them were given freedom upon posting bonds. One of their number, Joshua Gidney, wrote home to his father, "On our arrival and ever since we have been treated with civility and by some with Respect. I verily believe that Exeter is made up of as kind Hospitable People as in [any] Town in America, even to strangers."[19] By the end of 1777 all of these New York Loyalists had left the state.

On January 17, 1777, the New Hampshire legislature began the enactment of a long series of acts against the Loyalists. It was first resolved that all persons opposed to the Revolution should have ninety days to sell their property and to leave the state without molestation.[20] The crime of treason—aiding and conspiring with the enemy—was made punishable by death.[21] Lesser acts such as discouraging enlistment in the army and navy, speaking against the common cause, spreading false reports, refusing to obey the magistrates, were defined as misdemeanors punishable by fines or imprisonment.[22] On June 19, 1777, the legislature passed one of the most drastic laws of the entire war period—"An Act for taking up, imprisoning or otherwise restraining Persons dangerous to this State."[23] This act delegated to the state Committee of Safety, through its agents, the county sheriffs, the power of imprisoning indefinitely any suspected person without granting bail or trial. Furthermore the act granted to the Committee jurisdiction in the trial of Loyalists. Such types of imprisonment were authorized as the Committee "may judge necessary for the public Good." A definite time limit was set for the life of this act, and it was allowed to lapse in 1779.

Trials before the New Hampshire Committee of Safety in 1777 could not have differed much from the procedure in the French Revolutionary Tribunals. Certainly the Committee exercised a sweeping power over human behavior. The members of the Committee were politicians, members of the legislature, perhaps all seeking prominence. From their very character they were probably not qualified to conduct a judicial inquiry. All types of evidence—hearsay, gossip, irrelevant and prejudicial details—were allowed. In fact there were no rules on the admission of evidence before the Committee. Persons were often convicted of Loyalism on good grounds, it is true, but just as often on prejudice or flimsy proof. As examples the following types of evidence deserve inclusion here. In the case of the State *vs.* Elijah Willard of Winchester, a Mr. Sanderson made the following statement: "Elijah Willard says he had as leive risque his Estate in the Regulars hands as ours."[24] As an example of hearsay, Dr. Richard Bartlett, informing on Captain Ebenezer Frye of Pembroke, wrote: ". . . . Capt. Ebenr Frye has Publicly asserted (as I am told by Mr. Aaron Whittemore) that our Court is asleep, and he is determined not to go into the service untill they pay him his money. Likewise he has no Estate to depend and will joyn the strongest side if our Court don't do better."[25] On the other hand, in the case of the State *vs.* Abner Sanger of Keene, William Barran gave the following incriminating evidence: "Says, That when the Committee order'd him and some others of the Militia to bring Sanger in order to examination, that he swung his Axe at them and told them to Disperse you Damn'd Rebels; and when they had taken him, that on the way he drank a toast to the King and success to his Majesty's Arms and confusion to Americans."[26] It is interesting that the Committee of Safety was lenient as a rule in the punishments meted out to Loyalists. The worst punishment was indefinite imprisonment in one of the state's foul and overcrowded jails. Yet this sentence was only passed on the most dangerous and violent Loyalists, those most clever in organizing political opposition to the Revolution. Far more common were such restrictions as removal of residence from a strategic military area, confinement to the limits of the town, or release upon posting bond for future good behavior.

On July 19, 1777, the state legislature continued its campaign for the suppression of Loyalists. On that date the legislature passed an act empowering the colonels of the militia regiments to disarm all Loyalists and to appropriate their armament for the use of the state after payment of a fair price for the same.[27] On November 29 the legislature passed an act to prevent Loyalists from transferring the ownership of their property before fleeing from the state.[28] The property of all deserting Loyalists was to be held in trust by the selectmen of the towns. This act was, therefore, only a preliminary to confiscation.

In nearly every war there has been a move on the part of one or both of the belligerents to confiscate the property of such of the enemy's nationals as may be within their power. Early in the Revolution there was under way such a move to confiscate the property of the Loyalists. This program was popularized by the fact that it involved a redistribution of wealth—a breaking up of some of the large Loyalist estates. On November 27, 1777, the Continental Congress resolved "That it be earnestly recommended to the several states, as soon as may be, to confiscate and make sale of all the real and personal estate therein, of such of their inhabitants and other persons who have forfeited the same, and the right to the protection of their respective states. . . . . ."[29] It was urged that the funds so obtained by the sale be loaned to the Continental government. As a forerunner to confiscation the New Hampshire legislature passed a proscription act on November 19, 1778.[30] This act proscribed by name seventy-six persons who had already deserted to the British lines or to British soil and all others who should do so in the future. The act probably applied to about one hundred persons and their families at the end of the Revolution. Under the provisions of the act, if any proscribed person returned to the state without the permission of the legislature, he was liable to deportation for the first offense and death for the second. At the head of the proscribed list was the name of the late governor, John Wentworth. Also included were members of Wentworth's Portsmouth clique and a large number of the more prominent country gentry from the central and western portions of the state.

On November 28 the legislature passed its long awaited Confiscation Act.[31] This act confiscated outright the estates of twenty-five persons on the proscription list and those of three other persons who were nonresident landowners. These twenty-eight persons were sharply differentiated from the remainder of the proscription list. Mere desertion to the British lines was not at this time considered sufficient ground for confiscation. Confiscation fell on those who, in addition to having deserted, were in a civilian or military capacity actively aiding the British government to subdue the colonies. Trustees were appointed in each county to sell and liquidate the confiscated estates for the benefit of the state treasury. All creditors' actions at law against the confiscated estates were barred. Two years later on March 18, 1780, the legislature passed a supplementary act reforming the administration of the confiscated estates.[32] This act provided that the judge of probate in each county should choose an administrator for all the confiscated estates within that county, who upon posting bond might assume his duties. It was to be the duty of each administrator to pay all just debts against each estate and to turn the balance over to the treasury. For determining what debts should be allowed, the separate judges of probate were to choose commissions of three members each, who were to rule on the validity of all claims.

The Confiscation Act, contrary to the common impression, was not received throughout the state with joy and unanimous approval. Portsmouth held a town meeting in 1779 to remonstrate against confiscation of the Loyalist estates. It was urged that Portsmouth merchants were owed large debts by British trading houses, which might seize upon the Confiscation Act as a pretext for cancelling those debts. The town reasoned that "the real estate belonging to British subjects was permanent, and increasing in value, and always under the controul of the state; but when sold, the proceeds would be liable to embezzlement, or to be otherwise lost." It was resolved that "with respect to the absentees, it was unjust to condemn them unheard; and to confiscate their property without a trial, was contrary to the principles of civil liberty, for which we were contending."[33]

Throughout the Revolution it was suspected that the Connecticut River valley was the location of a line of Loyalist espionage stations. The valley was a convenient avenue of communication from Canada to New York. It adjoined the New Hampshire Grants (now Vermont) whose people were supposed to be continually dealing with the British. The suspicion was heightened by the large number of Loyalists in Cheshire County, particularly near Keene and Claremont. In May, 1779, Captain Elisha Mack of Gilsum organized a raid on some of the more prominent Loyalists in Keene hoping to discover incriminating evidence.[34] His designs, however, were forestalled when someone notified the militia authorities. As the raiders descended on Keene, they were confronted by a company of militia and forced to disperse. In Claremont the zealous Revolutionists were more successful in detection.[35] In 1780 they discovered a secret Loyalist rendezvous, known as "Tory Hole," in a neighboring swamp. This spot was one of a chain of hiding places from Canada to New York. Here refugees were sheltered and meetings held.

In the latter part of 1781 the New Hampshire legislature for some unknown reason renewed its anti-Loyalist crusade. On November 28 two additional acts were passed.[36] The first barred all Loyalists from acquiring property within the state. The second provided that no person might prosecute a legal action (except for assault and battery), serve as a juror or public official, or operate a tavern, unless he took an oath renouncing allegiance to Britain and swearing allegiance to the United Colonies. On June 21, 1782, a further restriction was imposed in an act which required all taxpayers to take a similar oath as a prerequisite to voting.[37]

The Confiscation Act of 1778 had confiscated the property of twenty-eight Loyalists who had joined or were aiding the British forces and had left the state. On March 25, 1782, the state legislature passed an act confiscating the property of all Loyalists who had left the state, regardless of whether they had been aiding the British, and also the property of all British subjects.[38] The enforcement of the act was placed under the attorney general of the state and the judiciary in each county. Where a Loyalist had deserted his family and had made no provision for their support, the act provided that the probate judges were to assign a certain portion of the estate for their use. Fortunately the provisional treaty of peace was signed before proceedings under this act had been initiated. Some time after receiving news of the treaty in 1783, Attorney General John Sullivan declared his intention of not bringing any actions against the estates of the Loyalist absentees.[39] Discussion of this subject, however, is reserved for a later chapter.

During the entire Revolution a conservative estimate would indicate that approximately one hundred Loyalists and their families left the state because of persecution or other reasons. Many of these refugees fled to the British lines in Boston in 1775 and later accompanied the army to Halifax. Many fled directly to Britain. Others took refuge on Long Island or in New York City. Quite a number joined the British army. John Stinson of Dunbarton served in the "Royal American Reformers." Stephen Holland of Londonderry joined the "Prince of Wales American Volunteers." Robert Robertson of Portsmouth was an ensign in the "Loyal American Regiment." John Stark of Dunbarton, a nephew of the Revolutionary general, enlisted as a lieutenant in the "Royal Guides and Pioneers." One of the most interesting Loyalist military organizations was a company formed by Governor John Wentworth on Long Island in 1776. This company, known as "Wentworth's Volunteers," was originally composed of a small nucleus of New Hampshire Loyalists. Among its officers were First Lieutenant Benjamin Whiting of Hollis and Second Lieutenant Elijah Williams of Keene. The company served throughout the war and was attached to a regiment known as the "Associated Refugees."[40]

At the end of the war in 1783 most of the New Hampshire refugees still on American soil emigrated to Nova Scotia. Some obtained land grants near Digby; others settled in the St. John River valley in New Brunswick. Former Governor Wentworth became chief executive of the province of Nova Scotia. Only a few of the Loyalist refugees dared to return to New Hampshire.[41] In 1784 Elijah Williams returned to Keene but was arrested and ordered by the court to leave the state. Feeling was still bitter. On March 4, 1784, several of the Claremont Episcopalians petitioned the governor of Quebec for grants in his province near the American border. They complained that they were still "overburdened with Usurpation, Tyrene, and opression from the Hands of Violent Men." The state statutes against the Loyalists were only gradually repealed. The Disenfranchisement Act and the act disqualifying Loyalists from holding public office were repealed in 1784. The Proscription Act was repealed in 1786, and the remaining acts in 1792.

Despite the repeal measures only a few Loyalist refugees saw fit to return to the scene of their persecution. One of the most interesting of the returning stragglers was Robert Lewis Fowle, a printer of Exeter, who had fled in 1777, while under indictment for Loyalist counterfeiting activities. Soon after his return he ran an advertisement in the *American Herald of Liberty* of August 13, 1793. This advertisement requested all persons who had owed him money in 1776 and 1777 for newspaper subscriptions to settle their accounts and warned those who "plundered him of his printing office, books of account, papers, book-shop etc., in 1777, to make satisfaction, or they will be called upon before the Court of the United States."[42] War emotions were a long time in subsiding. For years the term "Tory" stigmatized a person and caused social ostracism.[43] Some Loyalists recovered their standing by sheer brilliant ability or attractive personality. Joshua Atherton, a Loyalist of Amherst, led the opposition to the ratification

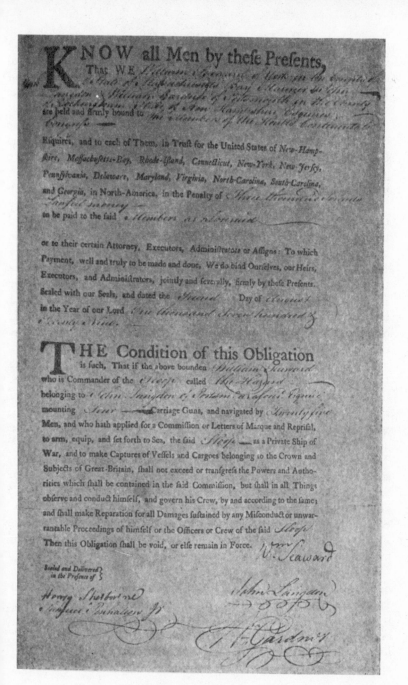

KNOW all Men by these Presents,

That WE _William Treadwell Clerk in the County of the State of Massachusetts Bay Mariner & the Captain William Gardner of Portsmouth in the County of Rockingham State of New Hampshire Esquire_ are held and firmly bound to _the Members of the Hon'ble Continental Congress_ ————

Esquires, and to each of Them, in Trust for the United States of _New-Hampshire, Massachusetts-Bay, Rhode-Island, Connecticut, New-York, New-Jersey, Pennsylvania, Delaware, Maryland, Virginia, North-Carolina, South-Carolina, and Georgia,_ in North-America, in the Penalty of _Three thousand pounds Lawful money_ to be paid to the said _Members as aforesaid_

or to their certain Attorney, Executors, Administrators or Assigns: To which Payment, well and truly to be made and done, We do bind Ourselves, our Heirs, Executors, and Administrators, jointly and severally, firmly by these Presents. Sealed with our Seals, and dated the _Second_ Day of _August_ in the Year of our Lord _One thousand Seven hundred & Seventy Nine._

THE Condition of this Obligation

is such, That if the above bounden _William Treadwell_ who is Commander of the _Sloop_ called _the Hazard_ belonging to _John Langdon of Portsm. aforesaid Esquire_ mounting _Four_ ——— Carriage Guns, and navigated by _Twenty five_ Men, and who hath applied for a Commission or Letters of Marque and Reprisal, to arm, equip, and set forth to Sea, the said _Sloop_ —— as a Private Ship of War, and to make Captures of Vessels and Cargoes belonging to the Crown and Subjects of Great-Britain, shall not exceed or transgress the Powers and Authorities which shall be contained in the said Commission, but shall in all Things observe and conduct himself, and govern his Crew, by and according to the same; and shall make Reparation for all Damages sustained by any Misconduct or unwarrantable Proceedings of himself or the Officers or Crew of the said _Sloop_ Then this Obligation shall be void, or else remain in Force. _W. Treaward_

Sealed and Delivered }
in the Presence of }

Henry Sherburne
Samuel Penhallow Jr

John Langdon

T. Gardner

Bond of the Privateer HAZARD Owned by John Langdon of Portsmouth.

of the Federal Constitution in 1788 and later became attorney general of the state. James Sheafe, a Loyalist of Portsmouth, was elected United States senator in 1802 on the Federalist ticket. In 1816 he came within 2,000 votes of being chosen governor.[44]

Much has been said by various historians of the deterioration of the quality of the American population caused by the banishment of the Loyalists during the American Revolution.[45] Some estimates have gone so far as to indicate that the Loyalist refugees from some colonies included the majority of the cultured and better educated people. In New Hampshire, at least, this cannot be said to have been entirely the case. The New Hampshire Loyalist refugees probably occupied the highest social positions and as a group were among the richer men in the colony. Nevertheless it must be remembered that New Hampshire was not, relatively speaking, a highly cultured section at the time of the Revolution. Only on the seacoast was society sharply divided into classes; in the greater part of the colony people were on a basis of democratic equality. Except for the clergy few men, Loyalist or Revolutionist, possessed more than a rudimentary education. Because of the general equality in the colony no one group had a monopoly of ability. Among the approximately one hundred New Hampshire Loyalist refugees and their families there were few outstanding men. Governor John Wentworth was a giant among his fellow-citizens; of that there can be no question. His secretary, Thomas McDonough, seems to have been a very capable man. New Hampshire sustained a great loss, too, when it exiled Benjamin Thompson of Concord.[46] Thompson later became prominent in British society as a leader in social reforms and scientific experiments. For his services to the Elector of Bavaria he was knighted and took the title "Count Rumford," after the original New Hampshire settlement which later became Concord. Among the remaining Loyalist refugees Colonel John Fenton of Plymouth and Colonel Stephen Holland of Londonderry were men of more than average ability.

The treatment of the Loyalists by the American Revolutionists can be considered from two viewpoints. All of the traditional rights and safeguards considered necessary to prevent one group in society from trampling on another, about which the colonists had shown such inexpressible concern in their petitions to England, were tossed to the four winds. A nation founded on the principle that free discussion and extensive deliberation will evolve the best governmental policy, had not enough faith in that principle to employ it in a time of great stress.

On the other hand, it must be remembered that the Revolutionists were fighting for their very existence. The great end which they were seeking to attain appeared in their eyes to justify the most severe means. Admittedly the Loyalists could and did hinder the efficiency of the Revolution. They spread false rumors; they discouraged enlistments in the Continental forces; they circulated underground propaganda; they counterfeited the money of the revolutionary governments; they acted as spies for the British intelligence service; and they served in great numbers in the British army. In time of peace a certain degree of inefficiency in democratic government, which is concomitant with absolute freedom of speech and extensive personal liberty, can be tolerated for the sake of the liberal principles involved. But in wartime the necessity of winning the war becomes the highest law. Democratic governments have nearly always found it necessary to sacrifice their principles in order to prosecute most efficiently their military struggles.

The real tragedy of the treatment of the Loyalists was not the fact that they were deprived of freedom of speech, that they were disarmed, that they were imprisoned, that they were exiled, and that their property was confiscated. The real tragedy lay in the fact that the Loyalists were brutally persecuted, that law and order surrendered supinely to mob psychology, that fair trials could not be had. The procedure in the detection and trial of the Loyalists was more at fault than the penalties devised for conviction. Yet it is doubtful if, in any time of war hysteria, political groups opposing the policies of the established government can obtain true justice.

Paper money always has promoted, and ever will promote corruption, and a multitude of other concomitant evils.

RESOLUTION OF PORTSMOUTH TOWN MEETING, 1786.[1]

But this depreciation, though in some circumstances inconvenient, has had the general good and great effect of operating as a tax, and perhaps the most equal of all taxes, since it depreciated in the hands of the holders of money, and thereby taxed them in proportion to the sums they held and the time they held it, which generally is in proportion to men's wealth.

BENJAMIN FRANKLIN.[2]

Revolutionary Finance in New Hampshire

REVOLUTIONARY governments have always been faced by the vexing problem of finance. They usually find themselves arrayed against a relatively well-established political and administrative system which enjoys superior advantages with respect to financial credit and resources. The historian has only to recall the days of the French Revolution, with its inflationary *assignats* and the wholesale repudiation of 1797, to perceive to what extremities revolutionary governments have frequently been driven. Within modern times the vast currency inflation of the Communist Revolution in Russia serves as a vivid example of the principle that the end justifies the means. This is the method of all violent revolutions, and it must be expected that revolutionary governments will adopt every expedient for the sake of their own survival.

It was not different in the case of the American Revolution. The revolting colonists were fighting a nation possessed of tremendous financial resources. There was in 1775 probably not enough money within the colonies to prosecute a successful war. Specie was continually being drained off by an unfavorable balance of trade. The British imperial system imposed narrow restrictions on colonial issues of paper money. Ready currency in America approximated twenty-two million dollars in paper and between six and twelve million dollars in specie.[3] This amount of currency was not sufficient to handle adequately the ordinary volume of business in peacetime without deflation and hardship to certain classes of society.

In New Hampshire the middle of the eighteenth century had been marked by wrangling between the royal governor, Benning Wentworth, and the provincial Assembly on the subject of the issuance of bills of credit.[4] The British government had reluctantly allowed New Hampshire to expand its currency during the Seven Years' War to meet military expenditures. After the war the bills of credit had been gradually called in by redemption and by taxation. By 1775 paper currency had practically ceased to exist. Specie was the circulating medium at an exchange standard of six shillings to one Spanish dollar. The provincial treasury had a slight surplus, and with an annual budget of only £3500 the public credit was sound and taxes were light. But from the viewpoint of the farmer, the debtor, and even the merchant, conditions were far from satisfactory. Money was scarce, and prices were intolerably low. As early as March 25, 1768, Governor Wentworth wrote to Lord Shelburne and the Lords of Trade, "In this Province the scarcity of money is so great—that it is totally impossible to collect near sufficient for Common Circulation."[5] Barter often became necessary as a method of exchange. Debtors frequently found the falling price level an insurmountable handicap in face of mortgages and debts contracted at a higher level. On May 21, 1774, the Assembly passed a more lenient bankruptcy law entitled— "An Act for Ease and Relief of Prisoners for Debt."[6]

With the advent of the Revolution New Hampshire might have resorted to three possible methods of financing her revolutionary activities—(1) taxation, (2) emission of bills of credit or treasury notes, (3) borrowing. The provincial system of taxation in New Hampshire was continued in force throughout the Revolution.[7] The tax law of July 2, 1776, stated that "all publick Rates and Taxes" should be "made and assessed in proportion to the amount of each Person's Poll, Ratable Estate and faculty."[8] The rates of assessment of 1776 give a fair idea of the character of the tax. All male polls 18 years of age and over were assessed at 12 shillings each. Rateable estate included male slaves, from 16 to 45 years of age, assessed at 10 shillings each; female slaves, from 16 to 45 years of age, assessed at 5 shillings each; live stock, classified as to species and age, assessed at from 6 pence to 3 shillings per animal; improved lands assessed according to quality at from 5 pence to 1 shilling and 6 pence per acre; all houses, mills, warehouses, wharves, and ferries, evaluated at one-twelfth their annual income; and all stock whether monies at hand, at interest, or in trade, invoiced at the rate of one-half of 1 per cent. The value of a person's "faculty" (his relative ability in his profession) was annually estimated at an amount not to exceed £10. Each year the selectmen in the towns were required to take an inventory, which included the total assessed value of all polls, estates, and faculties in their respective towns. Each town's quota of the annual state tax was apportioned according to the amount of its inventory.[9]

On November 29, 1777, there was passed an additional tax law, which classified unimproved land under rateable estate, assessable at one-half of 1 per cent of its value.[10] A royal tax on proprietary rights in towns was continued during the Revolution.[11] On September 1, 1781, an excise on the sale of intoxicating beverages by "Tavernors, Innholders and retailers" was imposed. As was the custom under royal government this excise was "farmed out" or sold to the highest bidder in each county, who then proceeded to collect it himself at a reasonable profit.[12] After 1778 a naval officer stationed at Portsmouth harbor collected tonnage and registration fees on all vessels entering or clearing the port.[13] No state tariff on imports was imposed until after the Revolution. Such in brief were the main sources of New Hampshire's tax revenue.

The administration of the state's finances was vested in the office of treasurer and receiver-general, which was filled by Nicholas Gilman until his death in 1783. Upon the treasurer fell the duty of ascertaining each town's share of the state tax according to the proportions established by law and of forwarding each town's tax warrant to its selectmen. The selectmen were then required to determine each taxpayer's share of the total amount of the tax according to the assessed value of his poll and estate. The individual taxes were then collected by the town constable or other designated collector and forwarded to the state treasury.

Revolutionary Finance in New Hampshire

At the beginning of the Revolution economic conditions made it inexpedient for the revolutionary government to impose heavy taxes. New Hampshire was still suffering the throes of the post-Seven Years' War depression.[14] Because of the inadequacy of a circulating medium, large numbers of farmers, whose wealth consisted almost wholly of real estate, were unable to pay public dues except in produce. Then too, the psychology of the political situation was an obstacle to a policy of taxation. By the overturn of the royal government the iniquitous British tax measures had been eliminated. It would have been unwise and perhaps politically impossible for the Revolutionists to proceed immediately to adapt British policy to their own use. The American colonies seemed to object to "taxation without representation." But the fact is that the American environment and the influence of the frontier had developed a laissez-faire philosophy which objected to taxation in itself as an unwarranted restriction on personal freedom.[15]

It is, therefore, understandable that no considerable taxes were imposed during the first year of revolutionary government in New Hampshire. During this period governmental activities were financed by an expansion of the currency. Once the currency had been moderately expanded, however, there was no logical reason for abstaining longer from taxing to support the war. On December 23, 1776, William Whipple, New Hampshire's delegate in the Continental Congress and a sound money advocate, wrote from Philadelphia to Dr. Josiah Bartlett, "How does taxing go on! do you raise much money in that way? the People certainly were never so well able to pay a large tax as at this time."[16]

Throughout the war the total amount of the state tax increased with the depreciation of the paper money and the mounting military costs. The first state tax, levied on September 2, 1775, amounted to £4000.[17] The next tax levy, imposed on September 19, 1776, called for £3923.[18] But the state tax for the year 1777 totaled £40,000.[19] On November 22, 1777, the Continental Congress made its first requisition on the states, calling upon New Hampshire for $200,000 or £60,000. Consequently the state tax for 1778 rose to £80,000 of which £60,000 were ear-marked for the Continental government.[20] During 1779 the Congress made three additional requisitions upon New Hampshire, calling in the aggregate for the sum of $2,500,000 or £750,000. To meet these demands there were in this year two levies of state taxes, by which £700,000 were to be raised. Of this sum £600,000 were allocated to the Continental treasury.[21] On March 15, 1780, the annual state tax reached the wartime high of £2,160,000, one-half of which was to be used to meet congressional requisitions.[22]

During 1780 and 1781 the Congress resorted to the method of requisitioning the states for food supplies for the Continental army. A schedule was devised whereby a certain monetary credit in specie was given for each kind of provision to be supplied. New Hampshire's supply requisitions called for rum and beef. But the credit allowed on these articles was much less in proportion to their real value than the credit allowed on the produce of the Southern states. Indian corn, flour, and hay were valued at from 100 to 200 per cent in advance of the 1774 price level, whereas rum, which had to be imported, and beef were valued at only 50 per cent in advance of the same scale of prices. New Hampshire's delegates in the Congress were extremely disgruntled at this situation.[23] Nevertheless, the state proceeded to fill its quota in the best manner possible. On June 27, 1780, a direct state tax of 1,120,000 lbs. of beef was levied upon the towns, each town being required to supply a quantity in proportion to its annual state tax.[24] On January 27, 1781, a similar tax of 1,400,000 lbs. of beef was levied.[25] On August 31 a tax of 10,000 gallons of rum was imposed, each town being assigned a certain quota.[26] Major General John Sullivan wrote to Meshech Weare on September 16, 1780, "I rejoice that Genl. Washington Gives New Hampshire Credit for Complying with the requisitions of Congress better than any other State."[27] Yet the records show that New Hampshire supplied less than half of its full quota of rum.[28]

In 1781 New Hampshire started to retrench in the matter of its finances. On January 27 a state tax of £120,000 in currency of the new Continental issue of 1780 was levied, together with a specie tax of £4500 for purposes of currency redemption.[29] On August 31 a tax of $100,000 in bills of the new emission plus a specie tax of $5000 was imposed.[30] On January 16, 1782, there was laid a state tax of £110,000 which was payable in specie, state loan certificates, rum, beef, leather shoes, yarn, hose, cloth, felt hats, wheat-flour, or blankets.[31] The state tax for the year 1783 totaled £55,000 of which £38,000 was to be paid into the Continental treasury.[32] By 1784 the tax had sunk to the normal figure of £25,000 lawful money.

The Articles of Confederation had gone into effect on March 1, 1781.

Revolutionary Finance in New Hampshire

Under their provisions financial requisitions on the states were supposedly apportioned according to the value of each state's surveyed land. Actually this method of apportioning taxes was never put into operation. Instead the Congress continued to use the old method of devising the quotas in proportion to each state's population. In 1781 and 1782 New Hampshire protested in the Continental Congress that her quota of taxes was based upon a population figure in excess of her actual population. On April 1, 1782, however, the Congress by a vote of eight states to four refused to reduce her quota.[33] During the dispute delegate Samuel Livermore wrote home to Meshech Weare, "It is further held forth that if any state is *now* overburthened they shall be recompensed *hereafter*. I fear this word *hereafter* is to be taken in a theological sense."[34] From that time until 1789 New Hampshire only partially complied with the Continental requisitions. In 1790 the estimates of Alexander Hamilton, Secretary of the Treasury, showed that over this seven year period New Hampshire had paid into the Continental treasury only $122,104 (specie value) out of total requisitions of $591,875 (specie value). Only New Jersey, North Carolina, and Georgia had been greater delinquents. Pennsylvania had paid 53 per cent of the total requisitions and New York 66 per cent to lead all of the states.[35]

One of the greatest problems of Revolutionary taxation had been that of devising a tax which would have a just incidence. The tax on polls and estates, by which most of the tax revenue was raised, was relatively more of a burden on the farmer and the laborer than on the mercantile element. The collection of taxes was annually a scene of great tragedy in the rural districts and the poorer sections of the towns.[36] Each year the small homesteads of large numbers of people had to be sold for delinquency in taxes. Then too, the difficulties in the liquidation of property delayed tax collection greatly. The state taxes were often several years late in being paid into the treasury and frequently were never paid in full. The tax records in 1781 showed £399,877 outstanding in unpaid taxes, covering the years 1775 to 1780.[37] On April 6, 1781, the state legislature passed a more drastic act to enforce the collection of taxes.[38] Yet despite the hardships of property and poll taxation, the merchants and financial interests were opposed to a tax on trade or commerce. On May 21, 1779, William Whipple in the Continental Congress wrote home to Dr. Josiah Bartlett, "the people in this part of the Country are every where clamerous for heavy Taxes. the greatest difficulty appears to me is, the levying it on the proper persons. if the whole sum could be drawn from those speculating miscreants, who have been sucking the Blood of their country, it would be a most happy circumstance. . . . . He who increases in wealth in such times as the present, must be an enemy to his Country, be his pretentions what they may."[39] Apparently war profiteers were no more popular then than they have been in modern times.

With the delinquency in the collection of taxes, the reluctance to levy heavy taxes, and the increasing costs of the war, taxation was far from sufficient as a method of financing the state government. By June 12, 1777, the expenditures of the state government since the beginning of the Revolution totaled £184,903. State expenditures for the period June 13, 1777, to October 23, 1779, amounted to £645,766 in paper money. Reaching still greater heights, in the period October 24, 1779, to November 23, 1781, state expenditures amazingly totaled £4,839,229 in old paper currency and £214,047 in notes of the new emission.[40] Even when allowance is made for the depreciation of the currency, these figures indicate a large increase in governmental costs.

In the light of modern theories of finance, far too little of the cost of the Revolutionary War was paid by taxation. But this can probably be said of any war fought by a democratic government. The politically expedient policy is to spread the financial burden of the war over as long a period as possible. The major portion of the costs of the Revolution, exclusive of foreign loans, was met by the issuance of paper money in various forms.

With the exception of two minor tax assessments on the towns to pay the expenses of delegates in the Continental Congress, the issuance of paper money was the first method employed in New Hampshire to finance revolutionary activities. The Revolutionists were frankly novices in the art of finance. On May 23, 1775, Presiden Thornton of the fourth Provincial Congress wrote to New Hampshire's delegates at Philadelphia, ". . . . The circulating cash in this Province is very small . . . . We desire to have the benefit of some general plan for bills of credit, or that we may act with the advice of the Congress in issuing such ourselves. . . . ."[41] On June 9 the Provincial Congress voted to issue £10,050 in treasury notes at 6 per cent interest, redeemable by the taxes of the future years 1776, 1777, and 1778.[42] This was the first issue of currency by the revolutionary government in New Hampshire. Technically this currency was secured not by specie but only by faith and patriotism. Such backing might have been sufficient had only a moderate amount of the paper been issued and had the war been of short duration. At any rate the new money was not made legal tender; it was merely declared receivable at the treasury.

The next issue of paper currency was authorized by the Provincial Congress on July 6, 1775. At that time the Congress voted to emit £10,000 in treasury notes at 6 per cent interest, redeemable by taxes in the years 1777, 1778, and 1779.[43] On August 22 the Congress pursued its inflationary policy still further by deciding to discontinue the payment of interest on the new currency.[44] Discontinuance of interest reduced the treasury notes to the lowly status of bills of credit. On November 1 the Provincial Congress voted an additional currency expansion of £20,000 in such bills of credit to be redeemed by taxes in the years 1779-1782.[45] On the whole New Hampshire's monetary policy for the year 1775 was fairly conservative. A total of £40,050 in bills of credit had been placed in circulation. No confiscation had taken place by making them legal tender. The bills circulated very nearly at par value. The evidence indicates that the state government honestly intended to redeem them at the times fixed by law. Not everyone was satisfied with the monetary situation, however. On October 2, 1775, Dr. Josiah Bartlett and John Langdon, New Hampshire's delegates in the Continental Congress, wrote home, ". . . . It would ruin us to be emitting paper on every occasion."[46] They urged taxation as a means of financing the war.

On January 2, 1776, the fifth Provincial Congress chose a committee of five to devise "a Plan for sinking the Colony Debt."[47] Nothing appears to have been accomplished by this committee, although £1128 in paper notes were retired on January 24.[48] On January 26, 1776, the newly inaugurated state government authorized the emission of £20,008 in bills of credit to be redeemed by taxes in the years 1783-1786.[49] This series of bills was made legal tender for "all payments." On June 7, 1776, the state legislature empowered a committee of seven to endeavor to exchange paper money for specie, which was sorely needed by the army.[50] The committee was unsuccessful in raising any appreciable amount, as gold and silver tended to be driven out of circulation by the issuance of paper currency. According to Gresham's Law cheap money nearly always tends to drive dear money into hoarding or out of the country.

On June 27, 1776, the state legislature voted to emit £3400 in fractional currency.[51] This, too, was made legal tender for all debts and was to be redeemed by taxes in 1787-1788. On July 3 all issues of bills of credit of New Hampshire and all Continental notes were made legal tender by an act of the legislature.[52] This same act defined as a crime the acceptance of paper money at less than its par value in gold and silver. Violators of this act were liable to a £50 fine and disqualification from public office-holding. At the same time the legislature resolved to issue £20,160 in bills of credit to be redeemed by taxes in the years 1789-1792.[53]

By the end of 1776 New Hampshire had outstanding £83,618 in circulating bills of credit. There were also in circulation throughout the colonies some $25,000,000 in Continental notes issued by the Continental Congress.[54] Depreciation was apparently only just beginning to be severely felt. In December, 1776, chairman Meshech Weare of the Committee of Safety wrote to the state's delegates in the Continental Congress, "The plenty of Paper Money and the Depreciation thereof has such an effect we are fearful of making more."[55] As yet no appreciable effort had been made to redeem any of the paper by taxation. Encouraged by the wartime demand as well as by the expansion of the currency, prices of goods were rapidly rising. Price conventions, price regulations and laws against monopoly and extortion all alike failed to keep prices down. The failure of these measures was an excellent example of the fact that eventually statute law cannot alter economic tendencies. A more detailed discussion of the phenomenon of price inflation is reserved for the following chapter.

On January 15, 1777, the New Hampshire legislature resumed its inflationary policy by authorizing the issuance of £30,000 in treasury notes at 6 per cent interest.[56] These notes were used to pay bounties for enlistments in the Continental army. On April 8, 1777, the legislature passed a law making paper money legal tender in satisfaction of all contracts.[57] · Refusal of Continental or New Hampshire notes at par value when tendered as full payment for contracted debts was punishable by forfeiture of the entire debt. All creditors bringing actions in court for recovery of debts, after having refused payment in paper, were to be penalized by being required to pay triple costs to the defendants. A contemporary historian, the Reverend Jeremy

Belknap, wrote, "The fraudulent debtor took advantage of this law to cheat his creditor, under colour of justice. . . . ."[58] Contracted debts requiring payment in gold and silver or the paper equivalent thereof might now be liquidated by the mere presentation of sheaves of depreciated paper money. A debt of £100 in silver incurred in 1774 could be paid off in £100 paper money, which at the end of 1777 was worth approximately £30 in silver.[59] Enterprizers engaging in business on borrowed capital could protect themselves from depreciation by charging tremendously high prices for their goods. But in repayment of their creditors they might liquidate their obligations by tendering money of less value than they had borrowed. A hawker or peddler could borrow capital of £100 paper money in 1778 (£25 in silver) and settle his obligation a year later by the presentation of £100 paper money (£8 in silver). One year's depreciation in this case could wipe out two-thirds of the debt. On November 18, 1779, this law concerning contracted debts was finally repealed as "unjust with respect to individuals."[60]

On February 15, 1777, the Continental Congress had urged the states to consolidate their finances. Accordingly on November 29, 1777, a law was passed empowering the state treasurer to call in all bills of credit of higher denomination than £5 and to issue in their stead treasury notes at 6 per cent interest.[61] During 1778 the treasurer issued new notes for the greater part of the outstanding bills of credit.[62] This policy, however, failed to change the monetary situation as the same amount of money still circulated, and the interest payments were never faithfully discharged. At the end of 1777 there was in circulation £111,746 of paper currency issued by New Hampshire. The expected redemption with the proceeds of taxation had failed to materialize. On April 10, 1777, the treasury had retired £1744 in paper currency, but this amount was insignificant.[63] To add to the woes of the state the amount of Continental notes in circulation throughout the colonies had risen to $38,000,000 which only accentuated the general depreciation. At the beginning of 1778 this mass of paper was worth less than one-third of its face value.[64]

Yet on March 5, 1778, the state treasurer was empowered to issue £40,000 in treasury notes at 6 per cent interest payable within four years.[65] This was the last issue of state paper currency, and it increased the total amount in circulation to £151,746. During 1778 the Continental Congress issued $63,500,300 in notes, thus raising the amount of outstanding Continental paper to $101,500,300.[66] Part of this, at least, circulated in New Hampshire and accelerated the depreciation of the state currency. At the beginning of 1779 paper money was worth less than one-seventh of its face value.

In 1779 New Hampshire entered upon a policy of borrowing from the public for short terms. On March 18 the treasurer was authorized to borrow £20,000 at interest for one year.[67] On December 22, 1779, the borrowing of an additional £50,000 for a short term was authorized.[68] On June 28, 1780, the legislature voted to borrow £300,000 for a limited period.[69] This transaction raised total authorized borrowings during 1779 and 1780 to £370,000. The treasurer, however, was unable to borrow nearly as much money as was authorized because of the weakness of the credit of the state. According to the treasury account books, state borrowings for the years 1777 to 1781 totaled but £96,539.[70] These obligations took the form of short term notes which probably circulated as currency.

By the end of 1779 the total amount of Continental paper money in circulation had reached $241,552,780. This paper was worth approximately one-fortieth of its face value. On March 18, 1780, the Continental Congress voted to issue new Continental notes to replace the old at the rate of $1 new money to $40 old.[71] Each state was assigned a quota of the old notes to collect by taxation and pay into the Continental treasury. New Hampshire's quota was fixed at $5,200,000.[72] Over a period of eighteen months the state collected and paid its quota in full. A specie credit of $130,000 was accordingly granted to New Hampshire by the Continental treasury. Against this central credit the state was enabled to issue $145,000 in new Continental money. Some of the old Continental notes continued to circulate, but in 1782 they became entirely worthless.

On July 4, 1781, the New Hampshire legislature repealed its legal tender laws, and on September 1 gold and silver were declared the only legal tender.[73] The same law set up a scale of depreciation of paper money for the years 1777-1781 to be used for the liquidation in terms of gold and silver of debts incurred during that period. A very bitter struggle occurred in the legislature over the passage of the gold and silver legal tender act.[74] It passed the House of Representatives by a majority of only one vote. Among those representatives voting for the act, the greater part came from large towns in Rockingham and Strafford, the two seacoast counties. Those opposing the act came mostly from towns in Hillsborough County and in western Rockingham County, the middle section of the state and a predominantly agrarian section.

On January 16, 1782, the legislature enacted a plan for the liquidation of the state's paper currency.[75] Holders of such currency or notes were enabled to bring them into the state treasury for exchange or redemption. There the principal of the currency or notes was liquidated according to the scale of depreciation of September 1, 1781. Interest was computed from the time of the issuance of each paper note. The amount of the liquidated principal was reissued as a new interest-bearing note payable in gold and silver upon demand. The computed interest on each old note was reissued as a gold and silver certificate receivable at the state treasury for taxes. This action amounted to theoretical repudiation of a substantial amount of the outstanding paper currency.

Even with the marking down of the amount of the principal of the state's paper currency, a very heavy debt was left with New Hampshire as a result of the Revolution. Timothy Pitkin estimated it to be an amount as high as $500,000 (specie), which was probably too large a figure.[76] At any rate within six or eight years a large part of the paper obligations was retired. Retirement was accomplished, strangely enough, not by redemption in gold and silver, but by an exchange of the paper notes for gold and silver certificates which were not secured by specie but were maintained at par value by being receivable at the state treasury for taxes. Upon the payment of these certificates into the treasury they were destroyed. In 1790 Alexander Hamilton, Secretary of the Treasury, estimated New Hampshire's total remaining debt at $300,000 (specie) representing a per capita debt of $2.15. As compared with New Hampshire in 1790, Massachusetts had a per capita debt of $14.00. Connecticut's per capita debt was $8.00; New York's was $3.30; Virginia's, $5.00; and that of South Carolina $21.50.[77] Under Hamilton's "Assumption Bill" $282,595 of New Hampshire's Revolutionary debt was assumed by the federal government.[78]

One of the most annoying problems of New Hampshire's monetary administration had been that of counterfeit money. With the large number and different types of monetary notes in circulation the counterfeiter's task was rendered relatively easy. Modern scientific methods of detection of forged notes were unknown during the Revolution.

The British and Loyalists frequently resorted to counterfeiting American money, which was a strategic method of weakening the revolutionary governments. By the placing of counterfeit notes in circulation the currency tended to become unstable and depreciate even more rapidly than it normally would have done. Because of the tremendous potential damage which could be and was caused by counterfeiting, drastic laws were passed and the offense was considered a political one, under the jurisdiction of the Committee of Safety as well as of the courts.[79]

On July 3, 1776, the New Hampshire legislature passed a law against "counterfeiting and forgeing."[80] Persons convicted of practising this "vile Cheat on unwary and less discerning Persons" were punished by "being set on the Gallows for the Space of one hour, with a Rope round the Neck," fined £50, imprisoned for six months, publicly whipped not exceeding thirty-nine stripes, disqualified from holding public office, and assessed treble damages for the benefit of those persons defrauded by the passage of counterfeit notes. On June 25, 1777, a supplemental law was passed declaring the property of fugitive counterfeiters forfeit to the state and preventing its transfer to other persons.[81]

Counterfeiters were often detected by local committees of safety upon popular suspicion. On March 23, 1776, Bezaleel Phelps of Norwich was brought before the Hanover Committee of Safety by virtue of a warrant "predicated on his having in his custody and detaining a certain Note of this Colony bearing the face of a six shilling Bill which is supposed to have been fraudulently altered and increased as to the value. . . . ."[82] Informers on counterfeiters were generally allowed a reward. In the records of the Council for November 28, 1776, appeared the following entry: "Allowed, John Ayer, £10 for detecting James Ryan in counterfeiting Bills of credit."[83] Detection of counterfeiting was not confined to state limits but was nationwide. On February 19, 1777, Governor Cooke of Rhode Island wrote to the New Hampshire Committee of Safety informing it that a man had been arrested in Rhode Island for forging New Hampshire notes.[84]

Perhaps the most famous counterfeiting scandal was exposed in 1777.[85] On January 9, 1776, the state had ordered a currency issue to be struck off by Robert Lewis Fowle of Exeter, a printer and a man of secret Loyalist sympathies. Fowle apparently printed many more paper notes than were desired before he destroyed his plates. These surplus notes were distributed by him among the Loyalists of Hillsborough County. Before long the state treasury discovered that there was in circulation an excessive number of bills of the series of January 9, 1776. An investigation was begun and on April 18, 1777, printer Fowle was summoned before the state Committee of Safety. He was offered immunity from prosecution if he would confess and name his associates. Upon his evidence the Committee issued warrants against five prominent Loyalists in Hillsborough County. Later, four more were shown to have been implicated. The evidence pointed strongly toward the existence of a Loyalist counterfeiting ring in Hillsborough County.

The financial chaos of the Revolution and Confederation periods demonstrated more than ever the need for a central or federal financial administration with more adequate powers. During the Revolution the Continental government had no authority over the states in the matter of finance. Scores of different types of currency circulated, and Continental tax requisitions carried no more force than a polite invitation for the states to appropriate money. There was, however, one organ of centralized financial administration. This was the Continental Loan Office which was established in each state.[86] In New Hampshire the duties of this office were vested in the state treasurer, Nicholas Gilman. He received such money as the public wished to loan to the Continental government and issued loan certificates bearing interest as security.

Economists and others with high ideals of public credit and a sense of the inviolability of private property are, no doubt, shocked at the "immorality" of the inflation and partial repudiation which took place during the Revolution. Yet one wonders how else the Revolution could have been financed. Benjamin Franklin, that shrewd dispenser of homely common sense, looked at the matter from another angle and observed, "This Currency, as we manage it, is a wonderful Machine. It performs its Office when we issue it; it pays and clothes Troops, and provides Victuals and Ammunition; and when we are obliged to issue a Quantity excessive, it pays itself off by Depreciation."[87]

The inflation of the currency and its partial repudiation at the end of the war constituted nothing less than an indirect tax, the burden of which was diffused over a long period. It was a tax of the widest possible incidence since it affected everyone who ever held currency. It was not, it is true, always a tax of just incidence. Creditors, as a rule, were paid back in money of less purchasing power than the money which they originally lent. Debtors, particularly farmers and laborers, were enabled to obtain higher prices for their goods and services, and to liquidate obligations which remained fixed in amount. Clever merchants protected themselves from loss through depreciation by charging prices well in advance of the existent money value of their goods. Consumers as a class were undoubtedly victimized. The group in society which suffered most included those persons living on fixed incomes and salaries. In this class was Dr. Eleazar Wheelock, President of Dartmouth College in Hanover. On April 25, 1778, Wheelock wrote to John Phillips, "I have thought it duty for me & my Family to live in as cheap & low a manner as would consist with bodily Health but the Iniquitous Sinking of our Medium outbids all my hopes of Surviving the evil and keeping my School together, without Some friendly assistance."[88] Perhaps the soldiers received the worst treatment as their wages were never revised upward with sufficient speed to keep pace with the rate of depreciation. On March 28, 1780, Meshech Weare wrote to Nathaniel Peabody that because of the depreciation, ". . . . The money we raised last year for the use of the State was not a quarter part sufficient to provide for our officers and soldiers."[89]

In New Hampshire at any rate the partial repudiation which took place at the end of the war was not in itself such a grave injustice as has commonly been supposed. The scale of depreciation by which the state's paper notes were liquidated contained an estimate of the specie value of the paper notes for every month during the years 1777 to 1781. In the process of liquidation of the paper notes the principal of each note was computed as equal to the specie value of the note at the time of its issuance. Thus paper notes dating before January, 1777, were computed as equal to their face value in specie while notes dating from October, 1778, for example, were computed as worth only one-fifth of their face value in specie. Provided the original holder of each New Hampshire treasury note had been able to hold this note until 1782, he might then have obtained a new note to the amount of the specie value of the goods and services which he had originally lent to the state government. However, it is extremely improbable that in 1782 many of the state treasury notes were still in the hands of the original holders. In most cases these notes had circulated from hand to hand during the war years. Each note had become worth a little less each time it had changed hands. One person might have received a certain amount of paper notes from the state government in payment for goods and services. Generally before he had been able to pass the paper on, it would have depreciated slightly. Thus the holder would not have been able to obtain quite as many goods and services in return for the money as he had given for the money upon first obtaining it. The net loss in purchasing power was an indirect tax on the holder of the currency. At the end of the war the currency in terms of purchasing power was worth only a small fraction of its original value. In 1782 the decision of the New Hampshire legislature to liquidate the amount of the principal of the state treasury notes according to the specie value of each note at the time of its issuance did not harm the current holders of these notes. In fact, where the notes were held by persons other than the original holders, these persons were unjustly enriched, for they received in exchange for their notes new currency of a higher value in specie than the value of their goods and services for which they had received the old notes. The real injustice of this plan of liquidation fell upon those original holders of state treasury notes who had not passed them on immediately before considerable depreciation had occurred but who had held their notes for months and years and then had been forced to dispose of them at a discount, having no knowledge that the state would eventually redeem the notes on a just basis.

Regardless of whether one considers the financial policies of the American Revolution to have been moral or immoral, which is really beside the point, certain practical benefits accrued from them. These policies aided in winning the war and setting up a new nation, but of greater and less questionable value was the experience gained from them. Nearly every person was made to feel the hardships of a chaotic and decentralized financial administration. The great majority of the people suffered from inflation, whether they understood the phenomenon or not. Many of them learned a valuable lesson in regard to efficiency of financial and monetary administration. The experience of the country in public finance during the Revolution undoubtedly laid the foundation for the sound public credit established by Alexander Hamilton, which has been maintained from 1790 to the present day.

CHAPTER I I

War is no longer Samson with his shield and spear and sword, and David with his sling; . . . . it is a conflict of smokestacks now, the combat of the driving wheel and the engine.

NEWTON D. BAKER, 1917.[1]

He who increases in wealth in such times as the present, must be an enemy to his Country, be his pretentions what they may.

WILLIAM WHIPPLE, 1779.[2]

Industry and the Revolution

THE American Revolution was characterized by the fact that during the conflict the greater part of the population was engaged in its ordinary economic pursuits. Out of a white population of two and one quarter millions in 1776 there were roughly 500,000 men of fighting age in the colonies. Yet, 1776, the peak year for military service, saw only 90,000 men under arms. Privateering and the Continental navy probably accounted for another 33,000. What were the remainder of the able-bodied men engaged in? Outside the few war industries they were pursuing their normal occupations, but by contributing to the support of the civilian population as well as the army, they were playing a part fully as necessary as that of the soldier in the prosecution of the war.

The principal industries of New Hampshire during the Revolutionary period, as before, were commerce, shipbuilding, fishing, lumbering and agriculture. The struggle had certain definite effects on each of these industries, and the resulting trends were important because they

[148]

marked the directions which certain types of American economic endeavor were to follow for many years to come.

Prior to the Revolution New Hampshire participated in the famed triangular commerce with the British West Indies and England.[3] Lumber, beef, fish, oil, and livestock were the principal exports, and rum, sugar, molasses, coffee, and naval stores the leading imports. New Hampshire merchants, employing ships of two or three hundred tons, exported cargoes to the West Indies where they were exchanged for the tropical products of the islands, which were sent back to New Hampshire in smaller vessels. The larger ships, in the meanwhile, took on cargoes of sugar as freight and sailed for England where the ships were sold and freight charges collected. The proceeds were used to buy cordage, anchors, canvas and other English goods which were shipped to New Hampshire. John Langdon, a merchant of Portsmouth, was engaged in this triangular commerce, and among his papers today can be seen his balance sheets made out by the London trading house of Lane, Son & Fraser.[4] Not all trade, however, followed this three-cornered route. Many vessels sailed directly from Portsmouth for London each year with cargoes of masts and spars. Portsmouth merchants also took part in a coasting trade with southern ports, exchanging their West Indian products for corn, rice, flour, pork, and naval stores, a part of which they reëxported to Newfoundland and Nova Scotia in order to obtain bills of exchange on England.

The foreign trade of the colony had been strictly limited by the British trade regulations.[5] Several vessels sailed annually for the free ports of the French and Dutch West Indies with cargoes of lumber, fish, oil, and provisions to exchange for sugar and molasses which could be distilled into rum.[6] One vessel each year went to the Azores or the Canaries with pipe staves and fish, returning with a cargo of wines. Frequently a ship which had sailed to England would there take on a cargo of freight for Lisbon or Cadiz and return to Portsmouth with salt and fruit.

The immediate effect of the Revolution on American commerce was to abolish the British trade regulations and to open possibilities for world-wide trade. Actually the war caused a partial suspension of foreign commerce. The British government, by an act of Parliament on December 22, 1775, declared the colonial ports closed. A partial blockade was maintained off the American coast, and because of the British control of the seas American commerce became an extremely hazardous activity. All American vessels taken on the high seas were liable to confiscation. Nevertheless, most of the merchants continued in commerce because of the great profits attendant upon even partial success in running the blockade. European goods commanded tremendous prices so great was the scarcity in the American market. Many merchants, as has been seen, engaged in privateering. Captured cargoes often furnished valuable articles for domestic trade. The former royal governor, John Wentworth, believed that commerce and privateering were the main incentives which kept up the revolutionary spirit in New Hampshire. On January 6, 1777, he wrote from New York to Lord George Germain, " . . . . Yet the leaders in the rebellion still continue very industrious to keep up an evil spirit among the people . . . . ,—among those Mr. John Langdon is one of the most violent and active, as he derives great advantages from the continuance of the rebellion."[7] Throughout the war Langdon and other Portsmouth merchants sent lumber cargoes to Bordeaux in France to exchange for military and naval stores and European goods.

The impetus which was given to foreign commerce by high profits and opportunities for speculation during the Revolution continued after the Treaty of Peace in 1783.[8] At first British colonial ports were closed to American goods, which caused a preliminary decline in commerce during the Confederation period. This situation gradually diverted American commerce farther afield to the Baltic, the Mediterranean, and the Far East. During the first half of the nineteenth century the United States became one of the leading maritime powers of the world, so rapidly did her commerce grow after the Revolution.

Not the least important factor in this astounding growth was the American shipbuilding industry. Before the Revolution many English enterprizers bought American ships, and thus a large part of the trade of the empire was carried in American-built vessels. The British trade regulations, in fact, gave the colonies a partial monoply of the carrying trade.[9] Portsmouth and the Great Bay region in New Hampshire were important centers of shipbuilding; not less than two hundred vessels of small tonnage were built there annually.[10] With the advent of the Revolution, however, the colonies lost their favored position in shipbuilding. Hundreds of American ships were destroyed, and the building industry sank to a low ebb because of lack of labor and materials.[11] Despite the fact that many British ships were captured by New Hampshire privateers, the amount of shipping owned at

Portsmouth sank from 12,000 tons in 1775 to 500 tons in 1780.[12] After the war New Hampshire shipyards regained much of their former prosperity, especially after the establishment of the Federal government in 1789, and continued to prosper well into the nineteenth century.[13]

Closely allied with the prosperity of the shipbuilding industry before the Revolution was the fishing industry. Excellent cod fishing prevailed all the way from the Isles of Shoals to Newfoundland, and salt fish had been the largest single article of export from New Hampshire. Each employer-fisherman annually organized three cruises to the Grand Banks.[14] His employees were enlisted on the share basis, being awarded a fixed percentage of the profits of each cruise. So vital was the fishing industry to New England as a whole that the closing of the coastal fisheries by the New England Restraining Act on March 30, 1775, was conceived by the British government as a fitting punishment for the revolutionary agitation which had permeated the district. During the summer and fall of 1775 the British navy ravaged the fishing fleet on a large scale.[15] The scarcity of labor and the rage for privateering finally caused the total suspension of the industry. At the end of the war fishing was resumed subject to a few minor restrictions imposed by the Treaty of 1783. However, the industry never afterwards flourished in New Hampshire to the same degree that it had before the Revolution. For one thing, the need for salt fish in the triangular trade to the West Indies had vanished, for many West Indian ports were closed to American commerce.

Next to fishing, lumbering was perhaps the oldest New Hampshire industry.[16] The white pine, which grew extensively in New Hampshire, was regarded as the most durable timber in America. Not only was pine lumber exported in bulk but also a large part of the cuttings was used for shipbuilding. Before the Revolution the mast trade with England employed large numbers of lumbermen. There were three principal centers of lumbering in New Hampshire—the Piscataqua River and Great Bay region, the Merrimack Valley system, and the Connecticut Valley. Lumbermen along the Piscataqua and on the tributaries of Great Bay floated their lumber in rafts down to Portsmouth. Those situated on the Merrimack River and its subsidiary streams floated their cuttings down the river to Newburyport in Massachusetts. The lumbering concerns in the Connecticut River valley floated their products down the river to Hartford, Connecticut, whence they were exported. During the Revolution lumbering operations were largely suspended because of the high cost of labor and the lack of a steady market. After 1783 the high price of lumber induced many lumbermen to resume their activities. Yet the demand for lumber fluctuated so widely in the post-Revolutionary years that only the largest enterprizers made profits. This situation caused many people to turn from lumbering to agriculture.

At the time of the Revolution agriculture was the largest single industry in New Hampshire.[17] The most common products were hay, clover, flaxseed, wheat, Indian corn, rye, barley, oats, peas, apples, and a few vegetables. Cattle, sheep, swine, and poultry were also raised in large numbers. Methods of farming were very crude. Crops were usually grown in fields of dead tree stumps, the land generally being cleared by burning the timber which, according to Jeremy Belknap, frequently scorched the soil and made it inferior. Very little use was made of fertilizer, and only a rudimentary system of crop rotation was practised. Before the Revolution the farmers were little disposed to experiment and very suspicious of new theories. Belknap wrote, "It is . . . . partly from the ideas of *equality* with which the minds of the husbandmen are early impressed, and partly from a want of education, that no spirit of improvement is seen among them, but every one pursues the business of sowing, planting, mowing, and raising cattle, with unremitting labor and undeviating uniformity."[18] For the most part the New Hampshire farmer had to be thrifty and economical to survive, and he was not eager to adopt new methods of farming which might have worked well in Europe. Furthermore, the good land in New Hampshire was limited to the intervale sections along the river valleys.

There have been various theories advanced as to the effect of the Revolution on agriculture. James Truslow Adams suggests that the industry suffered.[19] Many farmers fought in the army while their land grew up in weeds. Other farmers were caught by the high cost of living and high taxes; they incurred tremendous debts, causing them to join in the paper money agitation. Agricultural laborers charged extortionate wages, but the price level of agricultural products rose scarcely fast enough to keep pace with the depreciation of paper money. Thus agricultural production declined along with industry. Professor Ernest Ludlow Bogart, on the other hand, states that outside the military area, agriculture, so far as it was self-sufficing, was little affected by the Revolution.[20]

Industry and the Revolution

In New Hampshire the farmers without doubt suffered from the high taxes imposed in the latter years of the war. Agricultural laborers certainly demanded high wages. On July 12, 1778, William Whipple of Portsmouth wrote to Josiah Bartlett, "The Farmers cannot hire a laborer for less than 50 or 40 Dolls. pr. month, and in the neighbourhood of this town, 3 or 4 Dolls. pr. day, & very difficult to be had at that. This naturally raises the price of Provision—Indian Corn is not to be purchased, under 6 Dolls. pr. Bushel."[21] As a consumer the farmer suffered from high prices, although theoretically he should have been able to protect himself by demanding higher prices for his surplus produce.

There is no evidence to show that agriculture deteriorated in New Hampshire. Many of the farmers lived in the backwoods districts at a bare subsistence level and were undisturbed in their self-sufficiency.[22] Belknap maintained that the suspension of the lumbering industry during the war caused more people to enter into agriculture. The state exported large quantities of corn during the Revolution, whereas before it had been necessary to import this product. In 1770 there were imported at Portsmouth 16,587 bushels of corn but in 1778 New Hampshire exported 5,306 bushels and in 1780, 6,711 bushels.[23] This would indicate a great expansion of farming during the Revolution. The drouth in the year 1781 was an added impetus to the expansion of production in the following year.[24] After the Revolution agriculture continued to furnish a bare living to the great majority of the people. The post-Revolutionary years witnessed many internal improvements in New Hampshire such as the building of roads and bridges—all of which aided the farmer. New ideas were slowly beginning to be accepted by the agricultural population, although with misgivings.[25] It was not until 1812 that the New Hampshire Agricultural Society was founded with the avowed purpose "to Promote and encourage agriculture, economies in husbandry and useful domestic Manufactures," and to reward meritorious experiments and discoveries.[26]

Before the Revolution manufacturing was a minor industry in New Hampshire.[27] Potentially the state was in a position to manufacture various articles, but actually costs of production were so high, and demand was so low that these products could not be turned out at a profit. Furthermore the British government imposed severe restrictions on colonial manufactures in order that colonial markets might be reserved for British goods.[28] Nevertheless, a few products were manufactured in New Hampshire prior to the Revolution. The most important of these was linen, the making of which centered in the Scotch-Irish population at Londonderry.[29] These resourceful immigrants raised their own flax and wove it into linen cloth. They were noted as being among the best homespun artisans in the colonies. Iron works were started in New Hampshire at a very early date but were never very successful. The manufacture of tar was frequently resorted to, although the product could be made more cheaply in the South.[30] The refining of sugar, the distillation of rum, and the brewing of beer attracted a few enterprizers on the seacoast.[31] There were a few ropemakers but not enough to satisfy the demand. On some of the more accessible streams grist mills and fulling mills were operated. The manufacture of leather in tanyards and the making of shoes were industries of purely a minor importance.[32] Two valuable articles of export were potash and pearlash. In new towns where large quantities of forest timber were burned for clearance, the ashes were collected and boiled into lye which was in turn refined into the finished product at special works. Sail-cloth and tow-cloth, bricks and potter's ware were also objects of manufacture in various localities.

An immediate effect of the Revolution was to end all British restrictions on colonial manufactures and to throw the colonists largely upon their own resources for eight years. The British blockade acted as a barrier shutting out all but a few imports. Whereas the colonial population had hitherto depended upon many British manufactures, it now saw this supply cut off and a tremendous scarcity of manufactured goods created. Thus colonial manufacturing, which in normal times could not be carried on at a profit, was stimulated by the twin necessities of carrying on the war and supporting the population.[33] Homemade clothing and tools were the articles most widely manufactured. The iron and textile industries actually prospered because of the blockade and the scarcity of foreign imports. The arms and munitions industry experienced the greatest demand and the greatest stimulation. Saltpetre was collected from old cellars and stables. Sulphur was very scarce, and the supply was strictly economized. The manufacture of paper and salt also increased during the Revolution. Occasionally there were such shortages in necessary articles as to necessitate government bounties to bring certain marginal producers into the field in order to increase the supply.

On June 8, 1775, the fourth Provincial Congress of New Hampshire offered a bounty of £50 to that person who should manufacture the largest amount of saltpetre in excess of 100 pounds. This bounty was in addition to a basic price of 3 shillings and 6 pence per pound.[34] On January 12, 1776, the state legislature offered a price of £3 for every good firearm manufactured in New Hampshire.[35] On June 27 the legislature voted to lend Samuel Folsom £300 to build a powder mill in Exeter.[36] A powder mill was also constructed at Portsmouth in 1776. On September 2, 1776, Captain Peirce Long of that town wrote to Josiah Bartlett, "Our Mill has been to work this Week and I do assure you Its my opinion It Exceeds any Other on the Continent. It has only One Shaft which Carrys 44 pestles in Two Mortars. That Together with Every Necessary Required is Compleated. And is capable to Turning out at Least 24 or 2500 lbs. per week—its also Supplyed with Salt petre and Sulphur Sufficient to make Near Two hundred Barrels of Powder. I am a Little Concerned what we Shall do for Sulphur. As that appears to me to be the Only Article we Shall want Towards manufacturing any quantity."[37] On July 6, 1776, the state legislature advertised bounties on the production of sulphur of $2.00 per hundred weight and on the production of lead of £6 per hundred weight.[38] An extremely scarce article was salt which was used to preserve supplies for the army.[39] On June 28, 1777, the New Hampshire legislature offered a bounty of 3 shillings per bushel on salt manufactured from sea water. During the Revolution there was a greatly increased demand for paper. On November 28, 1777, the state legislature authorized the treasurer to lend £200 to Richard Jordan of Exeter for the purpose of building a paper mill. A year later the legislature urged the making of paper from rags and required the selectmen in each town to collect rags and to forward them to Jordan's paper mill at Exeter.[40] The war stimulated the raising of sheep for wool, and fulling mills came into operation. John Sullivan of Durham owned both a fulling mill and a cloth mill on the Lamprey River.[41] On March 4, 1778, the state legislature offered a bounty to manufacturers of "Wier and wool cards."[42] One of the most interesting forms of state aid was that granted to encourage the making of glass. On March 30, 1781, the state legislature authorized a public lottery for the purpose of raising £2000 to enable one Robert Hewes to carry on the manufacture of glass at Temple.[43]

The end of the Revolution saw the collapse of most of these artificially stimulated manufactures. British goods once again entered

American markets, and they drove many of these infant industries out of existence. Throughout the Confederation period the American states relied mainly on imported British manufactures. It was extremely difficult to accumuláte sufficient capital to start American enterprizes. One of the results of this situation was the protective tariff policy embarked upon by the Federal government in 1789 to enable American infant industries to become established.

During the Revolution the various state governments were forced to resort to the regulation of industry in view of the extraordinary economic emergency. These regulations consisted generally of restrictions on exports and imports and of restrictions on retail sales. In New Hampshire the regulation of exports and imports was vested at first in the state legislature and later in the Committee of Safety. On August 25, 1775, the fourth Provincial Congress forbade further exportation of fish in an effort to alleviate a sudden shortage.[44] On November 1 the Continental Congress urged all of the states to place embargoes on the export of provisions to foreign ports.[45] However, trade was permitted between the states. On January 3, 1776, Captain William Pearne of Portsmouth was allowed to send a vessel to Maryland upon posting bond that it would not visit any foreign ports.[46] On January 5 the state legislature resolved that the Isles of Shoals should be vacated lest the inhabitants commence trading with the enemy.[47] On March 19, 1776, the legislature, in dire need of munitions, allowed Captain Eliphalet Ladd to export produce to the West Indies to exchange for powder, arms, saltpetre, sulphur and "German Steel."[48] In the fall of 1776 a three months' embargo on the exportation of lumber was imposed by the state to enable the construction of a Continental naval vessel at Portsmouth to proceed without delay.[49] On December 10 the state legislature imposed a general embargo on all cargoes or shipments leaving the state except those approved by itself or the Committee of Safety.[50] This restriction was temporary but was revived for short intervals throughout the war. Thus one finds the following entry in the records of the Committee of Safety for 1778: "Thursday October 22d the Com'tee met & Permitted Robert Barton to carry 100 bushels corn to Falmouth in Casco Bay."[51]

On July 5, 1776, the office of maritime officer was established at Portsmouth.[52] The duties of the maritime officer were to enforce the trade regulations applying to ships entering or clearing out of Portsmouth harbor. In an act passed November 26, 1778, the duties of the office were further defined and enlarged.[53] The maritime officer was empowered to register all ships and to require a declaration of cargo and destination. No cargo of New Hampshire goods could leave the state without a certificate from the state legislature or the Committee of Safety. The naval officer was required to collect fees for registration, for entrance and clearance depending on the length of the cruise, and for permits to unload. Fishermen and wood-coasters were exempted from the provisions of the act.

During 1779 and 1780 New Hampshire and the other states were subject to requisitions for supplies by the Continental Congress. New Hampshire's supply requisitions called for rum and beef. To protect itself against a possible shortage the state legislature on April 29, 1780, passed a law prohibiting the export of live cattle, beef, rum, and molasses.[54]

The regulation of commerce by the several states during the Revolution and Confederation periods gave rise to an extremely vicious situation. State regulations were not uniform. Each state might establish tariff walls about itself which would effectively strangle interstate and foreign trade. The Continental government possessed no control over commerce, except by unanimous consent of the states. Thus it was deprived of an important source of revenue as well as of an opportunity to develop a uniform system of commercial regulations designed to promote the national economic welfare. On February 3, 1781, the Continental Congress resolved to recommend to the several states that they pass laws authorizing the Continental Congress to levy 5 per cent ad valorem import duties on all imports and condemned prizes brought into the United States.[55] Since New Hampshire had hitherto refrained from setting up a state tariff, the state eagerly accepted the congressional proposal. On April 6, 1781, an act was passed vesting the requested tariff powers in the Congress.[56] That body, however, was never able to impose import duties, because the unanimous consent of the states was not forthcoming. On February 13, 1783, Massachusetts proposed a convention of the New England states and New York to meet at Hartford to draw up state and regional tariffs. The New Hampshire legislature refused to send representatives to this convention. The report of the legislative committee which was adopted stated, ". . . . It is their opinion that the method of laying impost duties proposed in said Resolve will be unequal & hurtful to this State; and as this State impowered Congress to lay such Duties, which they still think preferable to the method proposed by said Resolve, that it is not best to appoint Delegates. . . . ."[57] Nevertheless, New Hampshire was unable to continue to stand by this sound principle. To meet its war obligations the state finally passed a general tariff on imports on April 17, 1784.[58]

It is a normal economic phenomenon for prices to rise enormously during wartime. There is a tremendous demand for goods, and the degree of scarcity varies with the state of the industrial development of the nation. During the Revolution this condition of scarcity, which would alone have caused a rise in the price level, was aggravated by a large expansion of the currency through the issuance of paper money. The result was that prices rose more rapidly than the rate of depreciation of the currency alone would have accounted for. On March 28, 1780, chairman Meshech Weare of the New Hampshire Committee of Safety wrote to Nathaniel Peabody, "I am in pain when I consider at what an enormous rate every thing has now got, 12 or 1300 dollars for a cow, 40 dollars per bushel for corn, 80 for rye, £100 per yard for common broadcloth, from 50 to 100 dollars per yard for linen, &c. &c. and still daily increasing—."[59] On May 26, 1781, a man paid the ludicrously high price of $1,000 for a felt hat in Norwich.[60] The fact that prices were so high caused many uninformed persons to believe that the correct remedy for the situation was to issue more paper money in order that they might have more cash to meet the high prices, and this despite the fact that the currency had already been inordinately expanded. On November 12, 1782, a petition signed by eighty-one yeomen and farmers in Hillsborough and western Rockingham counties was presented to the New Hampshire legislature. This petition stated in part, "That for want of a Currency the People of this State are really reduced to a most deplorable situation that with all their industry are unable to carry on any Commerce or Trade even with their Neighbors to pay any debt, tho' never so Just or trivial—And by reason of the scarcity & exhorbitant prices of Salt and other necessaries of Life the Small Quantity of Coin that was formerly amongst us is thereby taken away—And unless there can be some Medium for Trade Your Petitioners must of Consequence fall victims to their Creditors & both they and their Families a Sacrifice to Beggary & Want. . . . ."[61]

Jeremy Belknap wrote, "There was a disposition in the governing part of the people to keep out of sight the true cause of this growing mischief."[62] From this it would appear that politicians and men of affairs knew that the high prices were the result of the extreme inflation. But it was not politically expedient for them to criticize their own policies. Hence they hastened to fasten the blame upon the war profiteers and speculators. On November 24, 1778, William Whipple wrote to Meshech Weare, "The Spirit of Monopolizing under the name of Speculating rages with great violence through the United States the consequence of which must prove fatal unless the interposition of the Legislatures of the several States can check its fury."[63]

In November, 1776, a convention was held at Dracut to which the southern and western New Hampshire towns sent twenty-four delegates. This convention discussed, "ye Alarming Situation of our Public affairs at this Time on account of ye Exorbitant prices, that are demanded & Taken in Consideration for many of the Necessaries of Life, by which means our paper Currency is daily depreciating in its Value, and the Honest Mechanic & Labourer, very Much distressed, by the Extortion of the Trader, & farmer."[64] On December 25, 1776, upon the invitation of Rhode Island a convention of New England delegates met at Providence, New Hampshire being represented by Nathaniel Folsom, Josiah Bartlett, and Supply Clap. The convention discussed currency reform and better interstate coöperation in military affairs. Tentative schedules of fair retail prices were adopted.[65]

In accordance with these schedules the New Hampshire legislature, January 18, 1777, passed a drastic law setting up maximum prices for certain commodities.[66] For example, wheat was priced at 7 shillings 6 pence per bushel, Indian corn at 3 shillings 6 pence per bushel, peas at 8 shillings per bushel, salt pork at £5 per barrel, beef at 3 pence per pound, New England rum at 6 shillings 8 pence per gallon, sugar at 54 shillings per hundred weight, salt at 10 shillings per bushel, wool at 2 shillings 2 pence per pound, cotton and linen cloth at 3 shillings 8 pence per yard and bar iron at 40 shillings per hundred weight. Farm labor was allowed 3 shillings 4 pence per day, and the price of other labor was fixed proportionally. Any person demanding a higher price than the legal maximum might be fined the amount of the price demanded. The merchant's only escape was to refuse to sell any goods while prices remained fixed. On April 10, 1777, a supplemental act was passed empowering the local committees of safety to enforce price fixing.[67] The act also established the principle that a merchant could be forced to sell his goods at the legal maximum prices in paper money for the use of the government or of the poor and needy.

These price fixing measures soon failed. Not only were they an artificial attempt to maintain the purchasing power of the paper notes, but these laws ignored the fact that all prices were, in a measure, interdependent and that in order to fix one price, all prices had to be regulated. Faith and popular support failed to alter the economic situation. At a convention of New England delegates held at Springfield, Massachusetts, on July 30, 1777, the delegates resolved to recommend to their respective states that they repeal all price fixing laws and redeem their outstanding fiat money.[68] Thus on November 27, 1777, the New Hampshire legislature repealed its maximum price law. In its stead was passed an "Act to prohibit the Selling Goods at public Vendue."[69] In its own language this law forbade the selling of goods at public auction because it "has a Tendency to raise the Price thereof to the great Damage of the Public; and Some People have had the Meanness to bid upon their own Goods in order & with a View to raise the Price of the Same." On January 2, 1778, the legislature enacted an additional regulation entitled "An Act to Encourage Fair Dealing and to Restrain and Punish Sharpers and Oppressors."[70] By the terms of this act no person, with the exception of licensed dealers, was allowed to purchase certain basic commodities except in very small amounts for personal use. On the list of regulated commodities were coal, iron, steel, salt, rum, sugar, clothing, textiles, and staple foods.

It must not be supposed that the high prices demanded for goods by enterprizers were always justified. The Revolution had its share of war profiteers. For example, John Langdon of Portsmouth, merchant and Continental Agent, increased his fortune greatly during the war.[71] Necessary supplies frequently had to be impressed by government agents and their value appraised in order to prevent profiteering. Thus in February, 1777, the New Hampshire Committee of Safety appointed two appraisers of rum for Rockingham County.[72] These appraisers were to accompany the government purchasing agent and to estimate the value of rum. Should the retailers refuse to sell at a fair valuation, the agent was empowered with the aid of the sheriff to seize the goods, paying the appraised price. On January 15, 1778, New Hampshire was represented at a New England economic conference at New Haven, which had assembled upon the recommendation of the Continental Congress.[73] This conference attacked the principles of war profiteering which caused "the individuals of a community to exact and receive for their services or commodities, such prices as exceed that proportion, at which the army was raised and established, and to set no other bounds to their demands than what the necessity of the times will suffer them to receive; and to withhold and conceal their necessary commodities, unless their demands are complied with."

On November 16, 1779, New Hampshire empowered its delegates in the Continental Congress to represent the state in a price-fixing conference to be held in Philadelphia in January, 1780.[74] Meshech Weare wrote to the delegates concerning the proposed price regulation, ". . . . This is found to be attended with many difficulties, and it is feared will have little or no good effect, unless it be general. And what effect it may then have is problematical."[75] The Southern delegates refused to ratify the price regulations proposed at the conference, and the scheme accordingly had to be abandoned. On August 3, 1780, the state was represented at another New England economic conference at Boston. This conference attempted to devise a plan to promote uniformity of state purchasing and the speedier transportation of supplies.[76] The conference also urged the Continental Congress to establish executive departments for the more efficient conduct of the war.

Industrial activity in America carried on against the background of the Revolution brought into conflict two opposing theories. One theory held that during a war period all profits should be strictly regulated and that the civilian should not be in a more favored economic position than the soldier. The other theory held that unless prices were as a general rule allowed to follow their own course, there would not be sufficient incentive to cause enterprizers to produce those goods which were scarce, nor to cause the civilian population to economize in their consumption.

The various regional economic conferences held during the war demonstrated the fact that the states were aware that concerted action was necessary for effective regulation of economic activity. Concerted action, to be sure, failed because of state jealousies and overemphasis on state sovereignty, and this condition continued throughout the Confederation period. Out of the maze of conflicting state economic policies there finally rose a demand for the uniform regulation of certain phases of economic activity. The result was the Annapolis Trade Convention of 1786 culminating in the Constitutional Convention of

1787. There the states decided, in the interests of uniformity, to vest certain important economic powers, such as direct taxation, the laying of excises and imposts, the regulation of interstate and foreign commerce, the regulation of bankruptcy, and the coinage of money, in the Federal government.

CHAPTER 12

The humble petetyon of us whose names are under written beinge inhab-
ytants in this Jurisdiction, & beinge senceable of ye need of multeplyinge
of townshippes for ye inlargement of ye contrey And accommodateinge
of such as want opportunity to improve themselves, have taken into our
consideration a place wt is called pennecooke, wc by reporte is a place fit
for such an end, Now ye humble request of yor petetioners to this honred
Courte is yt wee may have ye grant of a trackte of land their to ye quan-
tyty of twelfe miles square. . . . .

Petition for Grant of Land at Penacook, 1659.[1]

The Revolution and Land Tenure

L AND was perhaps the most important single objective of the
first settlers of America. In the land they hoped to find
gold and silver. From it they hoped to derive its natural
products and on it they hoped to raise necessary foodstuffs.
Many of the English institutions carried over to America were originally based on the ownership of land. Inheritance, wealth, social
position, taxation, the franchise, were all closely connected with the
land. In New England, especially, the possibility of acquiring free
land to be held in fee simple was one of the principal inducements
causing the early settlement of that section.[2]

New Hampshire was originally granted to Captain John Mason in
1629 by the New England Council of which Mason was a member.
This grant was confirmed in 1635 when the Council surrendered its
charter to the Crown. Mason's grant was defined as bounded on the
south by the Merrimack River which was then believed to extend due
west, on the east by the Atlantic Ocean and the Piscataqua River,

then believed to extend due northwest, and on the west by a line connecting the Piscataqua and Merrimack rivers at points sixty miles inland from the mouths of each.[3]

Under Mason's direction settlements were begun near what is now Portsmouth in 1630. Mason died in 1635, and for many years none of his heirs showed any interest in the American grant. Nevertheless, new settlers kept coming in—dissenters from Massachusetts, stray parties of colonists, enterprizers of all sorts—so that in 1640 the population approximated one thousand persons. Most of these were legally squatters, having no deed from the Mason family. In 1641 the New Hampshire towns petitioned the General Court of Massachusetts to be included under its government and were received. In consequence Massachusetts proceeded to make grants north of the Merrimack River, which were technically invalid since the land was the property of the Mason family in England.

In 1660 the Mason title was revived by Robert Tufton Mason, who had the backing of King Charles II in his action. His first step was to attempt the eviction of all squatters then illegally occupying the Masonian grant. To facilitate his claims Mason challenged the authority of Massachusetts over his grant and succeeded in having New Hampshire made a separate province in 1679. Royal instructions were next issued to the New Hampshire government to aid Mason's actions. This partiality shown by the English government aroused the ire of the colonists who regarded it as an attempt on the part of the King to foist an unjust claim upon them. The existing inhabitants of New Hampshire had purchased or inherited their land from those who had occupied it for nearly fifty years without challenge to their title. Consequently they refused to pay rents to Mason and resisted eviction. Robert Mason died in 1688, and his sons, despairing of ever settling the dispute, sold the province to Samuel Allen of London in 1691 for £2750. Royal backing now went to Allen in his attempt to establish his titles. But he found legal action virtually impossible, since the New Hampshire Assembly was popularly controlled and all juries favored the cause of the inhabitants. The residents were willing to acknowledge Allen's right to all unsettled lands but contested his right to the lands in settled towns. Samuel Allen died in 1705, yet the Allen contests were carried on until 1715. Despite the requests of the Queen for special findings of fact and nothing more, the local New

Hampshire juries nearly always brought in general verdicts for the defendants in Allen's eviction suits.

Popular resentment against the attitude of the English government during the land litigation increased. James Truslow Adams writes, "New England had originally been settled by emigrants to whom one of the greatest inducements had been the possibility of acquiring free land in fee simple. It had become a country preëminently of small landholders, tenaciously devoted to their title deeds, and naturally regarding any attack upon them as overturning the very foundation of their liberties. . . . ."[4] In the years following 1715 settlement proceeded very slowly because of the uncertainty over land titles. The population of the province was 9650 in 1715; by 1730 it had increased to but 10,000.[5] Gradually, however, the pressure for new lands mounted. The New Hampshire government made provisional grants of new townships. The Massachusetts government also granted land west of the Merrimack River on the erroneous assumption that the river was the western boundary of New Hampshire. These grants by Massachusetts finally caused a boundary dispute between the two provinces. The outcome was a royal order in council in 1740 which separated New Hampshire from Massachusetts on the south by a line following a course three miles north of the Merrimack River and parallel to the river from its mouth to Pawtucket Falls and thence due west in a straight line to the eastern boundary of the province of New York. On the north and east New Hampshire was separated from Massachusetts (now Maine) by a line following the middle of the Piscataqua River to its headwaters and thence north two degrees west in a straight line to the French boundary. At the same time New Hampshire was given a separate governor, the province having previously been under the authority of the governor of Massachusetts.

The boundary dispute between New Hampshire and Massachusetts brought the Masonian title to light again. It was argued that in the sale of the Masonian grant to Samuel Allen the entail had not been properly "docked," and that consequently upon Allen's death the property had reverted to the Mason family.[6] John Tufton Mason, the living heir, at once took the proper legal measures to revive his title. He was immediately approached by agents of Massachusetts and New Hampshire, and in 1739 he made a secret agreement to sell his lands to New Hampshire. Unfortunately the provincial Assembly could not agree upon a suitable price nor could it come to an understanding with the Council as to which body should grant the lands in the event of their purchase. In 1746 after several years of bickering Mason became irked at the delay, and realizing the dubious legality of his revived title, he sold his grant to a syndicate of twelve New Hampshire citizens for £1500. This syndicate, known as the Masonian proprietors, was composed of several men in the Wentworth family circle, royal officials and gentlemen of leisure. These persons undoubtedly used their knowledge as public officials to acquire for private use property which was vitally connected with the public interest. This action aroused the small landowners and the Assembly to a high pitch of indignation. Nearly two million acres inhabited by some thirty thousand settlers were under the control of twelve men! To quiet the uproar the proprietors immediately deeded the land in all settled towns to the inhabitants thereof, although refusing to recognize the validity of certain township grants made by Massachusetts. The proprietors then offered to sell their remaining unsettled lands to the province provided that the granting of these lands be vested in the Governor and Council and not in the Assembly. In reality a change in the granting power from the Masonian proprietors to the Governor and Council meant that the power would be in substantially the same hands. The Assembly, representing the people's interest and being the body which would have to appropriate the money for any purchase, refused to buy.

The Masonian proprietors thereupon proceeded to organize and to grant the land themselves. They demanded no quitrents but made their profits by increases in land values aided by a growth of the population from forty thousand inhabitants in 1750 to fifty-two thousand in 1767.[7] Shares in the propriety were in great demand. In each township granted, the proprietors reserved selected lots for themselves so that the value of their land would increase no matter which section of the province grew fastest. Occasionally the shadow of the dead Allen claim appeared to worry the poor settler about his title.

At the outbreak of the Revolution there were on the Loyalist side ten Masonian proprietors or shareholders including Governor John Wentworth, Councillor Theodore Atkinson, secretary of the province, Mark Hunking Wentworth, father of the Governor, George Jaffrey, treasurer of the province, John Fisher, naval officer, George Meserve, collector of customs, Colonel Stephen Holland, Peter Pearse, Daniel

Rindge, and John Pierce. For several years the proprietors suspended activities. The government was in hostile hands although, curiously enough, only a few of the holdings were confiscated. In 1788 a boundary dispute between the proprietors and the state as to the western limits of the Masonian grant resulted in the proprietors' humbly quit-claiming to the state the segment in dispute for $40,800. In 1790 the Allen family settled their claims on the Masonian grant in return for 8500 acres of unsettled land. The proprietors continued in business until 1807 by which time their land had all been granted.

The hostility arising out of the various disputes concerning the Masonian title was one of the dominant characteristics of eighteenth century history in New Hampshire, involving as it did all land within a line sixty miles from the sea between the boundaries of the province of Massachusetts and the district of Maine. At first the royal support given to the Mason family in its efforts to assert its ownership aroused popular ire. Then the purchase of the grant by the Masonian proprietors, members of the Wentworth clique, several of whom were royal officials, was regarded as a corrupt bargain. The constant dickering between the Mason interests and the Allen claimants did little to allay the anxiety of those settlers who were uncertain of their land rights. James Truslow Adams writes, "The constant litigation and the uncertainty surrounding the inhabitants' titles to the lands they were improving could not fail to arouse a feeling of resentment, a contempt for law, and a rebellious attitude toward 'vested interests.' What with the recognized illegal trading in commerce, the lawless treatment of the woods, and the conflicts over land titles, it is little wonder that legal precedents should carry slight weight in New Hampshire, ... and that 'the rights of man' to 'life, liberty and the pursuit of happiness' should not only become popular but develop an extremely inclusive meaning in that sparsely settled and outlying portion of the British empire."[8] The matter of the Masonian title was inextricably woven into New Hampshire's revolutionary psychology.

The Masonian grant extended only sixty miles inland between the Maine and Massachusetts boundaries, but by the royal order in council of 1740 New Hampshire's western limits were set at the eastern boundary of the province of New York. Thus a vast tract west and north of the Masonian line was adjudged to be Crown land belonging to New Hampshire and under the control of the Governor and Council. At first it was not known whether the eastern boundary of New York was Lake Champlain or the Connecticut River. Nevertheless, Governor Benning Wentworth speedily proceeded to grant townships as far west as Lake Champlain. Not a few friends of the Wentworth family and gentlemen of leisure were awarded large tracts in the western part of the province. Landed estates, however, never assumed large proportions in New Hampshire because more grants were made in the form of corporate townships than were given to individuals. The soil was relatively poor; communication was difficult; Indian raids were a constant threat; and the settling of tenants was expensive. In 1764 a royal order in council declared the western boundary of New Hampshire to be the Connecticut River thus putting a check upon the Governor's proclivities for rapid and haphazard granting of lands.

One practice resulting from Benning Wentworth's land policy aroused popular antagonism.[9] In each township granted, he reserved for himself a choice plot in a favorable location. In over twenty years he thus accumulated 100,000 acres of valuable land. Furthermore every land grant meant a fee for the Governor, the size of which varied with the income of the grantee. The result was that Crown land often went to the highest bidder who was sometimes an absentee proprietor, to the anger of the poorer aspirants. Most objectionable also was the provision in each new town's charter requiring the reservation of a section of land for the Society for the Propagation of the Gospel in Foreign Parts, an Anglican missionary organization. When Benning Wentworth retired from office in 1767, his nephew and successor, John Wentworth, apparently hoped to fall heir to the extensive gubernatorial landholdings.[10] Benning Wentworth died in 1770, but to the surprise of everyone he left all his property to his wife. John Wentworth thereupon succeeded in persuading the Council that his uncle's reservations of land for himself had been illegal and that the land should revert to the Crown. Peter Livius, one of the Councillors, suspected that the Governor was planning a coup to seize the lands for himself and brought charges against him before the Board of Trade in England. Ultimately the Privy Council acquitted John Wentworth of all these charges. On April 7, 1773, a royal order in council was promulgated which forbade the granting of further Crown lands by all colonial governors without the King's express permission.[11] This measure put a stop to any land schemes which John Wentworth

Notice by Committee of Safety of Londonderry to Apprehend Adam Stuart, a Loyalist.

may have had, and in addition angered the frontiersmen and free land advocates.

Quitrents never seem to have been much of a problem in New Hampshire. The Masons and Allens tried to collect them but were unsuccessful, giving up the attempt in 1715. Land was most commonly held in fee simple and was generally free to original settlers, provided they settled within certain time limits and made certain improvements. On the earliest townships granted by the province in the decade 1720-1730 there was levied a quitrent of one pepper-corn a year—a nominal obligation.[12] In later town charters, 1730-1740, the quitrent varied; the charter of Nottingham called for one ear of Indian corn annually, that of Chester one pound of hemp annually, that of Gilmanton one pound of flax, that of Rochester one pint of turpentine.[13] The inclusion of extensive western Crown lands within the limits of the province of New Hampshire in 1740 brought specific instructions from England for the Governor to exact quitrents. Accordingly all town charters granted by Benning Wentworth and his successor, John Wentworth, required the payment of one ear of Indian corn annually for the first ten years and thereafter one shilling annually for each hundred acres.[14] These quitrents were carelessly collected by Governor Benning Wentworth. John Wentworth was instructed to collect them in full including the arrears. Realizing that these land taxes were "suggestive of oppression" even if the sums were nominal, the new Governor obtained permission to spend the quitrent money on road-building. In 1771 he devoted £500 to this project and built two hundred miles of road, thus eliminating much popular dissatisfaction.[15]

Perhaps the most irksome restriction on the land was the royal white pine law. Several Parliamentary statutes, supplemented by a New Hampshire law of 1708, reserved all white pines of twenty-four inches or more in diameter, which were not located on land already granted to private persons, as mast trees for the royal navy.[16] The colonial governors were instructed to reserve for the Crown the ownership of mast trees in all future land grants.[17] Throughout the colonies the surveyor-general of His Majesty's Woods and his four deputies were supposed to survey all timber lands and to emblazon the royal mark in the form of the "broad arrow" on the King's trees. Violators of the law were tried before courts of admiralty without juries, and conviction occurred upon probable guilt. The maximum penalties in-

The Revolution and Land Tenure

cluded confiscation and sale of the timber illegally cut, imprisonment for a term varying from three months to one year, and a fine of £100, one half for the Crown and one half for the informer.

An American idea popularly expressed was that the trees were "gifts of God and Nature" and that the King's right was merely nominal. People looked upon the law as foolish because it reserved more trees than the navy could ever use. Actually the law was probably a wise conservation measure, but it was practically impossible to enforce because of the popular disrespect for it. The surveyors could not hope to survey all the timber land, and the colonies' territorial extent was so large that they could not exercise proper vigilance for the detection of offenders.

In 1741 Governor Benning Wentworth of New Hampshire became surveyor-general of the King's Woods in North America with four deputies to assist him. He was lax in enforcing the law, and this was one of the reasons for his removal from office in 1767. His successor as governor, John Wentworth, also received the position of surveyor-general. Although the new governor was strict and firmly tactful, and prosecuted many offenders, he was really unable to check the numerous illegal depredations on the King's Woods. On July 12, 1775, he wrote to the Naval Commissioners in England, "The suppression of his Majesty's right to Mast timber & the unrestrained private appropriation of it, to the inhabitants of the Country is a popular object, as they find it impossible to trespass with safety & are so constantly visited by the Surveyors; to avoid which every method of discouragement is practised, & produces many difficulties; altho' violence I have generally suppress'd that there does not remain much personal danger, yet ev'ry artifice, fraud obloquy & secret combination to evade the operation of the Laws is so universal, That the utmost vigilance & steady support is peculiarly necessary to preserve Mast timber from Destruction."[18]

In the interior sections of New Hampshire where lumbering was an important industry, Wentworth's deputies were especially unpopular and were often subjected to physical violence at the hands of the loggers and sawyers. In the winter of 1772-1773 the Piscataquog River in Hillsborough County was under Wentworth's surveillance, especially Clement's Mills in Weare.[19] On April 13 Sheriff Benjamin Whiting and his deputy, John Quigley, both later notorious Tories, were instructed to proceed to Weare to enforce the law. Upon their arrival they were attacked by a mob and driven out of town. The provincial militia was finally called out to restore order, but no person appears to have suffered punishment. This affair was typical of the "swamp law" which often prevailed in the interior districts.[20]

The outbreak of the Revolution resulted in the scrapping of the entire British land policy. The white pine law became a thing of the past. Quitrents were abolished. The royal edict of 1773 forbidding the granting of further lands was ignored. In many states the confiscations of large Loyalist estates and their subsequent division and resale to numerous buyers resulted in a more equitable distribution of land. In New Hampshire approximately twenty-eight Loyalist estates were actually confiscated. The largest of these, that of Governor John Wentworth, contained 27,000 acres of land and a substantial interest in the Masonian propriety. Nearly as large as Wentworth's holdings was the confiscated estate of George Meserve which contained 30,000 acres. Other large Loyalist estates which were confiscated were those of Benning Wentworth and Colonel Stephen Holland, which contained 10,000 acres each.[21] Most of these large Loyalist land holdings consisted of grants in various townships throughout the state. These grants were, in most cases, sold by the state trustees to single individuals without any subdivision. As a whole the sale of the confiscated estates resulted in no wide redistribution of land in New Hampshire.

The Revolution caused all the ungranted Crown lands in New Hampshire to vest in the revolutionary government, and the state proceeded to incorporate new townships during the war years and after the treaty of peace. In the meanwhile the population had increased rapidly. In 1767 a rudimentary census had fixed the figure at 52,700. By 1770 the population had risen to 64,000. The Revolution retarded the growth somewhat. Yet the population grew from 82,200 in 1775 to 103,000 in 1780 and to 142,000 by the Federal census of 1790.[22] By 1800 nearly all of the state except for the wildest sections had been marked off into townships, concomitantly with this increase in population. In 1806 many remaining odd lots of land, still the property of the state, were sold at public auction at Concord with the minimum price fixed at forty-eight cents per acre.[23]

Closely connected with the general land problem were the English laws of inheritance, because they had an important effect upon the evolution of the American system of land tenure. Among the most

The Revolution and Land Tenure

common of these English institutions were those of primogeniture and entail. Under the rule of primogeniture it was customary upon the death of the father to transmit all his property to his eldest son. The law of entail required that all entailed estates should be limited to the grantee or devisee and the heirs of his body and should not be conveyed to any other person. It can readily be seen how suitable these institutions were for the maintenance of a permanent landed aristocracy.

Both primogeniture and entails in some form or to some degree were introduced into all of the American colonies. In New Hampshire primogeniture never gained full acceptance. Prior to the Revolution the general custom required each person making a will to bequeath a double share of his estate to his eldest son and equal shares to the remaining children. A provincial act of May 14, 1718, provided that the estates of all persons dying intestate should be thus divided.[24] After the Revolution the custom of favoring the eldest son seems to have been ignored. On February 3, 1789, the state legislature passed an act which provided that the estates of persons dying intestate should be divided equally among all of their children.[25]

Entails seem to have been a prevalent institution in New Hampshire before the Revolution. Any person holding an estate in fee simple could grant or devise it to another person and his lineal heirs under the restrictions of fee tail. Land held in fee tail passed directly down the designated line of heirs in the family and was not liable for the debts of the holder. Theoretically this land could not be conveyed to any person outside of the select line of heirs. Actually there were three cumbersome methods of conveying such land. The first was through an act of the legislature for "docking" the entail. Such acts were sometimes passed to enable creditors to salvage some of their claims from insolvent estates which would otherwise escape any levy.[26] The second method of conveying entailed estates was known as "common recovery." By this process the holder of land in fee tail could be engaged in a "fictitious suit" at common law by the purchaser of his land, and the resulting judgment of the court could effectively bar the entail forever.[27] The third method of conveyance was known as the levying of a fine. The holder of an entailed estate could be engaged in fictitious litigation by the purchaser, and the matter could reach an agreement outside of court upon the payment of a nominal fine, which agreement was recognized by the courts and regarded as a final barring of the entail. Upon the barring of the entail all land reverted to the status of fee simple, but nothing prevented the new owner from entailing the estate to his own heirs.[28]

In the greater number of the American states entails were abolished along with primogeniture during and after the Revolution.[29] In New Hampshire entails were not at once abolished by law, although the custom was gradually passing out of use by 1780. People found it much more convenient to hold land in fee simple because it could be freely conveyed and could be inherited with few restrictions. However, for those estates which had originally been entailed in the period prior to the Revolution, the only mode of conveyance was still either a fine or a common recovery. Curiously enough this antiquated system was allowed to continue until 1837. At that time a law was passed which legalized the conveyance of entailed estates by a common property deed, which transaction was declared as forever barring the entail.[30]

Thus the American Revolution furnished the impetus for the overthrow or the modification of many of the English landed institutions which had been introduced into the colonies. This revolution was merely the triumph of the philosophy of economic democracy, as taught by such men as Thomas Jefferson and Tom Paine, over the philosophy of propertied aristocracy which held that the ownership of real property was the best index of ability to rule society. It is true that in conservative New Hampshire, dominated by its seacoast commercial class and characterized by small land holdings, this overturn was not so extensive. The provincial institutions, except for the franchise and office holding, had been relatively democratic before the Revolution. Furthermore Jeffersonian equalitarian theories carried little weight in what was later to be a strong Federalist state. Yet the radical extremes to which some of the agrarian leaders resorted in their attack upon propertied institutions in other states during the years 1776-1786 resulted in a conservative reaction in 1787 and the evolution of a Federal Constitution containing ample safeguards for property rights.

*All men are born equally free and independent; therefore, all govern-
ment of right originates from the people . . . .*

CONSTITUTION of 1784.[1]

Government is a SCIENCE, *and requires education and information, as
well as judgment and prudence. . . . . The deficiency of persons qualified for the various departments in Government, has been much regretted,
and by none, more than those few, who know how public business ought to
be conducted.*

JEREMY BELKNAP.[2]

The Evolution of State Government

THE American state governments were the first tangible results of the great experiment in democracy which resulted
from the American Revolution. In 1775 while the New
Hampshire Provincial Congress was deliberating over the
first state constitution, General John Sullivan wrote to Meshech
Weare, ". . . . All governments are, or ought to be, instituted for
the good of the people . . . . No danger can arise to a State from
giving the people a free and full voice in their own government."[3]
This statement was typical of the political philosophy of the Revolutionists. It is true that the forms of state government which were
finally established represented an evolution from the British provincial governments. Nevertheless, there was a distinct displacement of
the classes which had hitherto held the ruling power. Consequently
the state governments, established as a result of independence, were

the result of the process of evolution in one sense and of revolution in another.

The history of the evolution of New Hampshire's state government is unique, since New Hampshire was the first of the new states to adopt a constitution or form of government after the opening of the Revolution. During the greater part of the year 1775 the state was governed by a unicameral legislature, the Provincial Congress. There was no separate executive, and the judiciary system had collapsed and decayed. Governmental administration was carried on by temporary committees of the Congress. Poor enforcement of the law, inefficiency in the conduct of the public business and the lack of a stable system of public finance—these conditions operated to convince many people that a definite form of government should be established. Throughout the fall of 1775 the Provincial Congress discussed the matter and finally sought the advice of the Continental Congress. After much evasion and delay the Continental Congress on November 3, 1775, resolved, "That it be recommended to the provincial Convention of New Hampshire, to call a full and free representation of the people, and that the representatives, if they think it necessary, establish such a form of government, as in their judgment will best produce the happiness of the people, and most effectually secure peace and good order in the province, during the continuance of the present dispute between G[reat] Britain and the colonies."[4] The first state government, then, was to be a temporary affair pending the adjustment of the disputes with the British government.

The initial problems confronting the Provincial Congress in the setting up of a new government were those of the franchise and the apportionment of representation in the legislative body. Before the Revolution the franchise in New Hampshire had been very restricted. In fact, it had not been altered since the election law of 1728 which declared that all voters for representatives to the Assembly must possess real estate to the value of £50 and that all representatives must own real estate to the value of £300.[5] This law imposed a decided limitation upon the number of candidates eligible to hold the office of representative to the Assembly as well as upon the number of voters. The outbreak of the Revolution and the overthrow of the royal government resulted in the overthrow of this franchise system. The members of the revolutionary provincial congresses were elected by the towns and were presumably chosen by those voters whom the select-

The Evolution of State Government

men adjudged as qualified to vote. It was in the fourth Provincial Congress that the question of the franchise under the proposed new constitution was first discussed. On November 4, 1775, the Congress voted that all electors for future representatives must possess real estate to the value of £20 and that all representatives in future provincial congresses must possess real estate to the value of £300.[6] This arrangement must have aroused some protest. At any rate on November 14 the fourth Congress voted to enlarge the franchise to include all taxpayers and to reduce the property qualification for representatives from £300 to £200.[7] This franchise system was continued throughout the Revolution. It certainly could not be defined as universal manhood suffrage. Furthermore the representatives of the people were definitely required to be men of some wealth. But the new system enabled many more people to participate in government than had done so under the royal governors.

The problem of apportioning representation in the legislative body among the several towns in the province had been vexatious long before the Revolution. The royal provincial government had been established when New Hampshire consisted of only a few towns on the seacoast. As the population had expanded westward and new towns had sprung up, the representation in the Assembly had not always been proportionately increased. Accordingly in 1775 only thirty-six towns out of a total of approximately one hundred and fifty in the province were represented in the Assembly. There was also much inequality in the basis of representation.[8] Four towns—Hopkinton with a population of 1085, Concord with a population of 1052, Brentwood with 1100, and Epping with 1569—were unrepresented while Plymouth with a population of 382, Orford with 222, and Lyme with 252 were each accorded one representative in the Assembly. Hampton on the seacoast with a population of 862 had two representatives while Londonderry with a population of 2590 had only one.

With the overthrow of the royal government this system was abolished. The apportionment of representation to the towns in the provincial congresses was apparently under the direction of the provincial Committee of Correspondence. In summoning the first Congress the Committee asked all of the towns to select "one or more" representatives.[9] The third Congress represented seventy-one towns. The fourth Congress represented one hundred towns and was called the "fullest representative body" the province had hitherto had.[10] Upon this fourth Congress fell the task of devising a plan for the future representation of the towns in the legislative body of the province. It was decided that every town containing one hundred freeholders should be entitled to one representative; that all towns containing less than one hundred freeholders might combine until they made up that number and then elect a representative; that all towns containing more than one hundred freeholders should be entitled to send one representative for each additional hundred.[11] Upon this general principle a plan of representation for the entire province, providing for a legislative body of eighty-nine members, was approved on November 14, 1775.[12] This apportionment of representation was based upon a recent census and was accurately proportional to the population of the towns. Nevertheless, it still permitted the more populous seacoast district, including Rockingham and Strafford counties, to dominate the provincial government. The small western towns along the Connecticut River found themselves denied the prerogative of sending individual representatives to the provincial legislature, being joined together in groups for the purpose of electing representatives. Although the new plan was perfectly just on the basis of the population as a whole, it angered the western towns, which saw in the plan an unfair discrimination. This friction over representation caused many of these western towns in Grafton County to withdraw entirely from participation in the state government and was one of the causes of a minor secession movement which will be discussed in the next chapter.

The fifth Provincial Congress was elected upon the basis of the franchise system and the plan of representation which had been evolved by the fourth Congress. It met at Exeter on December 2, 1775. On December 28 the Congress voted to establish a form of government.[13] There seems to have been some difference of opinion among the representatives in the Congress as to what form the new government should take. The conservatives favored a temporary arrangement of government by the Congress, giving that body a few additional functions. They feared that the establishment of a more permanent government savored too much of independence of Great Britain.[14] The more radical group in the Congress, however, succeeded in overcoming the majority, and on January 5, 1776, a form of "Civil Government" was adopted.[15]

The preamble of this rudimentary constitution stated that the new government was to last for the duration of the war. Under its provisions the fifth Provincial Congress resolved itself into a house of representatives. The house was empowered to elect a second body of the legislature, the council, to consist of twelve members,—five from Rockingham County, two from Strafford, two from Hillsborough, two from Cheshire, and one from Grafton County. All bills for the raising of money were to originate in the house of representatives, and the assent of both houses was required to pass a law. All state officers including a secretary and all general and field officers of the militia were to be elected by a joint convention of both houses. All county officers, except the county treasurers and the recorders of deeds who were popularly elective, were to be chosen by both houses. State elections were to be held annually. Such in brief was the machinery set up by the first state constitution, and it continued in force throughout the Revolution.

The new government had many obvious faults. There was an absence of an independent executive, although the committee of safety, an extra-constitutional body, filled that gap in many respects. There was no provision for a judicial department of the government. The new organic law lacked even the semblance of a bill of rights. Furthermore no provision was made for amendment of the constitution.

In addition to the faults inherent in the new constitution there was the unfavorable reception accorded it by the more conservative towns which opposed any new form of government. On January 18 petitions from the towns of Portsmouth, Dover, Newington, Rochester, Stratham, North Hampton, Rye, New Market, Kensington, Greenland, and Brentwood remonstrating against the new government, were read before the Council and the House.[16] The dispute was eventually referred to the Continental Congress for advice, but before that Congress had made any decision, sentiment for independence had reached such a stage that advice was no longer needed.

One of the first acts of the new government was the passage of a law formally abolishing the hated institution of appeals to Great Britain from the judgments of the New Hampshire courts.[17] On July 5 the Council and House passed an act establishing courts of law throughout the province.[18] The courts were to consist of one superior court of judicature to be the supreme court of appeals and to have original jurisdiction in important civil and criminal cases; five inferior courts of common pleas, one in each county, to try minor civil cases; five courts of general sessions of the peace, one in each county, to hear minor criminal cases; and a probate judge in each county to hear such actions as were under his jurisdiction.

On September 10, 1776, the Declaration of Independence was read before the legislature, whereupon an act was passed by the provisions of which the province assumed the name of the "State of New Hampshire."[19] On September 18 as a further consequence of independence it was voted to place the council upon a popularly elective basis.[20] The Declaration of Independence also led many people to wonder whether the system of laws in force under the royal provincial government had not been thereby voided. Accordingly on April 9, 1777, the legislature passed "an Act for re-establishing the general system of Laws heretofore in force in this State."[21] Under the provisions of this act all provincial laws which had not been expressly repealed and were not repugnant to the new status of independence were declared to be still in force.

So serious were the defects of the Constitution of 1776 and so numerous were the objections to it among the various interior towns that in 1777 there was initiated a move to hold a constitutional convention. Several resolutions to this effect passed the House of Representatives, but the Council, the conservative body, withheld its concurrence. The seacoast section was well satisfied with the existing government, and well it might have been, for Rockingham and Strafford counties controlled fifty-one out of the eighty-nine representatives and seven out of the twelve councillors.[22] Finally, however, popular sentiment forced action, and on February 25, 1778, the Council and House met in joint session and voted to call a constitutional convention to meet at Concord on June 10.[23] Each town was invited to send delegates excepting that groups of small towns were permitted to unite in sending one delegate for each group. The constitution devised by the convention was to be submitted to the town meetings for rejection or approval, and a three-fourths' majority of the popular vote was declared necessary to ratify.

The convention met at Concord on June 10, 1778. The seacoast and central towns were well represented, but the western and frontier towns in Grafton County either were unwilling to send delegates or were ignorant of the holding of the convention.[24] Meshech Weare was elected president of the assemblage. The first subject for debate had to do with the apportionment of representation in the legislature among the several towns. After vigorous discussion the convention voted to continue the existing plan of representation. The convention was also divided on the question of establishing an executive department or of lodging the executive power in a sovereign legislature. Samuel Philbrick wrote to Josiah Bartlett concerning the proceedings, "[It was] Voted that the Suprem Executive Authority Shall not be wholly Seprate from the Legislative—this was argued all most two half days: a Large number Insisting upon having the Supreem Executive Authority Lodged in one man with the advice of a Prive Counsel—and Some few thought it most Proper to be Lodged in one man only; he to be Elected Annually: but the Greater Part thought it most Safe in the Hands of the Counsil and Assembly. . . . ."[25] There existed a strong popular suspicion of powerful executives which was a reaction against the old institution of the British provincial governor. The executive power was therefore placed in the hands of the people's representatives.

The proposed constitution was not finally drawn up until 1779, and then it differed little from the Constitution of 1776.[26] There was a rudimentary bill of rights in the new organic law, which declared the sacredness of life, liberty and property, guaranteed freedom of conscience and the right to a jury trial, established the validity of the English common law principles, and vested sovereignty in the people. The council and the house of representatives were preserved with all their previous powers. Catholics were disqualified from voting or holding office. The property qualification for representatives and councillors was raised from £200 to £300, although all male inhabitants of lawful age and paying taxes were to be allowed to vote. The president of the council was given a few minor executive functions such as corresponding with other states, commissioning state officers, calling sessions of the council and of the house of representatives with the consent of three councillors, and reprieving criminals under sentence with the advice of the council. Amendment of the constitution was made possible by the assent of the house and council and of a majority of the electorate.

The principal faults of the new frame of government were those of its predecessor. It lacked strong, independent executive and judicial departments. Judges were appointable and removable at the will of both legislative houses. Supreme executive power was lodged in both houses or in persons to be designated by them. The executive and judicial departments had been most unpopular under British rule, and public sentiment now wished to guard against a recurrence of former experience by making both of these departments of government directly subservient to the popular will. Nevertheless, upon being submitted to the towns the new constitution was overwhelmingly rejected.[27] It probably offered too little change to suit the great majority. Consequently the old Constitution of 1776 continued in operation.

On April 5, 1781, the House of Representatives resolved to call another constitutional convention, and on the following day the Council concurred in this resolution.[28] Precepts or election writs were issued, calling upon the towns to elect delegates to a convention to meet on the first Tuesday in June at Concord. The convention met as scheduled, although many western towns and small parishes again declined to send delegates. George Atkinson of Portsmouth was elected president of the body. The first business was the preparation of an address to the people explaining the proposed new constitution. The convention continued in session until September 14, 1781, at which time a new constitution was submitted to the towns for revision, expression of sentiment, or ratification by a necessary two-thirds' majority of the popular vote.

The proposed constitution of 1781 was largely influenced by the recently adopted Massachusetts constitution, the work of John Adams, who was greatly admired in New Hampshire. It was headed by a ponderous bill of rights containing thirty-eight articles.[29] These were largely a statement of popular ideas of equality and ancient British rights of the people. The convention in its address to the people stated, "We have endeavored therein to ascertain and define the most important and essential natural rights of man."[30] The new document first defined the principles of separation of powers and of checks and balances. In its address to the people the convention observed that it was opposed to setting up a single department of government as "legislator, accuser, judge and executioner" all in one. The address further stated, "These several powers should also be independent; in order to which they are formed with a mutual check upon each other."[31] The constitution proposed a legislative department to consist of a senate and a house of representatives, an executive department to consist of a governor and a council, and a judiciary department consisting of judges holding office during good behavior.[32] No Catholics could qualify to hold office.

The Evolution of State Government

The senate was to consist of twelve members elected annually and apportioned among the counties according to the amount of taxes paid in each county. All voters for senator were required to own property to the value of £100, and all senators were required to own property to the value of £400. The house of representatives was to consist of fifty members apportioned among the counties according to the number of taxpayers in each county. The male taxpayers of legal age in each town were empowered to elect one representative for every fifty taxpayers in the town to meet in a county convention. Members of the county convention were required to possess real estate to the value of £200. The county conventions were to choose annually the county's delegation to the house of representatives from among their own members. All laws required the assent of both houses, money bills originating in the lower house. The governor possessed a veto power over all bills, which might be overridden by a three-fourths' majority in both houses.

The governor was to be elected annually by all legal taxpayers.[33] He was required to own an estate to the value of £1,000. Unless elected by an absolute majority of those voting, the choice of the governor was thrown into the legislature. A council of five members, elected by the legislature and having the same property qualifications as senators, was constituted to advise the governor. The governor was commander of the state militia, and he also had extensive appointive and pardoning powers with the consent of the council. No man was to be eligible for the governorship for more than three years in seven.

All judges were to be appointed by the governor and council.[34] They were to hold office during good behavior but could be removed by the governor and council upon address by the legislature. Delegates to the Continental Congress were to be chosen annually by the two houses of the legislature and were required to have the same property qualifications as the governor. Provision was also made for amendment of the constitution.

This constitution was, to say the least, a very conservative document. Rockingham County under its plan of representation controlled five of the twelve senators and twenty of the fifty representatives, thus giving the seacoast oligarchy substantial ruling power. The high property qualifications and the indirect election of the house of representatives were all designed to prevent the government from becoming too popular and to keep the control in the hands of the propertied class. The political leaders were determined to suppress effectively any agrarian radicalism. The property qualifications were, however, hated by the western towns. As early as November 27, 1776, the towns of Hanover, Canaan, and Cardigan had voted unanimously not to elect a representative under the Constitution of 1776 because, "It limits us in our choice to a person who has real estate of two hundred pounds, lawful money; whereas we conceive that there ought to be no pecuniary restriction, but that every elector is Capable to be elected."[35]

It was the very merits of the projected constitution of 1781, judged by modern standards, which destroyed its chances of ratification. A strong executive, an independent judiciary, and a division of powers were features which New Hampshire government had previously lacked and which the new constitution proposed to supply. Nevertheless, the people were still suspicious of strong executives, smacking of the monarchical tendencies of British rule. They were suspicious of a separation of governmental powers as tending to make the government less amenable to the will of the people. A contemporary observer, William Plumer, wrote concerning the newly drafted constitution, "The task was arduous: for the prejudices which the revolution had engendered against the arbitrary government of Great Britain, made the people jealous of giving to their own officers so much power as was necessary to establish an efficient government."[36] When the constitutional convention reconvened at Concord in January, 1782, to count the returns from the towns, it found the constitution of 1781 rejected by a large vote. The town of Concord had even cast a unanimous vote in opposition.[37] Less than half of the towns had been interested enough to send returns of their votes.

The convention met again in August, 1782, and proceeded to amend some of the objectionable features.[38] The property qualification for senators was reduced from £300 to £200, and all poll-tax payers were made eligible to elect senators. The indirect system of election of the house of representatives was abolished. All towns containing one hundred and fifty male polls were to be allowed to elect one representative and another representative for each additional three hundred male polls. All towns of less than one hundred and fifty male polls were to be classed with other small towns, until they made up that number, for the purpose of electing a representative. Yet if any small towns were so situated that it was very inconvenient to carry out this classification, such small towns were to be allowed to elect individual representatives. This was a distinct concession to the western towns, which objected to being grouped together in such a way that often several towns were electing only one representative. As a further compromise the property qualification for representatives was reduced from £200 to £100 and that for governor from £1000 to £500. On August 21, 1782, the revised constitution was submitted to the towns.

The convention met in December to analyze the returns. The two-thirds' majority of the popular vote necessary for ratification was again found to be lacking. The town of Concord had again cast all its votes against ratification. There still existed a strong prejudice against the powerful executive created by the proposed constitution, and the Concord town meeting resolved,"That the Governor and Privy Council be left out and that there be a President a Legislative Council and a House of Representatives, and that the Powers which are Vested in a Governor and Council be Vested in the Council and House of Representatives."[39]

Accordingly the convention again met at Concord in June, 1783, and revised the constitution a second time.[40] Perhaps the most important change was in the powers of the executive whose name was changed from governor to president. He was to have no veto power and was to preside over the meetings of the senate. But his appointive, military, and pardoning powers were preserved intact. The executive council was to consist of two senators and three representatives elected by the legislature. The revised constitution also contained expression favoring the encouragement of schools, agriculture, manufacturing, and arts and sciences.

In a lengthy bill of rights the constitution declared that no office should be hereditary and that the number of terms of office which a single man might serve should be strictly limited. Pensions were declared contrary to sound public policy. The civil establishment was stated to be at all times superior to the military. All penalties for crimes were to be proportional to the nature of the offense. Excessive bail and cruel, unusual punishments were forbidden, and the purpose of punishment was declared to be reformation rather than extermination.

The constitution of 1781 in its third form was submitted to the towns in the summer of 1783. On October 31, 1783, the convention assembled at Concord to count the returns. This time the constitution was found to be ratified by the necessary majority. The date for its taking effect was fixed as the first Wednesday in June, 1784. On that date the Constitution of 1776 passed out of existence, and the new constitution, which had required five years for its evolution, was established.

Alexander Johnston has said, "The new constitutions were the natural outgrowths of the colonial system, established by charters, or by commissions to royal or proprietary governors; and the provisions of the constitutions were only attempts to adopt such features as had grown up under the colonial systems, or to cut out such features as colonial or State experience had satisfied the people were dangerous."[41] The political theories evolved during the Revolution were, then, either logical developments of British political institutions or reactions against them.

The institutions of judicial appeal from the colonial courts to England and review of colonial laws in England were heartily disliked by the American colonists. These methods of procedure were automatically abolished by the Revolution. The extensive powers of the provincial governors had also been hated during the colonial era. The early revolutionary movement witnessed a reaction against independent executives in the new governments. One of Samuel Adams's aims in the pre-Revolutionary days had been to render the independent colonial judiciary subservient to the legislature. In the first revolutionary governments, this principle was carried to consummation. The British limitation of the franchise in the colonial governments had been regarded as oppressive, and the Revolution saw the franchise widened. In New Hampshire at any rate the old system of apportionment of representation which had prevailed under the royal provincial government was discarded. The conservative seacoast towns were forced to accord more voice in the state government to the interior and western towns. The early years of the Revolution witnessed an extensive revision of the political philosophy originally derived from England. In New Hampshire under government by the Provincial Congress and by the Council and House of Representatives under the Constitution of 1776, new heights of popular and responsible government were reached. The people through their elected representatives were sovereign.

Yet the New Hampshire government under the Constitution of 1776 was in many respects not unlike the preceding royal provincial government. A bicameral legislature consisting of a council and a house of representatives had been carried over from the British system. Money bills were required to originate in the lower house—an ancient British constitutional custom. The general system of colonial laws, which had prevailed under British rule, was adopted practically *in toto* by the new government. The old system of town and county government was left unchanged. The colonial system of provincial courts was reëstablished by the revolutionary government.

In the latter years of the Revolution when a conservative reaction set in against the extremely popular governments of the early years, more and more features of the British political system were incorporated into the state governments. Property qualifications for legislators were raised. The process of impeachment in the lower house of the legislature and trial in the upper house was adopted. An independent executive was established, a governor with extensive legislative, military and judicial powers, a direct counterpart of the royal governor. The judiciary was made independent during good behavior. To advise the governor an executive council was constituted in New Hampshire, being an outgrowth of the British institution of the Privy Council.[42] Each house of the legislature was to be the judge of the qualifications of its own members—an old British legislative prerogative. Even the institution of review of colonial laws and review of the judgments of colonial courts in England, which had passed out of existence in 1776, ultimately found its analogy in part in the American institution of judicial review by a supreme court.

The period of evolution of state governments was in a large sense an era of trial and error in which the American leaders gained experience in governmental theory and practice. The extremes to which popular government had been carried during the early years of revolutionary excess awakened a desire for a system of checks and balances and for a statement of political rights safeguarding the minority from the oppression of a majority. The spirit of the later state constitutions, designed to check popular control and radical democracy, was carried over into the Federal Constitutional Convention of 1787. James Bryce wrote, "The spirit of 1787 was an English spirit, and therefore a conservative spirit, tinged, no doubt, by the hatred to tyranny developed in the revolutionary struggle, tinged also by the nascent dislike to inequality, but in the main an English spirit, which desired to walk in the old paths of precedent. . . . . ."[43]

From the West swift Freedom came,
Against the course of Heaven and doom,
A second sun arrayed in flame
To burn, to kindle, to illume.

SHELLEY.

Secession Movement in the West

THE problem of disunion in New Hampshire during the Revolution was not unique. From New Hampshire to Georgia in fact the Revolutionists were frequently at odds with each other. Pennsylvania and South Carolina were harassed by factionalism. Massachusetts saw its intrastate sectional bitterness culminate in Shays's Rebellion. Many Virginians hated those "radical westerners," Thomas Jefferson and Patrick Henry, far more than the British.[1] In New Hampshire, however, the division was not fundamentally one of the propertied men of the seacoast aligned against the "democratic pirates" of the frontier. The dispute rested upon a political basis—the desire of the western towns to break the monopoly of state governmental control hitherto held by the eastern towns.[2]

The origin of the sectionalism as between east and west in New Hampshire lay in the details of the Masonian grant and its aftermath.[3] The limits of New Hampshire as originally granted to Captain John Mason were circumscribed on the west by a line running sixty miles from the seacoast between the Massachusetts and Maine boundaries. This line was known as the "Masonian curve." In 1740 the King in Council decided that all land between the Masonian curve and the eastern boundary of the province of New York was also included within the limits of New Hampshire. But this decision neglected to determine whether the eastern boundary of New York followed the line of Lake Champlain or of the Connecticut River. When Benning Wentworth became governor of New Hampshire in 1741, he proceeded to grant townships west of the Masonian curve and on both sides of the Connecticut River, even as far west as Lake Champlain. By 1764 he had granted in the neighborhood of one hundred and thirty townships west of the Connecticut River in addition to those which he had granted east of the river. This territory (now Vermont) was known as the "New Hampshire Grants."[4] In 1749 New York entered a claim to all territory west of the Connecticut River and north of Massachusetts, protesting the validity of Wentworth's land grants. This claim was allowed by the King in Council in 1764 when the eastern boundary of New York, north of Massachusetts, was fixed at the Connecticut River, despite the vehement protests of New Hampshire.

This order in council effectively voided all of Benning Wentworth's land grants west of the river. The inhabitants of the New Hampshire Grants were now liable to be dispossessed by New York grantees. This situation led to open revolt against the New York provincial authorities. The Grants reverted to a state of anarchy, the leading element in which was the so-called "Bennington mob" led by Ethan and Ira Allen, later of Ticonderoga fame, who were large landowners. This rabble terrorized the countryside and threatened violence to all who disobeyed its edicts. To meet the menace the New York provincial legislature passed "Twelve Acts of Outlawry." In answer to this legislation the Allens held a violent protest meeting at Manchester in 1775.

The western towns in New Hampshire bordering upon the Connecticut were more or less in sympathy with their neighbors immediately across the river. They came from the same stock, lived in the same kind of country and faced the same economic conditions. On the whole they had far more in common with the towns on the western side of the river than they had with the remainder of New Hampshire. Being under New Hampshire's royal government, their particular grievance was that they had little or no representation in an assembly and council located far away from them on the seacoast and controlled by Governor Wentworth's party and the eastern towns.

Upon the outbreak of the Revolution the western towns in New Hampshire, isolated as they were, did not send delegates to the first three provincial congresses and only a few to the fourth and fifth, although they probably acquiesced in government by the provincial congress because of the emergency. When the Constitution of 1776 was adopted, the delegates in the Congress from Grafton and Cheshire counties were outvoted in their protests against the system of representation. Under the new apportionment the thirty-five towns in Grafton County were awarded six representatives in the House of Representatives and one member of the Council. The thirty-three towns in Cheshire County were awarded fifteen representatives in the House and two members of the Council. Many of the towns in these two western counties, it will be recalled, objected to being classed with other towns for purposes of electing representatives and refused to participate in the new government, despite the requests emanating from Exeter, the new capital. The towns also became delinquent in the payment of state taxes.

In July, 1776, the western towns of Hanover, Canaan, Cardigan, Lyme, Lebanon, Plainfield, Acworth, Marlow, Alstead, Surry, Chesterfield, Haverhill, Lyman, Bath, Gunthwaite, Landaff, and Morristown issued an address to the people of eastern New Hampshire explaining their grievances.[5] They asserted that the Revolution had meant little change to them, since the control of the government was still in the hands of the seacoast towns. The address stated, ". . . . This new mode of government is a little horn, growing up in the place where the other was broken off."[6] The towns claimed that since they were west of the Masonian curve, New Hampshire's jurisdiction over them was based solely upon a royal commission issued from England. Upon the Declaration of Independence this commission had become void, and all towns west of the Masonian curve had reverted to a state of nature as corporate entities. The Constitution of 1776, set up by New Hampshire, was contingent for its validity outside the Masonian grant upon the consent of the towns in question. Accordingly the western towns asserted that because they had never consented to the new frame of government, they were not obligated to participate in it. During the fall of 1776 the various western towns held town meetings. Their objections to the state government were stated as follows: first, the new government was controlled by a certain oligarchy from among the Revolutionist party; secondly, contrary to the new system of apportionment, each town as a corporate entity was entitled to at least one representative in the House of Representatives; thirdly,

Resolution of the Continental Congress Recommending That New Hampshire Establish a Form of Government, November 3, 1775.

property qualifications for members of the legislature were contrary to true democracy; fourthly, the popular branch of the legislature should be sovereign and not checked by the Council; and fifthly, the new Constitution was lacking a bill of rights.[7] On January 3, 1777, a committee of the New Hampshire legislature was appointed to confer with the recalcitrant western towns.[8] This committee met with a convention of the towns at Lebanon on February 13 but was unable to arrange a compromise.

In the meantime on January 15, 1777, the towns west of the Connecticut River, throwing off the control of New York, had organized themselves as the sovereign state of New Connecticut and had petitioned the Continental Congress for recognition. In June the name was changed to Vermont. The towns on the eastern side of the river, still at odds with the New Hampshire government, viewed the new state with mixed emotions. On June 11, 1777, these western New Hampshire towns met in convention at Hanover and laid down three prerequisites for joining the New Hampshire government. They demanded that each town should be allowed at least one representative in the House of Representatives, that the seat of government should be moved from Exeter to a point nearer to the center of the state, and that a new constitution should be drawn up.[9] A committee of the western towns was appointed to go to Exeter to negotiate with the New Hampshire legislature. This committee arrived at Exeter in November, 1777, and was received by a committee of the state legislature, but again no agreement was reached. The legislative committee reported that the existing Constitution was sufficient for the war-time emergency "without any great Injury to any part of the State."

In the early part of 1778 a group of the disgruntled western towns determined to join the state of Vermont, and petitioned the Vermont legislature to be admitted.[10] The Vermont government, which was controlled by the Bennington party from west of the Green Mountains, was rather reluctant to receive an eastern addition. But those Vermont towns east of the Green Mountains and west of the Connecticut River threatened to secede to form a Connecticut Valley state unless the New Hampshire towns were received. On May 17, 1778, the Vermont legislature voted to receive the New Hampshire towns of Cornish, Lebanon, Hanover, Lyme, Orford, Piermont, Haverhill, Bath, Lyman, Apthorp (now divided between Littleton and Dalton), Enfield, Canaan, Cardigan (now Orange), Gunthwaite (now Lisbon),

Morristown (now Franconia), and Landaff upon the condition that a popular referendum of Vermont and of the sixteen towns in question should approve the union. The inhabitants of the sixteen New Hampshire towns were by no means unanimously in favor of joining the new state, but persuasion and propaganda were effectively used to combat the opposing minorities. The New Hampshire government at Exeter charged that the center of the secession movement was at Dartmouth College in Hanover. Although Dr. Eleazar Wheelock, President of the College, was probably neutral in the dispute, there can be no question that his son, Colonel John Wheelock, Colonel Elisha Payne, a trustee of the College, and Bezaleel Woodward, a member of the faculty, were active in the political machinations involving the secession movement.[11] On June 11, 1778, the Vermont Assembly ratified the admission of the sixteen New Hampshire towns by a vote of 37 to 12. In the meantime the New Hampshire government at Exeter was in a turmoil. On August 22, 1778, President Weare of the Council wrote a strong letter of remonstrance to Governor Thomas Chittenden of Vermont.[12] Upon the receipt of this letter Ethan Allen was sent to Philadelphia to represent the interests of Vermont before the Continental Congress.

In Philadelphia the strategy of the Allens first became apparent. They realized that the petition of Vermont to be recognized as a new state would be contested by New York and New Hampshire, both of which claimed the territory of the New Hampshire Grants. Accordingly the Allens had consented to the union with the sixteen New Hampshire towns, thinking to return them only upon the condition that New Hampshire should not push its claim for territory west of the Connecticut River. Apparently an agreement to this effect was worked out between the Allens and the New Hampshire leaders. On September 26, 1778, Josiah Bartlett, New Hampshire's delegate in the Congress at Philadelphia, wrote to President Weare, "On the 19th Colo. Ethan Allen Came to this City from said Vermont and understanding in what Situation the affair was and that their Conduct with Regard to the said Towns was universally condemned He earnestly Requested me not to press Congress to take up the matter till he had an oppertunity to Return to Vermont and lay the matter before their Assembly . . . . and he says he is persuaded they will Resind their vote for Receiving those Towns and Disclaim any pretensions to the East side of Connecticut River."[13] On October 8, 1778, Ethan Allen reported to the Vermont Assembly that the only obstacle to recognition of the state was the presence of the western New Hampshire towns within the Vermont government.[14] On October 20, however, the union was sustained by a vote of the Assembly. Yet on the very next day the Assembly by its refusal to extend county organization to the towns east of the river practically rescinded the union. The New Hampshire towns withdrew from the Vermont Assembly claiming breach of faith. On October 23, 1778, Ethan Allen wrote to President Weare of New Hampshire, "The Union I ever view'd to be Incompatible with the Right of New Hampshire, and have Punctually Discharged my obligation to Col. [Josiah] Bartlet, for its Dissolution; and that worthy Gentleman on his part assured me, that he had no directions from the Government of New Hampshire, to extend their claims to the westward of Connecticut River, to interfere with the State of Vermont; and I hope that the Government of New Hampshire will excuse the Imbicility of Vermont, in the matter of the union."[15]

On December 9, 1778, the western New Hampshire towns held a convention at Cornish to air their grievances.[16] They were joined by several Vermont towns from east of the Green Mountains who were more in sympathy with the New Hampshire valley towns than with the Vermont government controlled by the Bennington clique from west of the Green Mountains. The convention represented in all twenty-two towns from both sides of the river. These towns were no more favorable toward the Bennington government than toward the New Hampshire government but wished to be included in either state as a complete unit or to be an independent valley state. William Whipple of New Hampshire in the Continental Congress wrote to President Weare, "I am rather inclined to think that nothing will effectually settle the dispute but New Hampshire's opposing her claim to that of New York even if she should afterwards (supposing the decision to be in favor of New Hampshire) agree that the grant on the west side of the River should be a separate State, because in that case New Hampshire would have it in her power to settle the line to her satisfaction. . . . ."[17]

New Hampshire accordingly resolved to prosecute in the Continental Congress its claim that the territory of Vermont should be under the jurisdiction of New Hampshire. The state asserted that the royal order in council of 1764, fixing the eastern boundary of New York at the Connecticut River, was invalid and that all territory as far west as Lake Champlain should revert to New Hampshire, since it had been originally granted by Governor Benning Wentworth. Although New Hampshire had no real hope of gaining the full extent of this claim, the state hoped at least to have its western boundary fixed at the Connecticut River, thus ensuring its control over the disaffected western towns.[18] On November 17, 1779, in accordance with the request of the Continental Congress the New Hampshire legislature passed an act empowering the Congress to arbitrate its dispute with New York.[19] Samuel Livermore, a noted New Hampshire trial lawyer and former royal Attorney General, was sent to the Congress especially to argue the state's case. The Continental Congress appointed an investigating committee which was supposedly packed in favor of New York's claims, but the committee failed to file a report. Even Massachusetts entered a claim to some of the Vermont territory, hoping thereby to gain political leverage. The valley towns on both sides of the Connecticut River were represented at Philadelpha by Bezaleel Woodward of Hanover and Colonel Peter Olcott of Norwich. These two representatives had been instructed to urge that the towns on both sides of the river be formed into an independent valley state—allegedly the dream of Dr. Eleazar Wheelock— or that the boundary between New Hampshire and New York be fixed at the Green Mountains. The arguments before the Congress occupied the period from January to September, 1780, but at the latter date the Congress was no nearer a decision than in the beginning.[20]

At this point the struggle assumed a new aspect. Hitherto the only disaffected New Hampshire towns had been those north of Cornish on the Connecticut River. But now the towns in Cheshire County to the south became aroused at New Hampshire's dilatory policy in not pushing its claims to Vermont with more vigor. A convention of forty-three towns from both sides of the river met at Charlestown on January 16, 1781.[21] This convention at first favored extending the New Hampshire boundary westward to the Green Mountains so as to include the valley towns in Vermont. New York was agreeable to this division provided it received all territory west of the Green Mountain range. The division was also acceptable to New Hampshire. Had the convention formally ratified the proposal, it is probable that Vermont would have been divided between her eastern and western neighbors. Unfortunately for the plan of division, however, was the fact that Ira Allen, the leader in Vermont's move for independence, was present at the convention. By his masterful political strategy and diplomacy he succeeded in bringing about a reversal of sentiment almost overnight. The convention recommended that the western New Hampshire towns should again secede and join Vermont. On February 8, 1781, the Vermont Assembly approved the second projected union, and thirty-six New Hampshire towns from Cheshire and Grafton counties joined Vermont.[22] County organization was extended east of the river. Colonel Elisha Payne of Lebanon, a trustee of Dartmouth College, was elected deputy-governor of Vermont, and the Vermont legislature held a session east of the river at Charlestown. At the same time the Vermont government, dominated by the Allens, boldly entered a claim to a strip of territory twenty miles wide, west of the line of Lake Champlain and indisputably the territory of New York. The strategy of the Allens was now clear. By enforcing claims upon territory within the limits of New York and New Hampshire, they hoped to force those two states to agree to the territorial independence of Vermont.

New Hampshire was now thoroughly alarmed and resolved to submit the matter to the Continental Congress. On August 20, 1781, the Congress announced that as a prerequisite to recognition Vermont must give up all claims to territory east of the Connecticut River and west of the line of Lake Champlain, but the Vermont legislature, meeting at Charlestown on October 11, 1781, refused to abrogate the union with the thirty-six New Hampshire towns.

The result was rather bizarre and nearly caused civil war.[23] The thirty-six towns on the eastern side of the river under the jurisdiction of Vermont contained strong minorities in favor of the New Hampshire government. There was a conflict of governmental jurisdiction between two sets of civil officers—those representing New Hampshire and Vermont, respectively. In Chesterfield, one of the seceding towns, originated the spark which nearly set off an explosion. In November, 1781, a constable acting under a Vermont commission arrested two supporters of New Hampshire authority. These two men petitioned the New Hampshire legislature for relief, whereupon the legislature ordered its sheriff of Cheshire County, Colonel Enoch Hale, to release them. Hale in turn was arrested by Nathaniel Prentice of Alstead, the Vermont sheriff, for interfering with the course of justice. Immediately Hale sent word to Brigadier General Benjamin Bellows of Walpole, urging him to call out the New Hampshire militia. Vermont countered by preparing to mobilize its troops. On January 8,

1782, the New Hampshire legislature voted to raise one thousand men under the command of Major General John Sullivan to restore civil order in the western counties.[24] On January 12 the legislature issued a proclamation of rebellion and gave all citizens of the revolted New Hampshire towns forty days to subscribe to a declaration acknowledging the western boundary of New Hampshire to be the Connecticut River.

With hostilities imminent the Continental Congress resolved to intervene. The Congress was practically unanimous in its condemnation of Vermont's action. The feeling of the thirteen states toward Vermont was not softened by the recent discovery of Vermont's negotiations with the British authorities in the form of letters from the Allen brothers to Lord George Germain. On January 1, 1782, at the instance of the Congress, General George Washington wrote to Governor Thomas Chittenden of Vermont urging that his state rescind its late actions. Washington opened his letter by saying, "Now I would ask you candidly, whether . . . . the late extension of your claim upon New Hampshire and New York, was not more a political manoevre, than one in which you conceived yourselves justifiable." Washington continued, "The State of Vermont, if acknowledged, will be the first new one admitted into the confederacy; and if suffered to encroach upon the ancient established boundaries of the adjacent ones, will serve as a precedent for others, which it may hereafter be expedient to set off, to make the same unjustifiable demands." He concluded with a veiled threat, "There is no calamity within the compass of my foresight, which is more to be dreaded than the necessity of *coercion* on the part of Congress. . . . ."[25]

The Vermont Assembly met in a mid-winter session at Bennington in the latter part of January, 1782.[26] The seceding New Hampshire towns were not well represented because of poor traveling conditions. On February 20 the Assembly passed an act dissolving the union with the New Hampshire towns and fixing the eastern boundary of the state at the Connecticut River. In the Continental Congress, however, Vermont was adjudged to have delayed too long in its action, and immediate recognition was withheld. The new state was not finally admitted to the Union until 1790.

The thirty-six seceding towns then returned to the jurisdiction of New Hampshire. For a long period many of the inhabitants of Cheshire and Grafton counties were sullen over the final outcome and adopted an obstructionist policy in the courts. In the face of anarchy the lenient and understanding attitude of the circuit judges and of Attorney General John Sullivan helped to restore order.[27] A more liberal representation in the Senate and House of Representatives was accorded the western towns in the Constitution of 1784. More leading citizens from the western counties were selected for important state duties, and sectional bitterness gradually abated.

The secession movement entrenched more firmly than ever the idea of the town as the political unit of representation in the state legislature. This principle has not been fundamentally altered since 1784 and has operated to give New Hampshire today the largest House of Representatives among all of the forty-eight states, its membership varying from 419 to 422. Another result of the secession movement was the bitter feeling engendered in the New Hampshire government toward Dartmouth College.[28] The College was regarded in the southeastern section of the state as having instigated the whole affair. Thus the Constitution of 1784 stated, "No person holding the office of . . . . president, professor or instructor in any college . . . . shall at the same time have a seat in the senate or house of representatives, or council. . . . ."[29] This provision was not eliminated until the constitutional convention of 1791. This bitterness between the College and the state was carried over into the nineteenth century and was partly responsible for the state's attempt to assume control of the College in violation of its charter, an action which culminated in Daniel Webster's famous argument in the "Dartmouth College Case" before the Supreme Court of the United States in 1818 and John Marshall's opinion upholding the validity of contracts.[30]

It is indifferent who understands it. The deed is done; and a strong foundation laid for eternal amity between England and America.

LORD SHELBURNE.[1]

New Hampshire and the Peace Settlement

THE year 1781 found Great Britain at war with perhaps the most formidable combination of powers that she has faced in all modern history. France, Spain, Holland and the American states were actively fighting Britain on land and sea. Russia, Denmark, Sweden, and Holland were united in an armed neutrality to oppose British absolutism on the seas. It is not too great an exaggeration to call this alignment "Britain against the World." The surrender of Cornwallis at Yorktown on October 19, 1781, together with the general diplomatic situation, rendered it extremely improbable that Great Britain would ever be able to subdue her rebellious colonies. An American peace commission was appointed in 1781. Negotiations were opened at Paris and continued throughout the early part of 1782. The immediate British policy as directed by Lord Shelburne, the prime minister, was to induce the American commissioners to sign a treaty independently of their European allies. Shelburne accordingly granted almost all of the American terms, fully realizing that by doing so he would be better able to resist the peace demands of France and Spain.

The provisional treaty was signed at Paris on November 30, 1782. Article I of the treaty recognized the thirteen states severally as "free, sovereign, and independent."[2] Article II defined the boundaries of the new nation. The northeastern boundary, with which this discussion is more directly concerned, was described as extending "From the northwest angle of Nova Scotia viz. that angle which is formed by a line drawn due north from the source of the St. Croix River to the Highlands; from said Highlands which divide those rivers that empty themselves into the river St. Lawrence, from those which fall into the Atlantic Ocean, to the northwesternmost head of the Connecticut River; thence down along middle of said river to the forty-fifth degree of north latitude; from thence by a line due west on that latitude. . . . ." Article III acknowledged the American right to take fish on the Grand Banks off the Newfoundland coast and granted to American fishermen the liberty to participate in all of the inshore fisheries of the British territories in America, and also "the liberty to dry and cure fish in any of the unsettled bays, harbors, and creeks of Nova Scotia, Magdalen Islands, and Labrador, so long as the same shall remain unsettled." Article IV declared that there should be no legal impediment to the recovery of debts as between British and American citizens. Articles V and VI provided that there should be no future confiscation of Loyalist estates and that the Continental Congress should recommend to the legislatures of the several states the restitution of Loyalist estates already confiscated. This treaty was signed without the knowledge of Count Vergennes, in specific violation of the terms of the French alliance and of the instructions of the Congress to the American commissioners, but the terms secured from the British were so highly satisfactory and the position of the French and Spanish was so ambiguous that the American peace commission was willing to proceed without the latter.

News of the treaty reached the Continental Congress on March 12, 1783. On April 9 Sir Guy Carleton proclaimed the cessation of hostilities, and two days later the Congress did likewise. On April 15 after some criticism of the violation of the agreement with France touching the peace negotiations, the Congress ratified the treaty by a unanimous vote.[3] In England the terms were regarded as too conciliatory, and Shelburne's ministry was overthrown. Nevertheless, the terms were approved by Shelburne's successors, and the provisional articles became definitive on September 3, 1783. The final ratification of the treaty by the Continental Congress took place on January 14, 1784.

On March 12, 1783, John Taylor Gilman, New Hampshire's delegate in the Continental Congress, wrote to President Meshech Weare informing him of the treaty. Gilman declared, "The Articles respecting the Boundaries of the United States and that respecting the right of Fishery, are Ample and I believe Equal to the most Sanguine Expectation. These Two very Important Articles are highly pleasing, as are most of the others."[4] This letter from Gilman was the first authoritative news of the treaty to be received in New Hampshire, and it was printed in the *New Hampshire Gazette* of March 29, 1783.[5]

President Weare and the Committee of Safety immediately set aside April 28 as a day of thanksgiving. In Portsmouth the day was ushered in by cannon salutes and the ringing of bells.[6] At ten o'clock in the morning a religious service was held in the north meeting house presided over by the Reverend Doctor Samuel Haven. At noon President Weare, attended by high state officers, proceeded to the old province-house, from the balcony of which was read the proclamation of peace amidst a wild demonstration of cheering. A huge banquet then took place in the former royal assembly room, and in the evening there was a splendid ball, ornamented by a display of fireworks. On June 18, 1783, Portsmouth harbor was opened to British ships.[7]

The Treaty of 1783 left some question as to the exact location of the northern and northwestern boundary of New Hampshire. According to the provisions of Article II the boundary was to follow certain highlands until it reached the northwesternmost head of the Connecticut River and was to proceed thence down the middle of the said river to the forty-fifth parallel where began the northern boundary of Vermont. The difficulty lay in the determination of that branch of the Connecticut River which was the "northwesternmost head."[8] There were three principal branches—the main head of the river which flowed out of the Connecticut lakes, which was the easternmost branch, Hall Stream, which was the westernmost branch, and Indian Stream, which followed a course halfway between the other two. The province of Lower Canada maintained that the main head of the Connecticut River or at least the Indian Stream was the "northwesternmost head" defined in the treaty. The state of New Hampshire maintained that the Hall Stream was the northwesternmost branch and was accordingly the boundary established by the treaty. Thus there were roughly between 30,000 and 80,000 acres of land in dispute, comprised in what is now the township of Pittsburg. The Treaty of Ghent in 1814 established a boundary commission to define the whole northeastern boundary of the United States more accurately, but this commission was never able to reach a decision.

In the meantime the inhabitants of the New Hampshire territory in dispute, which became known as the "Indian Stream territory," were in a quandary, not knowing whether they belonged to the province of Lower Canada or were a part of Coös County in New Hampshire.[9] In 1832 the fifty-nine inhabitants drew up a constitution and founded the "Indian Stream Republic." For eight years they resisted all attempts of New Hampshire and Canada to establish authority over them. In 1840, however, the New Hampshire militia seized the territory, and it was incorporated as the town of Pittsburg, despite the protests of Canada. The Webster-Ashburton treaty in 1842 effectively ended further dispute by defining the "northwesternmost head" of the Connecticut River as the Hall Stream—a complete vindication of New Hampshire's claim.[10]

The question as to the debts which were owed to British subjects by American citizens and vice versa, and which had been contracted before the war, had an interesting aftermath. The treaty provided that neither Britain nor the United States should oppose any legal impediment to the full collection of these debts, this provision being in accord with international law of the period. Yet the Continental Congress could do no more than recommend to the various state legislatures the passage of acts enabling British citizens to bring legal action in the state courts, and not all of the states complied with this recommendation. In New Hampshire few persons owed money to English citizens. In fact many English subjects owed large balances to Portsmouth merchants.[11] Accordingly the state legislature had no qualms about passing a law empowering English citizens to bring actions in the New Hampshire courts for the collection of debts.[12] By the Constitution of 1787 the Federal District Courts were given jurisdiction in such cases, but British subjects still experienced great difficulty in gaining just verdicts before American juries. Finally the United States under the terms of Jay's Treaty of 1794 agreed to assume and to pay these debts as the only just and practicable method of settlement.[13]

The question of the restitution of Loyalist estates was an equally knotty one. The New Hampshire Confiscation Act of 1778 had confiscated the estates of twenty-eight Loyalists who were either serving in the British army or actively aiding the British government.[14] Nearly all of the estates sequestered under this act were sold for the benefit of the state after the payment of all debts against them. Unfortunately because of the size of these debts, the laxness in administration of the estates, the depreciation of paper money, and possibly even corruption, the sales netted the state treasury but little. The Wolfeborough estate of Governor John Wentworth was sold in 1781 for £354,470 in Continental currency, which was equal to approximately £9,000 in specie.[15] The final liquidation of the Wentworth property, which was the largest Loyalist estate in New Hampshire, brought only £10,000 into the treasury. But the estate owed £18,000 to various creditors, and after the payment of these debts there was naturally no ultimate profit for the state.

In 1782 the New Hampshire legislature had passed an act confiscating the estates of all Loyalists absent from the state,[16] and the attorney general was empowered to bring actions in court under the law. Fortunately few of these estates had been sequestered before the signing of the provisional treaty of peace, which in Article VI forbade any future confiscations. The Attorney General of New Hampshire, John Sullivan, correctly interpreted Article VI to mean that all actions for confiscation under the act of 1782 should be suspended. Sullivan was bitterly criticized for this attitude, and finally on August 2, 1783, he replied to a letter from one of his most vehement critics by publishing an address in the *New Hampshire Gazette*. He defended his actions under the terms of the treaty and wrote as follows concerning the confiscations under the act of 1778, ". . . . The property of absentees, which has been appropriated and sold in this state, though in itself of great value, has scarcely yielded to the treasury a sum sufficient to pay for the paper, which he has stained with his malicious pen; it is exceedingly fortunate for the inhabitants of New Hampshire, that they are not bound by the articles of peace, to make restitution for the estates of the late Governor Wentworth and Col. Holland. . . . ."[17]

Under the provisions of Article V of the treaty the Continental Congress agreed to recommend to the several states the restitution of the property of bona fide British subjects. The Congress also agreed to recommend to the states that they repeal their laws of confiscation and that they permit all Loyalists to return to their respective states for a period of one year to attempt to obtain restitution of their property. The Congress faithfully transmitted these recommendations to the states on January 14, 1784. Accordingly on September 15, 1786, an act repealing the Confiscation Act of 1778 and enabling the absentee Loyalists to return to the state for one year was passed by the New Hampshire legislature.[18] By repealing the Confiscation Act the legislature accomplished nothing in the way of restitution, since the confiscations were already an accomplished fact and the state had resold the estates to individuals, who had purchased them in good faith. In reality the Treaty of 1783 could not legally bring about a restitution of Loyalist property. The determination of qualifications for property ownership is not properly within the scope of international law but is considered a "municipal" regulation entirely within the power of a sovereign state. Accordingly the state legislatures were entirely within their legal rights in confiscating the Loyalist estates, since they possessed full power to determine what persons might own property within their respective jurisdictions.[19] Of course, the foregoing statement assumes that there were no provisions for the protection of property rights in the several state constitutions at the time when the confiscation acts were passed by the various states. In New Hampshire the state legislature was sovereign when it confiscated the Loyalist estates, and it will be recalled that there was no bill of rights in the New Hampshire Constitution of 1776. The Constitution of 1784 contained provision for the safeguarding of property rights but specifically declared that such provisions should not affect the Loyalist confiscations.[20]

Few if any Loyalists were able to gain restitution of their confiscated property in New Hampshire. Colonel John Fenton's estate was especially exempted from confiscation in order to pay his creditors.[21] From time to time in the post-war years parts of the confiscated estates of Benjamin Whiting, George Meserve, and William Stark were released to pay creditors of the estates.[22] On February 26, 1786, John Fisher's estate was restored to him *in toto* by a special act of the legislature.[23] On March 1, 1786, the legislature returned part of the confiscated Cummings estate in Hollis to the children of the former owner.[24]

The Loyalist refugees in England and Canada were left practically destitute by the confiscations. They fully expected the Treaty of 1783 to restore to them their property rights. When it was found that Lord Shelburne had been unable to secure adequate provision for restitution, the Loyalists demanded compensation from the British government for their losses, and this demand was favorably received by Parliament. In 1783 a royal commission was appointed to "enquire into the losses and services of all such persons who had suffered in their Rights, Properties and Professions during the late unhappy Dissentions in America in consequence of their loyalty to his Majesty and attachment to the British Government." This commission held hearings in London and also sent agents to Halifax in Nova Scotia to conduct hearings. Their work continued until 1788 by which time nearly nine million dollars, or about one-fifth of the total claims, had been paid by the British treasury.[25]

There were in all forty-nine Loyalist claimants, who had originally resided in New Hampshire.[26] Of these, forty-three had claims of real consequence and gained compensation. The New Hampshire Loyalists claimed total losses of £185,787. Parliament upon the recommendation of the commission finally granted compensation based upon twenty-four property claims to the amount of £27,029 and voted twenty-three annual pensions totaling £3,012. The largest confiscated estate was that of Governor John Wentworth, which he had valued at £47,116. He was compensated by a payment of £8,827 for his property loss and received an annual pension of £440. John Fisher was allowed £3,500 for property loss and received a position in the royal naval office with an annual salary of £888. Colonel Stephen Holland received £2,558 for property loss and a pension of £268. Several other Loyalists were less fortunate, being unable to prove their losses with the necessary documents, and consequently received little compensation. Thus was mitigated a certain amount of the injustice and hardship resulting from the American Revolution.

In 1783 the provisions relating to American participation in the northeastern fisheries, as defined in Article III of the peace treaty, were considered of great importance in New Hampshire. Fishing continued to be an important industry of the state for several decades after the Revolution. After the War of 1812, however, the British government declined to renew the fishing privileges granted in the Treaty of 1783. An agreement was not finally reached until 1818 when on October 20 there was negotiated a Convention on Fisheries. This convention limited American participation in the fisheries to certain parts·of the coasts of Newfoundland, Labrador, and the Magdalen Islands but specifically granted the liberty *forever*. The convention also granted in perpetuity the right to dry fish in the unsettled bays, creeks, and harbors of Newfoundland and Labrador. The latter provision occasioned international friction as the coasts became settled. The matter reached a crisis during the first administration of President Grover Cleveland, but a final settlement was not reached until the decision of the Hague Tribunal in 1910.[27] Long before this time fishing had ceased to have much importance among New Hampshire industries.

On the whole the Treaty of 1783 must be regarded as a great success for American diplomacy. The American states gained practically everything for which they were contending. The strongest commercial and naval power in the world had condescended to recognize their independence, and their territorial demands were fully complied with. They were forced to make almost no concessions to Great Britain in return for their gains. Perhaps the broad concessions accorded to the American states by this treaty established the basis for future relations between Great Britain and the United States which, despite many serious conflicts of interest between the two nations, have witnessed only one short period of hostilities since 1783.

CHAPTER 16

Even progress, which ought to superadd, for the most part only substitutes, one partial and incomplete truth for another; improvement consisting chiefly in this, that the new fragment of truth is more wanted, more adapted to the needs of the time, than that which it displaces.

JOHN STUART MILL.[1]

Advance in Liberal Ideas

A N impressive advance in liberal and progressive ideas and a revolution in social philosophy were aspects of the American Revolution which were fully as important as the political and economic overturn. These aspects, however, were more intangible and more elusive in that they were entangled in the social psychology of the period. The modern historian experiences difficulty in weighing the results of the new spirit of liberalism and humanity which was an aftermath of the Revolution, for he all too often cannot be sure of a definite connection between apparent cause and effect. It is probable that the revolutionary psychology was not the sole force behind the advance in liberal ideas during the last two decades of the eighteenth century. Nevertheless, it afforded a certain radical attitude and a lack of respect for precedent, which were necessary for an era of change. The Revolution also removed the influence of British interests and British tradition, which in several respects had hitherto served as a conservative brake upon any extensive alteration of the *status quo*. Thus, among the many enlightened changes which the new liberalism initiated, it succeeded in effecting thoroughgoing progress in four important fields, namely, religious tol-

[207]

erance, improvement in education, reform of the barbaric penal codes, and elimination of slavery.

In New Hampshire such religious tolerance as existed prior to the Revolution was dependent upon a legislative act of May 15, 1714.[2] This law provided that any town or parish at its meeting might choose a minister and enter into a contract for his support, a majority of the townspeople having a controlling voice in this matter. The selectmen were empowered to assess taxes upon all persons within the town or parish for the support of the chosen minister. The law further declared, ". . . . Nor shall any person Under pretence of being of a Different perswasion be Excused from paying towards the Support of the Settled Minister or Ministers of Such Town aforesaid, but onley Such as are Conscientiously soe, and Constantly Attend the publick Worship of God on the Lords day according to their own perswasion. . . . ." The result of this act was to create a situation whereby it was extremely difficult for a minority sect within a town to gain exemption from paying tithes to the church established by the majority. Minority sects could usually gain such exemption only by a special act of the general court.

In 1776 eighty-four of the one hundred and eighteen New Hampshire churches were Congregational.[3] Indeed, the Congregational Church was regarded as the established church or the "standing order." There were also fifteen Presbyterian churches, eleven Baptist, four Quaker, and three Episcopal. In many towns these minority sects had only gained exemption from the Congregational tithes after struggles covering many years—particularly the Baptists and the Quakers. The Presbyterian churches experienced less difficulty in gaining toleration, since the Scotch-Irish population, which had introduced this faith, was usually preponderant in the towns where Presbyterian churches were to be found. In any case, however, it was an arduous task for a new sect to gain recognition in the shadow of an established church. Dissenting ministers had to overcome great obstacles to obtain their share of the taxes. An agnostic belonging to no church was automatically taxed to support the established order. Furthermore a convert from the established church to a new sect was often unable to transfer his payment of tithes to his new faith. Thus the dissenters within each town keenly felt their disadvantages.

The religious revival of 1780-1781 and the years following the Revolution saw a large increase in new denominations in New Hampshire.[4] The Freewill Baptists gained access to the state in 1780. The Universalist faith was established in 1781. The Shakers and the Methodists appeared in 1792. The Christian sect originated in 1800. The rise of these new sects created tremendous dissatisfaction with the degree of toleration provided by the existing law. The Constitution of 1784 stated, "And no person of any one particular religious sect or denomination, shall ever be compelled to pay towards the support of the teacher or teachers of another persuasion, sect or denomination."[5] This declaration actually did little to improve the existing situation.[6] In order to escape paying taxes to the legally established church a person had to prove that he was a member of another faith. Usually he had to do this in court before prejudiced juries or partial judges.[7] Legal disputes centered about a person's views on the dogma and ritual of the various denominations. It was frequently impossible for a dissenter to prove membership in another faith. The only certain method by which a dissenting congregation could obtain exemption from the tithes of the town's established church was a special legislative act. These acts of exemption were difficult to obtain because the state legislature was usually controlled by the Congregationalists.

Not until the Toleration Act of 1819 were all denominations finally placed upon an equal basis. Four years of vigorous struggle were required to force this law through the state legislature, in the face of the united opposition of the Congregational clergy and the narrow-minded rural sections. The law as finally passed on July 1, 1819, provided that no person should be required to contribute to the support of any church of which he was not a member, and that no person should be required to be a member of any church but could resign upon giving written notice.[8] The Congregational clergy were very bitter toward the act. It was regarded as "a repeal of the Christian religion" and "an abolition of the Bible."[9] Nevertheless, a large part of the opposition could be traced to the fact that the act placed the dissenting churches on a basis of equality with the established churches.

Education had been placed upon an established basis fully as early as religion. The first public school in New Hampshire was authorized in 1708 when on May 10 the General Court passed an "act for a free school to bee kept at Portsmo."[10] On May 2, 1719, there was passed a general education law for the entire province.[11] This law provided that every town of fifty householders and over should be required to hire a schoolmaster to teach reading, writing, and arithmetic and that every town of one hundred householders and over should be required to maintain a grammar school taught by "Some Discreet person of good Conversation well Instructed in the Tongues." Failure of any town to maintain a school over a period of six months was punishable by a fine of £20. Selectmen who allowed the school to lapse for more than one month were liable to a fine of £20.[12] The enforcement of this act was placed under the Court of General Quarter Sessions, which upon application might excuse certain impoverished towns from compliance with the act. This law was in force without modification until the outbreak of the Revolution. It was widely evaded, the usual method being to hire a schoolmaster only during the period that the Court of General Quarter Sessions was sitting.[13] A hostile attitude among the greater part of the uneducated population toward attempts to alleviate illiteracy operated to defeat the purpose of the law. Governor John Wentworth repeatedly urged the Assembly to reform the educational system during his administration but was largely unsuccessful. On December 14, 1771, in his message to the Assembly he said, ". . . . The promoting of learning very obviously calls for Legislative Care. The insufficiency of our present Laws for this purpose, must be too evident, seeing nine-tenths of your Towns are wholly without Schools, or have such vagrant foreign Masters as are much worse than none; Being for the most part unknown in their principles & deplorably illiterate."[14] The Assembly, however, declined to impose an educational system upon the province which would entail further taxation.

In addition to the public schools there were numerous private tutors in the larger towns. The following advertisement taken from the *New Hampshire Gazette* is a typical example.

> *Vere Royse,*
> *Informs the Public, That he shall keep from 6 to 8 in the Morning, and from 11 to 1 at Noon, to teach young Ladies Reading, Writing and Arithmetic; the remainder of the Day shall be kept to teach young Men as above; also, the Mathematicks, and besides the common Methods of working Navigation, shall teach to work it expeditiously by Arithmetic, without Book or Instrument, only with a Pen or Piece of Chaulk.*[15]

The children of more wealthy parents usually patronized these private tutors.

Advance in Liberal Ideas

Prior to the Revolution the emphasis upon education was primarily religious, and the settled ministers frequently served as schoolmasters. In Claremont the Society for the Propagation of the Gospel conducted a school. In 1774 a Portsmouth Congregational minister, Dr. Samuel Langdon, was chosen President of Harvard College. Governor Benning Wentworth's commission authorized him to establish schools "in order to the training up of Youth to Reading and to a necessary Knowledge of the Principles of Religion."[16] Governor John Wentworth's commission also stated that all schoolmasters must possess proper religious qualifications.[17]

The Revolution disrupted what few educational facilities had hitherto existed in New Hampshire.[18] The heavy taxes rendered necessary for war purposes left little town money available for the support of the schools. They were forgotten in the face of the emergency. By 1781 scarcely a vestige of public school education remained. Dartmouth College, however, founded by Eleazar Wheelock in 1770 and in which Governor John Wentworth had shown great interest, sturdily survived the war.[19] Also in 1778 Phillips Exeter Academy, founded by John Phillips, began giving instruction, and in 1781 it was incorporated by the state legislature because "the Education of Youth has ever been considered by the wise & good, as an object of the highest consequence to the safety & happiness of a People."[20]

At the close of the Revolution new theories of education came into acceptance. Education tended to reflect political trends rather than to rest upon a basis primarily religious. Enjoyment of the rights of citizenship and of self-government made the people conscious of the handicaps of illiteracy. The Constitution of 1784 contained a clause praising the ideal of education and good schools. "Knowledge and learning" were declared "essential to the preservation of a free government."[21] In the following years assessments on the towns for purposes of education were repeatedly raised.[22] Finally in 1805 a law was enacted which established the rudiments of the present system of school districts.[23] The period from 1780 to 1800 also marked a time of great increase in private schools. New Ipswich Academy was incorporated in 1789, Chesterfield Academy in 1790, Atkinson and Charlestown Academies in 1791, Gilmanton and Haverhill Academies in 1794, and Salisbury Academy in 1795.

The post-Revolutionary period saw the springing up of numerous newspapers in New Hampshire.[24] Prior to the Revolution the province had had only one news sheet of importance—the *New Hampshire Gazette*, which began publication in Portsmouth in 1756 and continued well into the nineteenth century. The *Portsmouth Mercury* appeared for a few months in 1765, and the *New Hampshire Gazette and Exeter Morning Chronicle* published several issues in 1776 and 1777. During 1778 and 1779 the *Exeter Journal* made its appearance but lapsed for want of support. In Hanover the *Dresden Mercury* was published in 1779. During the years 1784 to 1788 the *New Hampshire Mercury and General Advertiser* circulated in Portsmouth. In 1787 the *New Hampshire Recorder and Weekly Advertiser* was printed in Keene, and in Portsmouth the *New Hampshire Spy* flourished from 1787 to 1793. Concord had two newspapers, the *Herald* and the *Mirrour*, in the 1790's. At Walpole was published the *New Hampshire Journal and Farmer's Weekly Museum* from 1793 to 1795. The *Amherst Journal* and the *Dover Phoenix* also appeared during these years. Although few of these newspapers had more than a temporary existence, they reflected an increasing popular interest in current events, especially national politics and foreign affairs. Nearly one-third of Portsmouth's weekly, the *New Hampshire Gazette*, was devoted to European conditions. An equal proportion of space in the paper contained descriptions of the activities of the national government. No longer was the press closely scrutinized by the political authorities for seditious outbursts. The Constitution of 1784 declared, "The Liberty of the Press is essential to the security of freedom in a state; it ought, therefore, to be inviolably preserved."[25]

The influx of new ideas which accompanied the rising degree of religious tolerance, the desire for education, and the increased demand for newspapers, was also the cause of liberal progress in the treatment of lawbreakers. Prior to the Revolution the penal code of New Hampshire was a reflection of conditions in England, where at the time of the Revolution two hundred crimes were punishable by death. In New Hampshire, to be sure, this marked severity did not prevail. Nevertheless, eleven offenses—idolatry, blasphemy, treason, wilful murder, manslaughter, murder "through guile," witchcraft, bestiality, buggery, perjury for the purpose of taking another man's life, and cursing of parents by a son—were punishable by death.[26] Six offenses—man-stealing, public rebellion, rebellion by a son against his parents, rape, arson, and a third conviction of burglary—were punishable by death or "other grievous punishment." Other minor offenses were punished by branding, committing to the stocks or the pillory, whipping or other corporal punishment, imprisonment, or fine.

It is difficult to determine how rigidly these penalties were enforced. On December 27, 1739, "Sarah Simpson and Penelope Kenny were executed for the murder of an infant child."[27] These were allegedly the first executions in New Hampshire. On December 30, 1768, Ruth Blay was hanged at Portsmouth for concealing the birth of a bastard child to prevent determination of whether it was born dead or alive.[28] The *New Hampshire Gazette* of November 28, 1766, contained an unconsciously ironical announcement of sentences meted out by the New York Supreme Court—Elizabeth Dent, a pickpocket, to be hanged, and John Dominy, convicted of rape, to suffer one hundred and seventeen lashes and undergo three months' imprisonment.[29]

During the Revolution the provincial penal code was continued in force in New Hampshire.[30] Yet few of the death penalties were actually enforced. Jeremy Belknap wrote, "In the trial of criminals, the courts proceed with great tenderness."[31] The Constitution of 1784 laid down an entirely new principle for the punishment of crime. Article XVIII of the Bill of Rights stated, "All penalties ought to be proportioned to the nature of the offence. No wise legislature will affix the same punishment to the crimes of theft, forgery and the like, which they do to those of murder and treason; where the same undistinguishing severity is exerted against all offences, the people are led to forget the real distinction in the crimes themselves, and to commit the most flagrant with as little compunction as they do those of the lightest dye: For the same reason a multitude of sanguinary laws is both impolitic and unjust. The true design of all punishments being to reform, not to exterminate, mankind."[32]

No actual reform was made in the old penal code until 1791. At that time the death penalty was restricted to eight crimes—treason, wilful murder, rape, homosexuality, breaking and entering, arson at night, forcible robbery, and counterfeiting state securities.[33] Lesser crimes such as manslaughter, forgery, drunkenness, libel, perjury, and assault and battery were punished by placing the convict upon the gallows or upon the pillory or in the stocks for a certain space of time, by whipping, by a fine, or by imprisonment.[34]

In 1812 the first state prison was built, replacing the filthy and unsanitary old province jail at Portsmouth. In the same year the penal code was further reformed, the death penalty being restricted to two offenses—treason and wilful murder.[35] The punishments of the pillory, the stocks, and the whip were abolished. Four crimes—arson, rape, breaking and entering, and forcible robbery—were made punishable by life imprisonment at hard labor. Lesser crimes were made punishable by terms of imprisonment at hard labor varying according to the gravity of the crime.

New Hampshire was much less tardy in providing for the relief of persons in debt.[36] By an act passed June 21, 1782, it was provided that any person imprisoned for debt, who upon commitment possessed less than £10 estate, might after two months in jail swear out a statement of bankruptcy, showing that he owned no more than £6 in personal or real property (excepting a suit of clothes). Upon the receipt of such a sworn statement any judge was empowered to order his release, unless his creditors agreed to pay five shillings per week for his board during the balance of his term. The act also allowed prisoners for debt the liberty of the jail yard and its immediate surroundings provided that they posted bond. The release of any prisoner for debt did not, however, extinguish the debt, for which the debtor was thereafter liable, should he acquire any property.

While passing legislation for the more humane treatment of erring citizens, New Hampshire also adopted an increasingly lenient attitude toward the black race. Slavery was never a widely prevalent institution in the state. On May 10, 1732, the Assembly in an address to the Governor declared, "We have considered his Majties Instruction relating to an Impost on Negroes & Felons, to which this House answers, that there never was any Duties laid on either, by this Governmt, and so few bro't in that it would not be worth the Publick notice, so as to make an act concerning them."[37] When Governor John Wentworth assumed office in 1767 there were 633 slaves in the province. By 1773 the number had risen to 674, but the returns of the census of 1775 showed a decline to 626.[38] Of this last number 533 were located in the two seacoast counties of Strafford and Rockingham.[39]

Anti-slavery sentiment originated in New Hampshire even before the Revolution. In July, 1774, Dr. Jeremy Belknap in a sermon at Dover said, "Would it not be astonishing to hear that a people who are contending so earnestly for liberty are not willing to allow liberty to others? Is it not astonishing to think that, at this day, there are in the several colonies upon this continent some thousands of men, women and children in bondage and slavery for no other reason than that their skin is of a darker color than our own? Such is the inconsistency of our conduct."[40] Another prominent New Hampshire man who opposed the institution of slavery was William Whipple of Portsmouth, who freed his own slaves during the Revolution. On March 28, 1779, Whipple wrote to Josiah Bartlett, "The last accts. from S. Carolina were favorable, a recommendation is gone thither for raising some regiments of Blacks this will I suppose lay a foundation for the emancipation of those poor wretches in that Country, & I hope be the means of dispensing the Blessings of freedom to all the Human Race in America."[41]

On November 12, 1779, the petition of twenty Portsmouth slaves asking for emancipation was forwarded to the state legislature. They pleaded "That the God of nature gave them life and freedom, upon the terms of most perfect equality with other men; That freedom is an inherent right of the human species, not to be surrendered, but by consent, for the sake of social life; . . . ."[42] The signers included such illustrious personages as Nero Brewster, Pharaoh Rogers, Seneca Hall, Cato Newmarch, Caesar Gerrish, and others. This petition was laid before the House of Representatives on April 25, 1780, and a hearing was granted on June 9. Upon the House Journal appeared the following notation:

> *According to the order of the day, the Petition of Nero Brewster and others Negro Slaves praying to be set free from Slavery, being read, considered and argued by Counsel on behalf of the Petitioners before this House, It appears to this house, That at this time the House is not ripe for a Determination in this matter; Therefore ordered that the further consideration & determination of the matter be postponed till a more convenient opportunity.*[43]

The question of emancipation, however, was never brought before the legislature again.

Importation of slaves had been forbidden by the Continental Association of 1774, and there is no evidence to show that any were ever brought into the state after that time. A number of New Hampshire slaves earned their freedom by military service during the war, while others were freed by their masters at the close of the war. Many declined to accept freedom, preferring the economic security of steady employment to the enjoyment of the proffered civil rights. Although the Constitution of 1784 contained an inherent rights clause, slavery was never actually abolished by law in New Hampshire.[44] Slaves were taxed as property on the tax inventories of 1783, but when the new inventory forms were issued in 1789, they were no longer mentioned. The Federal Census of 1790 showed but 158 slaves in the state, and this number declined to 8 in the Census of 1800.[45] Thereafter slavery ceased to exist in New Hampshire. The institution was economically unprofitable, and its end was merely hastened by the liberal philosophy of the Revolutionary period.

The foregoing analysis has merely touched upon some of the more obvious of the liberal movements which, following the general trend of the American Revolution, so fundamentally altered many American institutions. The thought and feeling of the time certainly had much larger and wider implications, which are somewhat imponderable today. The forces of the Revolution, despite their manifestations in so many fields of human endeavor, exhibit a surprising degree of unity. Men were swept along enthusiastically in a great tide of philosophizing. Society underwent a momentous "re-charging" process—something which it seems to require periodically before turning with fresh vigor toward a new epoch. As Charles A. Beard has fittingly said, ". . . . the American Revolution was more than a war on England. It was in truth an economic, social, and intellectual transformation of prime significance—the first of those modern world-shaking reconstructions in which mankind has sought to cut and fashion the tough and stubborn web of fact to fit the pattern of its dreams."[46]

* * * * * *

A summary of the course of the Revolution in New Hampshire can scarcely avoid appearing to be an over-simplification and an attempt at broad generalization, at once abstract and unreal. The more one studies history and human behavior, the more he appreciates the complexity of these fields and is forced to recognize the fact that the formulation of generalizations without a multitude of exceptions can lead to serious error. Yet one cannot escape the conclusion that the citizen of New Hampshire and to a greater or less degree the American of 1784 led a far different life from that which was possible in 1774. In many instances the differences were concrete and tangible;

in other cases the changes, while important, were less palpable, and it is difficult to attribute them definitely to the Revolution.

In the political field, New Hampshire in 1784 had a government of separated powers in which the executive, the legislative, and the judicial branches were largely independent of each other. No longer, as in 1774, were the judicial and legislative departments subject to executive interference. Furthermore, by 1784 new classes had come to the fore to participate in government. The restricted franchise of 1774 based upon property ownership had been abolished. For a time there had flourished the popular philosophy that all government, far from being a benevolent institution to be administered by a propertied oligarchy, originated with the common people. Despite the conservative reaction which followed the initial ardor of the Revolution and tended to undermine this democratic doctrine, there had occurred a substantial enlargement of the franchise, applying to many in the middle and lower classes. A political consequence of even greater importance was the growth of national unity among the states. This idea had been discouraged by the British government prior to the Revolution because it had been regarded as a possible forerunner of revolt. The Revolution had united the states in a war against Great Britain, and for political, social, and economic reasons the union was brought to a consummation after the Revolution.

It also appears that in the field of material development the Revolution had freed American enterprise from British control. No longer was the American economy subordinated to the British imperial scheme. New England, including New Hampshire, had perhaps suffered more than the other colonies under British regulation. The separation from England opened the way for an eventual industrial revolution in this section. Rapid expansion in the fields of commerce and manufactures ultimately resulted from the newly established economic independence. Then too, New Hampshire had gone through a process of evolution in the realm of public finance. The early days of the Revolution had witnessed an orgy of agrarian and debtor financial schemes which were in the nature of a reaction against the deflationary tendencies resulting from British monetary policies. The post-Revolutionary period, however, saw the establishment of the federal government in 1789, when the state was enabled for the first time to benefit from a sound national currency more nearly equal to the requirements of the volume of trade.

Revolutionary New Hampshire

With respect to social change, one encounters the difficulty of determining the exact relationships between new ideas and new institutions. Yet no institution can be totally independent of the thoughts and philosophies of the persons who live under it. The ideals of the Revolution must be regarded as powerful influences responsible for the evolution of many of the new institutions of the post-Revolutionary years. Chief among such innovations was the overthrow of British landed institutions and land regulations, which from the very beginning had seemed incompatible with an environment, in the main expansive rather than static. Indeed, the Revolution for the time being really destroyed the authority of conservatism. Thus were made possible reforms of the penal code, the liberalization of public education, the growth of a more tolerant spirit in religion, and the beginning of skepticism toward the institution of slavery.

One must resist the temptation to try to explain the subsequent history of New Hampshire and New England on the basis of the American Revolution. Statesmen and leaders today are still actuated, consciously or unconsciously, by the same principles and motives which actuated those who participated in the Revolution. The "Tories" and "Revolutionists" of the twentieth century really vary but little in temperament from their prototypes of the eighteenth century. History still seems to approximate a cycle which includes a period of reform and change followed by an era of readjustment, reaction, and satisfaction with the *status quo*. Perhaps one wishes that there might be a little less fluctuation from one extreme to another and that the evolution of human society might advance in orderly fashion along a charted course, with changes occurring scientifically and in due time. One could also wish that civilization might follow with some degree of consistency an even path between exaltation of the past and worship of the present, constantly rejecting those precedents which are static and retaining those traditions which are dynamic, thus establishing an equilibrium between the fundamental need for order and the demand for institutional transformation. The experience of history, however, seems to suggest that perhaps this is expecting too much of human nature, failing to allow for the eccentricities of individualism, overlooking the existence of the fortuitous, and disregarding the likelihood that human actions must largely be classified as tendencies since they do not conform to a known body of laws.

Notes

NOTES

Chapter 1. Prelude to Conflict

1 Wentworth to Dr. Belham, August 9, 1768, *Wentworth Letter Book*, transcripts in New Hampshire Historical Society.

2 E. B. Greene and V. D. Harrington, *American Population Before the Federal Census of 1790*, p. 72.

3 Wentworth had just returned to New Hampshire after a visit in England, and he had landed in South Carolina, journeying up the coast to Portsmouth.

4 L. S. Mayo, *John Wentworth*, p. 34.

5 J. Belknap, *History of New Hampshire*, vol. III, pp. 191, 192.

6 Tax records and census of 1767, *New Hampshire Provincial Papers*, vol. VII, pp. 166-170.

7 N. Adams, *Annals of Portsmouth, passim.*

8 Mayo, *op. cit.*, p. 32.

9 *N. H. Provincial Papers*, vol. VII, pp. 168-170.

10 This theory is substantiated by the following references. O. G. Libby, *The Geographical Distribution of the Vote of the Thirteen States on the Federal Constitution*, pp. 7-11; J. F. Burns, *Controversies Between Royal Governors and Their Assemblies in the Northern Colonies*, pp. 267 ff.

11 J. T. Adams, *New England in the Republic*, p. 170.

12 For a comprehensive study of the royal government, see W. H. Fry, *New Hampshire as a Royal Province.*

13 Wentworth to Stephen Apthorp, August 18, 1767, *Letter Book.*

14 Mayo, *John Wentworth*, p. 124; A. I. Harriman, *Praises on Tombs*, p. 5.

15 J. Belknap, *History of New Hampshire* (edited by J. Farmer), pp. 326-329. This book is a one-volume condensation of Belknap's history, edited by John Farmer of Dover.

16 C. W. Alvord, *The Mississippi Valley in British Politics*, vol. II, pp. 249, 250. Professor Alvord presents an able exposition of this theory.

17 C. H. Van Tyne, *The Causes of the War of Independence*, p. 246.

18 Nathaniel Whitaker to Eleazar Wheelock, April 19, 1767, *Wheelock Manuscripts*, in Dartmouth College Library. Whitaker was in London attempting to raise funds for Wheelock's projected Indian School.

19 *Memoirs of the Marquis of Rockingham* (edited by G. T. K. Albemarle), vol. II, p. 254.

20 W. MacDonald, *Select Charters and Other Documents Illustrative of American History, 1606-1775*, pp. 320 ff.

Notes

21 Letter dated April 19, 1767, *Wheelock Manuscripts*.

22 Van Tyne, *op. cit.*, p. 248. (Quoted by courtesy of Houghton Mifflin Co.)

23 *New Hampshire Gazette*, July 15, 1774.

24 Adams, *Annals of Portsmouth*, pp. 223, 224.

25 *New Hampshire Gazette*, September 30, 1768.

26 Wentworth to Dr. Belham, August 9, 1768, *Letter Book*.

27 *The Writings of Samuel Adams* (edited by H. A. Cushing), vol. I, pp. 184-188.

28 *Documents Relative to the Colonial History of the State of New York* (edited by E. B. O'Callaghan and B. Fernow), vol. VIII, pp. 58, 59.

29 For a general account, see Van Tyne, *op. cit.*, chap. XI.

30 *N. H. Provincial Papers*, vol. VII, pp. 152, 153.

31 Wentworth to the Earl of Hillsborough, June 25, 1768, *Letter Book*.

32 *N. H. Provincial Papers*, vol. VII, pp. 180, 187, 188, 248.

33 A. M. Schlesinger, *The Colonial Merchants and the American Revolution*, p. 194.

34 *N. H. Provincial Papers*, vol. VII, pp. 186, 188, 189.

35 *Ibid.*, p. 190.

36 For a general account, see Van Tyne, *op. cit.*, chap. XI.

37 *N. H. Provincial Papers*, vol. VII, pp. 232, 254, 255.

38 General account in Van Tyne, *op. cit.*, chap. X.

39 Mayo, *op. cit.*, p. 125.

40 *New Hampshire Gazette*, March 16, 1770.

41 *New Hampshire Gazette*, March 23, 1770.

42 Letter dated April 12, 1770, *Letter Book;* the petition is in *N. H. Provincial Papers*, vol. VII, p. 248.

43 Adams, *Annals of Portsmouth*, pp. 226, 227.

44 Letter dated October 28, 1770, *Letter Book;* Schlesinger, *op. cit.*, pp. 216, 217.

45 Wentworth to Lord Shelburne and the Lords of Trade, March 25, 1768, *Letter Book*. Wentworth wrote, "At present ye Inhabitants in ye Western part of the Province daily increasing labour under great disadvantages in obtaining Justice—in ye probate of Wills—Settlement of Estates and Registry of Conveyances; wch are now brot & accomplished at Portsmouth from Ev'ry part of the Province. . . . . An Action of Debt for Five pounds Sterlg. by reason of long travels of principals, Evidences &c. may frequently & justly be loaded with ten pounds Costs."

46 Mayo, *op. cit.*, p. 36.

47 Belknap, *History of New Hampshire*, vol. III, p. 193. The dissension over county division is an excellent example of Frederick Jackson Turner's thesis concerning frontier attitudes.

48 Van Tyne, *Causes of the War of Independence*, p. 369.

49 Wentworth to Trecothick and Apthorp, May 2, 1769, *Letter Book*.

50 *New Hampshire Gazette*, February 8, 1771.

51 This act of Parliament placed a duty on sugar and molasses imported into the British colonies from foreign colonies. It was designed to protect the sugar growers of the British West Indies from the competition of cheaper foreign sugar and molasses.

52 *New Hampshire State Papers*, vol. XVIII, pp. 606, 607.

53 Van Tyne, *op. cit.*, pp. 370-372.

54 *N. H. Provincial Papers*, vol. VII, pp. 315, 316.

55 *Ibid.*, pp. 329-331.

56 *Ibid.*, pp. 331, 332.

57 Van Tyne, *op. cit.*, p. 374.

58 *N. H. Provincial Papers*, vol. VII, p. 334.

59 Van Tyne, *op. cit.*, pp. 386, 387.

60 Adams, *Annals of Portsmouth*, pp. 239-242.

61 Newspaper accounts in *New Hampshire Gazette*, December 17, 24, 31, 1773.

62 Schlesinger, *The Colonial Merchants and the American Revolution*, p. 302.

63 *New Hampshire Gazette*, December 31, 1773.

64 F. Moore, *Songs and Ballads of the American Revolution*, pp. 62, 63; *New Hampshire Gazette*, July 22, 1774.

65 *New Hampshire Gazette*, February 18, 1774.

66 Mayo, *op. cit.*, pp. 133, 134; Adams, *Annals of Portsmouth*, pp. 243, 244; Wentworth to Lord Dartmouth, July 4, 1774, *N. H. Provincial Papers*, vol. VII, pp. 409, 410.

67 Wentworth to Lord Dartmouth, September 13, 1774, *N. H. Provincial Papers*, vol. VII, pp. 413, 414; Adams, *Annals of Portsmouth*, pp. 244, 245.

68 Letter dated September 13, 1774, *N. H. Provincial Papers*, vol. VII, p. 414. The italics are mine.

Notes

Chapter 2. The Downfall of Royal Government

1 *Correspondence of George III* (edited by Sir John W. Fortescue), vol. III, p. 131. Communication to Lord North dated September 11, 1774.

2 MacDonald, *Select Charters and Other Documents Illustrative of American History, 1606-1775,* pp. 337-356.

3 This view is that of C. W. Alvord in *The Mississippi Valley in British Politics,* vol. II, chap. VIII.

4 *N. H. Provincial Papers,* vol. VII, p. 361.

5 Letter dated June 8, 1774, *ibid.,* p. 369.

6 *New Hampshire Gazette,* May 13, 20, 1774.

7 Letter dated May 19, 1774, *American Archives* (edited by Peter Force), 4th series, vol. I, p. 337.

8 *N. H. Provincial Papers,* vol. VII, pp. 365, 366; John Wentworth to Lord Dartmouth, June 8, 1774, *ibid.,* p. 369.

9 For a general account, see letters of John Wentworth to Lord Dartmouth, July 6, 13, August 29, 1774, *N. H. Provincial Papers,* vol. VII, pp. 410, 411.

10 *New Hampshire Gazette,* July 29, August 5, 19, September 9, 1774.

11 John Sullivan to John Langdon, September 5, 1774, *Letters and Papers of Major-General John Sullivan* (edited by O. G. Hammond), vol. I, p. 48.

12 Van Tyne, *Causes of the War of Independence,* p. 404.

13 Letter dated October 28, 1774, New Hampshire Historical Society, *Collections,* vol. IX, p. 77.

14 John Wentworth to Lord Dartmouth, August 29, 1774, *N. H. Provincial Papers,* vol. VII, p. 411.

15 John Wentworth to Lord Dartmouth, November 15, 1774, *N. H. Provincial Papers,* vol. VII, p. 417.

16 J. B. Walker, "The New Hampshire Covenant of 1774," in *Granite Monthly,* vol. XXXV, pp. 188-197.

17 Mayo, *John Wentworth,* pp. 137-139; Adams, *Annals of Portsmouth,* p. 246; *American Archives,* 4th series, vol. I, p. 981.

18 *American Archives,* 4th series, vol. I, p. 974.

19 *New Hampshire Gazette,* October 28, November 11, 1774.

20 *New York Colonial Documents,* vol. VIII, p. 509.

21 For a general account of the attack on the fort, see undated letter of John Wentworth to Lord Dartmouth, December 20, 1774, *New England Historical and Genealogical Register,* vol. XXIII, p. 276; Mayo, *op. cit.,* pp. 140-144; New Hampshire Historical Society, *Proceedings,* vol. IV, pp. 18-47.

22 Letter dated December 14, 1774, *Letter Book.*

23 These cannon were later transported to Boston on the *Canceaux* in June, 1775.

24 Letter dated December 24, 1774, *American Archives*, 4th series, vol. I, p. 1063.

25 *Letter Book.*

26 Mayo, *op. cit.*, p. 147; John Wentworth to Lord Dartmouth, March 10, 1775, *Letter Book.*

27 Adams, *Annals of Portsmouth*, pp. 251, 252.

28 *N. H. Provincial Papers*, vol. VII, p. 372.

29 *Ibid.*, pp. 374, 375.

30 "Petition of John Fenton" in *Records of the Committee for Enquiring into the Losses and Services of the American Loyalists*, transcripts of claims of New Hampshire Loyalists in New Hampshire State Library.

31 *N. H. Provincial Papers*, vol. VII, pp. 378-381.

32 Mayo, *op. cit.*, pp. 155, 156.

33 *N. H. Provincial Papers*, vol. VII, p. 384.

34 See population and seating in *N. H. Provincial Papers*, vol. VII, pp. 370, 780; Belknap, *History of New Hampshire*, vol. III, p. 192.

35 The Assembly and Council had passed an act in 1764 which would have allowed all towns containing 100 persons who possessed real estate to the value of £50 to send a representative to the assembly. This act would have taken the prerogative of calling new representatives out of the governor's hands and placed it under the automatic operation of a fixed rule. This act was disallowed by the King in Council. Hence arose the popular suspicion of executive influence over new members. *Laws of New Hampshire* (edited by H. Metcalf), vol. III, p. 343.

36 *Wheelock Manuscripts.*

37 *N. H. Provincial Papers*, vol. VII, p. 384.

38 *Ibid.*, p. 385.

39 *Ibid.*, p. 376; Mayo, *op. cit.*, pp. 150, 151.

40 *N. H. Provincial Papers*, vol. VII, p. 382.

41 Hunking Wentworth to the Provincial Congress, June 2, 1775, *ibid.*, p. 502.

42 *Ibid.*, pp. 387-390; Mayo, *op. cit.*, pp. 158-160.

43 Wentworth to Tristam Dalton, July 31, 1775, *Letter Book.*

44 *N. H. Provincial Papers*, vol. VII, p. 390.

45 Mayo, *op. cit.*, pp. 161, 162. The original proclamation is preserved in the New Hampshire Historical Society.

Notes

Chapter 3. Revolutionary Organization

1 J. T. Adams, *Revolutionary New England*, p. 404. (Quoted by courtesy of Little, Brown and Co.)

2 Van Tyne, *Causes of the War of Independence*, p. 375.

3 These extracts are from Jefferson's "Autobiography," written in 1821. *The Writings of Thomas Jefferson* (edited by P. L. Ford), vol. I, pp. 7, 8.

4 *N. H. Provincial Papers*, vol. VII, pp. 329-332.

5 *Ibid.*, p. 334.

6 Adams, *Annals of Portsmouth, passim.*

7 These towns passed resolutions against the importation of teas. The resolutions seem to have contained provisions establishing committees of correspondence. Schlesinger, *The Colonial Merchants and the American Revolution*, p. 302.

8 *N. H. Provincial Papers*, vol. VII, pp. 366-368.

9 *Ibid.*, p. 369.

10 Anonymous letter to Wentworth, March 17, 1775, *American Archives*, 4th series, vol. II, p. 159.

11 Adams, *Revolutionary New England*, p. 402; Van Tyne, *op. cit.*, chap. XVII; J. Fiske, *The American Revolution*, vol. I, pp. 122-124; Jefferson, *Writings*, vol. I, p. 11.

12 *American Archives*, 4th series, vol. I, p. 516. Wentworth's proclamation is in *N. H. Provincial Papers*, vol. VII, p. 400.

13 Letter dated July 13, 1774, *American Archives*, 4th series, vol. I, p. 536.

14 Journal of the first Provincial Congress, *N. H. Provincial Papers*, vol. VII, pp. 407, 408.

15 *Collections, Topographical, Historical and Biographical Relating Principally to New Hampshire* (edited by J. B. Moore and J. Farmer), vol. I, p. 147.

16 *N. H. Provincial Papers*, vol. VII, p. 407.

17 Letter dated August 29, 1774, *American Archives*, 4th series, vol. I, p. 745.

18 Walker, "The New Hampshire Covenant of 1774," in *Granite Monthly*, vol. XXXV, pp. 188-197.

19 S. Hale, *Annals of the Town of Keene*, p. 40.

20 Proceedings of the Hillsborough County Congresses in *N. H. Provincial Papers*, vol. VII, pp. 447-451.

21 *Ibid.*, p. 448.

22 *Ibid.*, p. 449.

23 *Journals of the Continental Congress* (edited by W. C. Ford), vol. I, pp. 75-80.

24 Schlesinger, *op. cit.*, p. 442.

25 *American Archives*, 4th series, vol. I, p. 888.

26 *N. H. Provincial Papers*, vol. VII, p. 419.

27 Adams, *Annals of Portsmouth*, pp. 246, 247.

28 *Ibid.*

29 *N. H. Provincial Papers*, vol. VII, p. 424.

30 Letter dated December 2, 1774, *ibid.*, p. 419.

31 For a general account, see Schlesinger, *op. cit.*, pp. 483, 484.

32 *N. H. Provincial Papers*, vol. VII, p. 445.

33 Quoted in Schlesinger, *op. cit.*, p. 484.

34 *N. H. Provincial Papers*, vol. VII, p. 425.

35 Journals of the second Provincial Congress, *ibid.*, pp. 442-444.

36 Wentworth to Thomas Waldron, January 27, 1775, quoted in C. E. L. Wingate, *Life of Paine Wingate*, vol. I, p. 153.

37 L. W. Leonard, *History of Dublin, New Hampshire*, p. 166.

38 *Bartlett Manuscripts*, in Dartmouth College Library.

39 *N. H. Provincial Papers*, vol. VII, p. 422.

40 Letter dated December 28, 1774, *Letter Book.*

41 *N. H. Provincial Papers*, vol. VII, p. 446.

42 *Ibid.*, p. 448.

43 C. Bell, *Facts Relating to the Early History of Chester*, p. 28.

44 Journals of the third Provincial Congress, *N. H. Provincial Papers*, vol. VII, pp. 452-467.

45 Journals of the fourth Provincial Congress, *ibid.*, pp. 468-664.

46 Weare to the Continental Congress, *ibid.*, p. 561.

47 *Ibid.*, pp. 657-660.

48 General account of the Committee of Safety—A. Hunt, *The Provincial Committees of Safety*, pp. 19-33; Letters and Orders of the Committee of Safety in *N. H. Provincial and State Papers*, vol. X, pp. 501-620; Journal of the Committee of Safety in *Laws of New Hampshire* (edited by H. Metcalf), vol. IV, appendix.

49 Metcalf, *Laws of New Hampshire*, vol. IV, p. 576.

50 Hunt, *op. cit.*, p. 33.

Notes

Chapter 4. Clash of Political Opinion

1 M. C. Tyler, *Literary History of the American Revolution, 1763-1783*, vol. II, p. 111.

2 Brewster names several prominent Portsmouth men who opposed the Stamp Act but were later Tories at the outbreak of the Revolution. C. W. Brewster, *Rambles about Portsmouth*, 1st series, p. 236.

3 Adams, *Revolutionary New England*, p. 405. (Quoted by courtesy of Little, Brown and Co.)

4 Beard, C. A. and Mary R., *Rise of American Civilization;* Van Tyne, *The Loyalists in the American Revolution;* J. F. Jameson, *The American Revolution Considered as a Social Movement;* F. J. Turner, *The Frontier in American History.*

5 Association Test in *New Hampshire State Papers*, vol. VIII, pp. 204-296; Proscription Act in Metcalf, *Laws of New Hampshire*, vol. IV, pp. 171 ff.

6 O. G. Hammond, *Tories of New Hampshire in the War of the Revolution*, pp. 3-7.

7 The Wheelock correspondence mentions no difficulties with Loyalists in Grafton County. *Wheelock Manuscripts.*

8 Register of province officials in Belknap, *History of New Hampshire* (Farmer ed.), appendix.

9 *Plumer Biographies*, manuscripts in the New Hampshire Historical Society, vol. IV, p. 484.

10 *N. H. Provincial Papers*, vol. VII, p. 320.

11 Hunking Wentworth to the Provincial Congress, *ibid.*, p. 502.

12 Van Tyne, *The American Revolution, 1776-1783*, p. 35.

13 Brewster, *Rambles about Portsmouth*, 1st series, p. 165.

14 Forty-six out of eighty-two Congregational ministers were college graduates. H. Worthington, *The New Hampshire Churches and the American Revolution*, manuscript thesis in Dartmouth College Library, appendix A, pp. III-VI.

15 *N. H. State Papers*, vol. VIII, p. 713.

16 Hammond, *Tories of New Hampshire*, p. 8.

17 *N. H. State Papers*, vol. VIII, p. 235.

18 Worthington, *op. cit.*, pp. 94-97.

19 *Ibid.*, appendix A, p. XVII.

20 Meshech Weare, John Langdon, William Whipple, and Ebenezer Thompson.

21 Mayo, *John Wentworth*, chap. IX.

22 Worthington, *op. cit.*, pp. 83-89.

23 Mayo, *op. cit.*, chap. ix.

24 Worthington, *op. cit.*, p. 86.

25 *Ibid.*, pp. 89-92.

26 This computation assumes a family of four or five persons.

Chapter 5. Independence and Confederation

1 Paine Wingate to Timothy Pickering, quoted in Wingate, *Life of Paine Wingate*, vol. i, p. 156.

2 *Letters by Josiah Bartlett, William Whipple and Others, Written Before and During the Revolution*, p. 10.

3 Letter dated April 23, 1775, *N. H. Provincial Papers*, vol. vii, p. 456.

4 Letter dated April 25, 1775, *N. H. Provincial Papers*, vol. vii, p. 459. James Sullivan was the brother of John Sullivan of Durham, New Hampshire. Both Sullivans were revolutionary leaders in their respective states.

5 Letter dated May 2, 1775, *Letter Book*.

6 Wheelock to John Thornton, April 29, 1775, *Wheelock Manuscripts*.

7 *N. H. Provincial Papers*, vol. vii, p. 477.

8 *Ibid.*, p. 497.

9 Wentworth to Timothy Ruggles, July 3, 1775, *Letter Book*.

10 Adams, *Revolutionary New England*, p. 427.

11 Adams, *Annals of Portsmouth*, pp. 255-257.

12 Hunking Wentworth to Washington, October 19, 1775, *N. H. Provincial Papers*, vol. vii, p. 629.

13 John Sullivan to the Committee of Safety, October 26, 1775, *Sullivan Papers*, vol. i, p. 115.

14 *N. H. Provincial Papers*, vol. vii, p. 561.

15 *Letters by Josiah Bartlett, William Whipple and Others*, p. 20.

16 Ford, *Journals of the Continental Congress*, vol. iii, p. 319.

17 *N. H. State Papers*, vol. viii, pp. 2-3.

18 Adams, *Annals of Portsmouth*, p. 262.

19 *N. H. State Papers*, vol. viii, p. 14.

20 *Ibid.*, p. 33.

21 *New Hampshire Gazette*, January 9, 1776.

Notes

22 *N. H. State Papers*, vol. VIII, pp. 24-27. The issues of the *New Hampshire Gazette* ceased abruptly on January 9 and did not appear again until *Freeman's Journal* began publication, replacing the *Gazette* for a short period of time.

23 Schlesinger, *The Colonial Merchants and the American Revolution*, p. 593. (Quoted by courtesy of A. M. Schlesinger.)

24 Letter quoted in H. Pillsbury, *History of New Hampshire*, vol. I, p. 295.

25 *Wheelock Manuscripts.*

26 *Freeman's Journal*, June 22, 1776.

27 Ford, *Journals of the Continental Congress*, vol. V, p. 507.

28 *N. H. State Papers*, vol. VIII, pp. 138, 139.

29 *Ibid.*, p. 149.

30 Adams, *Annals of Portsmouth*, p. 263.

31 Letter dated August 14, 1776, *Bartlett Manuscripts.*

32 *Letters of Members of the Continental Congress* (edited by E. C. Burnett), vol. I, p. 456.

33 Letter dated July 28, 1776, *Bartlett Manuscripts.*

34 Whipple to Oliver Wolcott, August 12, 1776, Burnett, *Letters of Members of the Continental Congress*, vol. II, pp. 47, 48.

35 *N. H. State Papers*, vol. VIII, p. 755.

36 *Weare Manuscripts*, in New Hampshire Historical Society, vol. IV, pp. 54-119.

37 *Weare Manuscripts*, vol. IV, p. 54.

38 *N. H. State Papers*, vol. XIII, pp. 679, 680.

39 *Weare Manuscripts*, vol. IV, p. 82.

40 *N. H. State Papers*, vol. VIII, pp. 773, 774.

41 *Ibid.*, p. 778.

42 *Ibid.*, p. 753.

43 Burnett, *Letters*, vol. III, p. 329.

Chapter 6. New Hampshire in the Continental Congress

1 Peabody to Josiah Bartlett, August 6, 1780, Burnett, *Letters of Members of the Continental Congress*, vol. V, p. 312. Peabody was a New Hampshire delegate to the Congress.

2 Beard, C. A. and Mary, *Rise of American Civilization*, vol. I, pp. 234, 235.

3 Delegate Josiah Bartlett of New Hampshire wrote an interesting account of his travels to and from the Congress. *Itineraries of Josiah Bartlett, 1775-1779,* manuscript in New Hampshire State Library.

4 Letter dated November 24, 1778, Burnett, *Letters of Members of the Continental Congress,* vol. III, p. 507.

5 Letter dated April 27, 1777, *Bartlett Manuscripts.*

6 Letter dated October 30, 1777, Burnett, *Letters,* vol. II, p. 538.

7 Letter dated November 15, 1780, *ibid.,* vol. V, p. 448.

8 Letter dated May 8, 1781, *ibid.,* vol. VI, p. 84.

9 Letter dated July 27, 1778, *ibid.,* vol. III, p. 351.

10 Letter dated August 18, 1778, *ibid.,* vol. III, p. 379.

11 Letter dated March 13, 1780, *ibid.,* vol. V, p. 70.

12 Letter dated October 30, 1777, *ibid.,* vol. II, p. 538.

13 Letter dated August 18, 1778, *ibid.,* vol. III, p. 379.

14 J. B. Sanders, *Evolution of the Executive Departments of the Continental Congress, 1774-1789,* pp. 67, 68.

15 Burnett, *Letters,* vol. III, p. 4.

16 Letter dated July 29, 1776, *ibid.,* vol. II, p. 28.

17 Letter dated August 8, 1777, *N. H. State Papers,* vol. VIII, p. 662.

18 Letter from New Hampshire delegates, August 22, 1777, quoted in Ford, *Journals of the Continental Congress,* vol. VIII, pp. 656-658.

19 *Ibid.,* vol. IX, pp. 770, 771.

20 Burnett, *Letters,* vol. IV, p. 91.

21 Ford, *Journals of the Continental Congress,* vol. IX, pp. 779-782.

22 *Ibid.,* p. 801.

23 *Ibid.,* pp. 803, 804.

24 *Ibid.,* pp. 806-843.

25 Metcalf, *Laws of New Hampshire,* vol. IV, p. 379.

26 *Bartlett Manuscripts.*

27 Ford, *Journals of the Continental Congress,* vol. X, p. 177.

28 *Ibid.,* vol. XIV, pp. 946-949, 973-979; Hunt, *ibid.,* vol. XXIV, pp. 146-148, 207-210.

29 *Ibid.,* vol. XVI, pp. 171-200.

30 *Ibid.,* vol. XII, pp. 990, 999, 1000, 1224, 1231-1234, 1235-1238, 1266; vol. XIV, pp. 1013, 1014; vol. XVI, pp. 261-267.

31 E. Q. Hawk, *Economic History of the South,* p. 180.

32 Ford, *Journals of the Continental Congress*, vol. XIV, pp. 680-683, 766-770, 926; Hunt, *ibid.*, vol. XX, pp. 611-615.

33 A more detailed treatment of the peace terms is given in chapter XV.

34 Peabody to Josiah Bartlett, July 13, 1779, Burnett, *Letters*, vol. IV, p. 314.

Chapter 7. The Army and Its Administration

1 G. Bancroft, *History of the United States*, vol. V, p. 52.

2 Stark to Meshech Weare, June 8, 1778, *Weare Manuscripts*, vol. V, p. 39.

3 Letter dated September 30, 1776, *Bartlett Manuscripts*.

4 For a general account of the colonial militia laws, see C. E. Potter, *Military History of the State of New Hampshire*, pp. 38, 39, 114, 115; Belknap, *History of New Hampshire*, vol. II, pp. 298, 299.

5 Mayo, *John Wentworth*, pp. 45, 46.

6 *N. H. Provincial Papers*, vol. VII, p. 444.

7 *Ibid.*, p. 477.

8 Letter dated March 24, 1776, *Sullivan Papers*, vol. I, p. 190.

9 *N. H. Provincial Papers*, vol. VII, p. 460.

10 L. S. Mayo, "Colonel John Stark at Winter Hill," in Massachusetts Historical Society, *Proceedings*, vol. LVII, pp. 328-336. William Whipple and Matthew Thornton were New Hampshire's delegates in the Continental Congress in February, 1777. In January, 1776, Stark had bitterly criticized their conduct of the revolutionary government. Consequently they probably did not favor Stark's election to the vacant post.

11 Biographical information concerning New Hampshire officers has been taken from *The Dictionary of American Biography*.

12 Washington correspondence, in New Hampshire Historical Society, *Collections*, vol. II, p. 154.

13 *Ibid.*, p. 155.

14 A. Beveridge, *Life of John Marshall*, vol. I, p. 69.

15 Beard, *Rise of American Civilization*, vol. I, p. 252.

16 Ford, *Journals of the Continental Congress*, vol. II, pp. 187-190.

17 *N. H. Provincial Papers*, vol. VII, pp. 575-583; Metcalf, *Laws of New Hampshire*, vol. IV, pp. 39-57.

18 *N. H. State Papers*, vol. VIII, p. 393 n.

19 Metcalf, *Laws of New Hampshire*, vol. IV, p. 77; *N. H. State Papers*, vol. VIII, p. 760.

20 Metcalf, *Laws of New Hampshire*, vol. IV, pp. 219, 293.

21 *Ibid.*, pp. 345, 443.

22 *American State Papers, Military Affairs*, vol. I, pp. 14 ff.

23 Beard, C. A. and Mary R., *op. cit.*, vol. I, p. 252.

24 New Hampshire Historical Society, *Collections*, vol. IX, pp. 417-422.

25 Washington correspondence, in New Hampshire Historical Society, *Collections*, vol. II, p. 165.

26 For an example of the procedure in the negotiation of such contracts, see *N. H. State Papers*, vol. VIII, p. 794.

27 Metcalf, *Laws of New Hampshire*, vol. IV, p. 390.

28 *N. H. State Papers*, vol. VIII, p. 770.

29 Ford, *Journals of the Continental Congress*, vol. II, pp. 93, 94, 220, 221; vol. V, p. 853.

30 "Paymaster's account with John Sullivan," in unpublished folio of *Sullivan Papers*, in New Hampshire Historical Society.

31 L. C. Hatch, *The Administration of the American Revolutionary Army*, chap. V.

32 Letter dated November 7, 1777, *Correspondence of the American Revolution* (edited by J. Sparks), vol. II, p. 31; F. Kidder, *History of the First New Hampshire Regiment in the War of the Revolution*, p. 38.

33 Ford, *Journals of the Continental Congress*, vol. VI, p. 858.

34 Sanders, *Evolution of the Executive Departments of the Continental Congress*, chap. I.

35 Hatch, *op. cit.*, p. 123.

36 Adams, *New England in the Republic*, pp. 24-30.

37 Ford, *Journals of the Continental Congress*, vol. III, p. 322.

38 Hatch, *op. cit.*, pp. 86-98.

39 Sanders, *op. cit.*, p. 17.

40 "Journal of Major Henry Dearborn," quoted in Hatch, *op. cit.*, p. 92.

41 Sanders, *op. cit.*, pp. 3-5.

42 Washington correspondence, in New Hampshire Historical Society, *Collections*, vol. II, p. 176.

43 *Ibid.*

44 Rules and Regulations of the Militia and Articles of War, in Metcalf, *Laws of New Hampshire*, vol. IV, pp. 39-57.

45 *Ibid.*, p. 273.

Notes

46 Washington correspondence, in New Hampshire Historical Society, *Collections*, vol. II, p. 169. Letter dated October 18, 1780.

47 Letter dated June 8, 1778, *Weare Manuscripts*, vol. v, p. 39.

48 For a detailed account of the ranger service, see Potter, *Military History of the State of New Hampshire*, pp. 365-367.

49 Washington correspondence, in New Hampshire Historical Society, *Collections*, vol. II, p. 191.

50 Hatch, *op. cit.*, pp. 78-85; chap. VIII.

51 Letter dated December 22, 1781, *Stark Manuscripts*, in New Hampshire Historical Society, vol. II, p. 165.

52 "The Institution and Records of the New Hampshire Society of the Cincinnati," in *N. H. State Papers*, vol. XXII, pp. 758-820.

53 Ford, *Journals of the Continental Congress*, vol. v, pp. 702-705.

54 Metcalf, *Laws of New Hampshire*, vol. IV, p. 96.

55 *N. H. State Papers*, vol. VIII, p. 984.

56 Fitzpatrick, *Journals of the Continental Congress*, vol. XXVIII, pp. 435-438; Metcalf, *Laws of New Hampshire*, vol. v, p. 170.

57 Pension documents, in *N. H. State Papers*, vol. XVI.

58 *American State Papers, Military Affairs*, vol. I, pp. 14 ff.

59 *Ibid.*

60 Beard, C. A. and Mary R., *Rise of American Civilization*, vol. I, p. 274. (Quoted by courtesy of the Macmillan Co.)

Chapter 8. Privateering and the Continental Navy

1 *Compilation of the Messages and Papers of the Presidents* (edited by J. D. Richardson), vol. v, p. 276.

2 F. R. Stark, "The Abolition of Privateering and the Declaration of Paris," in *Studies in History, Economics and Public Law*, vol. VIII, pp. 118, 119.

3 Ford, *Journals of the Continental Congress*, vol. III, pp. 371-375.

4 *Ibid.*, vol. IV, p. 230.

5 Stark, *op. cit.*, p. 121.

6 *N. H. State Papers*, vol. VIII, pp. 53-55.

7 Metcalf, *Laws of New Hampshire*, vol. IV, pp. 25-32.

8 *Ibid.*, p. 238.

9 Bonds of privateers, in *Provincial and Revolutionary Papers*, one folio of miscellaneous manuscripts in New Hampshire Historical Society; see also list of privateers' bonds on file at the Library of Congress in *New Hampshire Genealogical Record*, vol. v, pp. 161-170.

10 Records of the proprietors, in *New England Historical and Genealogical Register*, vol. xxiii, pp. 47, 181, 289; Adams, *New England in the Republic*, pp. 49-51.

11 Letter dated July 12, 1778, *Historical Magazine*, vol. iv, pp. 74, 75.

12 Stark, *op. cit.*, p. 125.

13 Letter dated July 12, 1778, *Historical Magazine*, vol. iv, pp. 74, 75.

14 Potter, *Military History of the State of New Hampshire*, pp. 367 ff.

15 *Ibid.*, pp. 367-369.

16 Petition of Hugh Hunter, *Weare Manuscripts*, vol. v, p. 50.

17 A. T. Mahan, *Major Operations of the Navies in the War of American Independence*, p. 61.

18 Petition of several families of captured seamen to the Committee of Safety, *Weare Manuscripts*, vol. v, p. 44.

19 Adams, *New England in the Republic*, p. 16.

20 *New England Historical and Genealogical Register*, vol. xxii, pp. 393-402.

21 Sanders, *Evolution of the Executive Departments of the Continental Congress*, chap. ii.

22 Whipple later declined the office on account of ill health.

23 Sanders, *op. cit.*, pp. 29, 30.

24 Ford, *Journals of the Continental Congress*, vol. vi, p. 954.

25 Records of the proprietors of the "Privateer General Sullivan," *New England Historical and Genealogical Register*, vol. xxiii, pp. 291, 292.

26 Thomas Thompson to the Committee of Safety, February 6, June 4, 1777, *N. H. State Papers*, vol. viii, pp. 482, 483, 574, 575; Committee of Portsmouth to the Committee of Safety, July 7, 1777, *ibid.*, p. 621.

27 *Statement of the Cause of the McClary Owners and Doane and Doanes' Administrators*, anonymous pamphlet in New Hampshire Historical Society; *Reports of Cases Ruled and Adjudged in the Several Courts of the United States and Pennsylvania* (edited by A. J. Dallas), vol. iii, pp. 54 ff.

28 *Journals of the Senate and House of Representatives*, 1794.

29 Letter dated June 20, 1778, Burnett, *Letters of Members of Continental Congress*, vol. iii, p. 309.

30 Mahan, *Major Operations of the Navies in the War of American Independence*, p. 61.

31 Stark, *op. cit.*, p. 127.

Notes

Chapter 9. The Suppression of the Loyalists

1 *New England Quarterly*, vol. II, pp. 75, 76.

2 Van Tyne, *Causes of the War of Independence*, p. 456.

3 *Ibid.*, p. 478. (Quoted by courtesy of Houghton Mifflin Co.)

4 Letter dated May 28, 1777, *Bartlett Manuscripts*.

5 *New Hampshire Gazette*, May 11, 1770.

6 *N. H. Provincial Papers*, vol. VII, p. 636.

7 *Concord Town Records*, p. 154.

8 *The Diary of Matthew Patten*, p. 330.

9 Hammond, *Tories of New Hampshire in the War of the Revolution*, p. 13.

10 *New Hampshire Gazette*, January 20, 1775.

11 E. D. Boylston, *Historical Sketch of the Hillsborough County Congresses*, p. 30.

12 *Ibid.*, p. 22.

13 Ford, *Journals of the Continental Congress*, vol. IV, p. 205.

14 *N. H. State Papers*, vol. VIII, pp. 324-331, 413.

15 *Ibid.*, p. 327.

16 Hammond, *op. cit.*, p. 26.

17 Mayo, *John Wentworth*, pp. 116-118.

18 John Peters to Samuel Peters, July 20, 1778, quoted in Hammond, *op. cit.*, p. 27.

19 Letter dated January 30, 1777, *N. H. State Papers*, vol. VIII, pp. 475, 476.

20 *N. H. State Papers*, vol. VIII, p. 468.

21 Metcalf, *Laws of New Hampshire*, vol. IV, p. 71.

22 *Ibid.*, p. 75.

23 *Ibid.*, p. 97.

24 *N. H. State Papers*, vol. VIII, p. 596.

25 Bartlett to David Gilman, May 25, 1777, *ibid.*, p. 565.

26 *Ibid.*, p. 596.

27 *Ibid.*, p. 638.

28 Metcalf, *Laws of New Hampshire*, vol. IV, p. 128.

29 Ford, *Journals of the Continental Congress*, vol. IX, p. 971.

30 Metcalf, *Laws of New Hampshire*, vol. IV, pp. 177 ff.

31 *Ibid.*, pp. 191 ff.

32 *Ibid.*, pp. 286 ff.

33 Adams, *Annals of Portsmouth*, pp. 268, 269.

34 Hale, *Annals of the Town of Keene*, p. 54.

35 Hammond, *op. cit.*, pp. 25, 26.

36 Metcalf, *Laws of New Hampshire*, vol. IV, p. 427.

37 *Ibid.*, p. 473.

38 *Ibid.*, p. 456.

39 Open letter by John Sullivan in *New Hampshire Gazette*, August 2, 1783.

40 For a general account of Loyalist war services, see W. H. Siebert, "Loyalist Refugees of New Hampshire," in *Ohio State University Bulletin*, no. XXI.

41 *Ibid.*, pp. 22, 23.

42 C. H. Bell, *History of Exeter*, p. 302.

43 Robert Stinson writing in his *Record and Journal* sometime after 1800 mentions the shame which he felt for his grandfather, John Stinson, who had been a Loyalist.

44 Siebert, *op. cit.*, p. 23.

45 J. T. Adams, C. H. Van Tyne, J. F. Jameson.

46 *Dictionary of National Biography* (edited by S. Lee), vol. LVI, pp. 205-208; *Dictionary of American Biography* (edited by Allen Johnson and Dumas Malone), vol. XVIII, pp. 445-452.

Chapter 10. Revolutionary Finance in New Hampshire

1 Adams, *Annals of Portsmouth*, p. 287.

2 *Complete Works of Benjamin Franklin* (edited by J. Bigelow), vol. VII, pp. 137, 138.

3 R. V. Harlow, "Aspects of Revolutionary Finance," in *American Historical Review*, vol. XXXV, p. 47.

4 J. F. Burns, *Controversies Between Royal Governors and Their Assemblies in the Northern American Colonies*, pp. 270-276; Belknap, *History of New Hampshire* (Farmer ed.), pp. 321, 322.

5 *Letter Book.*

6 Metcalf, *Laws of New Hampshire*, vol. III, p. 619.

7 M. H. Robinson, *History of Taxation in New Hampshire*, p. 86.

8 Metcalf, *Laws of New Hampshire*, vol. IV, p. 14.

9 *Ibid.*, p. 118. Reapportionments of the town tax quotas were made, on the average, once in every three years by the state legislature according to changes in the town inventories.

10 *Ibid.*, p. 131.

11 *Ibid.*, p. 132.

12 *Ibid.*, pp. 421, 494.

13 *Ibid.*, p. 184.

14 *N. H. Provincial Papers*, vol. VII, p. 502; *N. H. Town Papers*, vol. XIII, p. 276.

15 E. L. Bogart, *Economic History of the American People*, p. 193.

16 *Bartlett Manuscripts.*

17 *N. H. Provincial Papers*, vol. VII, p. 609.

18 *Treasurer's Tax Book, 1775-1781*, manuscript volume in vault of New Hampshire State Treasurer.

19 Metcalf, *Laws of New Hampshire*, vol. IV, p. 113.

20 *Ibid.*, p. 153.

21 *Ibid.*, pp. 203, 215.

22 *Ibid.*, p. 261.

23 Nathaniel Peabody to Meshech Weare, March 13, 1780, Burnett, *Letters of Members of the Continental Congress*, vol. V, pp. 68, 69.

24 Metcalf, *Laws of New Hampshire*, vol. IV, p. 307.

25 *Ibid.*, p. 353.

26 *Ibid.*, p. 415.

27 Burnett, *Letters*, vol. V, p. 378.

28 For a schedule of the state quotas, see Ford, *Journals of the Continental Congress*, vol. XVI, p. 196; Hunt, *ibid.*, vol. XVIII, p. 1011.

29 Metcalf, *Laws of New Hampshire*, vol. IV, p. 357.

30 *Ibid.*, p. 414.

31 *Ibid.*, p. 437.

32 *Ibid.*, p. 505.

33 Hunt, *Journals of the Continental Congress*, vol. XXII, pp. 160, 161.

34 Letter dated November 6, 1781, Burnett, *Letters*, vol. VI, pp. 257, 258.

35 *American State Papers, Finance*, vol. I, p. 57.

36 J. Smith, *Peterboro, New Hampshire, in the American Revolution*, p. 151.

37 *Treasurer's Tax Book, 1775-1781*, appendix.

38 Metcalf, *Laws of New Hampshire*, vol. IV, p. 386.

39 Burnett, *Letters*, vol. IV, p. 223.

40 *Treasurer's Account Book, 1775-1791*, manuscript volume in vault of New Hampshire State Treasurer.

41 *N. H. Provincial Papers*, vol. VII, p. 483.

42 *Ibid.*, p. 510.

43 *Ibid.*, p. 549.

44 *Ibid.*, p. 575.

45 *Ibid.*, p. 638.

46 *Ibid.*, p. 615.

47 *Ibid.*, p. 706.

48 *Treasurer's Account Book, 1775-1791*.

49 *N. H. State Papers*, vol. VIII, pp. 60, 61.

50 *Ibid.*, p. 136.

51 *Ibid.*, p. 169.

52 Metcalf, *Laws of New Hampshire*, vol. IV, pp. 21-23.

53 *N. H. State Papers*, vol. VIII, p. 190.

54 Harlow, *op. cit.*, see chart opposite p. 50.

55 Letter dated December 14, 1776, *Letters by Josiah Bartlett, William Whipple and Others*, p. 65.

56 Metcalf, *Laws of New Hampshire*, vol. IV, p. 70.

57 *Ibid.*, pp. 85-87.

58 Belknap, *History of New Hampshire*, vol. II, p. 327.

59 See scale of depreciation, in Metcalf, *Laws of New Hampshire*, vol. IV, p. 420.

60 *Ibid.*, p. 237.

61 *Ibid.*, p. 126.

62 Harlow, *op. cit.*, p. 60 n..

63 *N. H. State Papers*, vol. VIII, p. 537.

64 Metcalf, *Laws of New Hampshire*, vol. IV, p. 420.

65 *N. H. State Papers*, vol. VIII, p. 779.

66 Harlow, *op. cit.*, see chart opposite p. 50.

67 *N. H. State Papers*, vol. VIII, p. 823.

68 *Ibid.*, p. 842.

Notes

69 *Ibid.*, p. 868.

70 *Treasurer's Account Book, 1775-1791.*

71 Ford, *Journals of the Continental Congress*, vol. XVI, pp. 261, 267.

72 C. Bullock, *Essays on the Monetary History of the United States*, p. 269.

73 Metcalf, *Laws of New Hampshire*, vol. IV, pp. 411, 420.

74 *N. H. State Papers*, vol. VIII, p. 913.

75 Metcalf, *Laws of New Hampshire*, vol. IV, p. 439.

76 Bullock, *op. cit.*, p. 271.

77 These figures were obtained by dividing the total state debt by the white population of the state. *American State Papers, Finance*, vol. I, pp. 28, 29; Greene and Harrington, *American Population Before the Federal Census of 1790, passim.*

78 Bullock, *op. cit.*, p. 271.

79 Hunt, *Provincial Committees of Safety*, p. 27.

80 Metcalf, *Laws of New Hampshire*, vol. IV, pp. 21-23.

81 *Ibid.*, p. 101.

82 *N. H. State Papers*, vol. VIII, p. 115.

83 *Ibid.*, p. 404.

84 *Ibid.*, p. 494.

85 Smith, *Peterboro, New Hampshire, in the American Revolution*, p. 139; *N. H. State Papers*, vol. VIII, pp. 544-546, 558, 703.

86 Ford, *Journals of the Continental Congress*, vol. V, pp. 845, 846.

87 *Writings of Benjamin Franklin* (edited by Albert H. Smyth), vol. VII, p. 294.

88 New Hampshire Historical Society, *Collections*, vol. IX, p. 108.

89 *Ibid.*, vol. II, p. 70.

Chapter 11. Industry and the Revolution

1 M. Sullivan, *Our Times*, vol. V, p. 372.

2 Whipple to Josiah Bartlett, May 21, 1779, Burnett, *Letters of Members of the Continental Congress*, vol. IV, p. 223.

3 Belknap, *History of New Hampshire*, vol. III, p. 151; Adams, *Annals of Portsmouth*, pp. 258, 259; see also a description of New Hampshire's pre-Revolutionary commerce in a letter of John Wentworth to Lord Shelburne and the Lords of Trade, March 25, 1768, *Letter Book.*

4 *Langdon Manuscripts*, in New Hampshire Historical Society.

5 Belknap, *op. cit.*, vol. III, p. 151.

6 The northern British colonies disliked to trade with the British West Indies because there was little demand there for northern goods. Then too, sugar and molasses could be purchased at a lower price in the French and Dutch West Indies where costs of production were lower and where there existed a demand for goods from the northern British colonies. Accordingly the French and Dutch trade laws had been relaxed enough to open several ports in the French and Dutch West Indies to permit such trade.

7 *Letter Book.*

8 J. F. Jameson, *American Revolution Considered as a Social Movement*, pp. 73-114.

9 All vessels carrying cargoes to or from the colonies were required to be built in either England, Ireland or the colonies under the provisions of the Navigation Act of 1696.

10 W. B. Weeden, *Economic and Social History of New England*, vol. II, p. 766.

11 Jameson, *op. cit.*, pp. 73-114.

12 F. Sanborn, *New Hampshire, an Epitome of Popular Government*, p. 236.

13 Belknap, *History of New Hampshire*, vol. III, p. 155.

14 *Ibid.*, pp. 157-160.

15 Adams, *New England in the Republic*, pp. 32, 116, 117.

16 Belknap, *op. cit.*, vol. III, pp. 150, 156, 157.

17 *Ibid.*, pp. 100 ff.; see also a description of the soil and produce in letter of John Wentworth to Lord Shelburne and the Lords of Trade, March 25, 1768, *Letter Book.*

18 Belknap, *op. cit.*, vol. III, p. 102.

19 Adams, *New England in the Republic*, pp. 54-57.

20 Bogart, *Economic History of the American People*, p. 228.

21 *Historical Magazine*, vol. IV, pp. 74, 75.

22 Belknap, *op. cit.*, vol. II, p. 327.

23 *Ibid.*, vol. III, pp. 156, 157.

24 Brewster, *Rambles About Portsmouth*, 2nd series, vol. II, p. 43.

25 Adams, *New England in the Republic*, pp. 189, 190.

26 *Laws of New Hampshire* (edited by E. C. Bean), vol. VIII, p. 178.

27 John Wentworth to Trecothick and Apthorp, May 20, 1769, *Letter Book.*

Notes

28 John Wentworth to Lord Shelburne and the Lords of Trade, March 25, 1768, *Letter Book*. Wentworth submitted a description of the few New Hampshire manufactures. He wrote, "But no small Work, scarcely to repair can be had without long delay, much difficulty & treble Cost." Wentworth added that as governor he discouraged all manufactures within the province and encouraged artisans to become farmers, hoping thus to increase the consumption of British goods.

29 Weeden, *Economic and Social History of New England*, vol. II, p. 494.

30 *Ibid.*, vol. I, pp. 394, 395.

31 Adams, *Annals of Portsmouth*, pp. 258-260.

32 Belknap, *History of New Hampshire*, vol. III, pp. 160, 161.

33 Jameson, *op. cit.*, pp. 73-114; H. U. Faulkner, *American Economic History*, pp. 170, 171.

34 *N. H. Provincial Papers*, vol. VII, p. 507; *N. H. State Papers*, vol. VIII, pp. 98, 109.

35 *N. H. State Papers*, vol. VIII, p. 16.

36 *Ibid.*, p. 171.

37 *Bartlett Manuscripts*.

38 *N. H. State Papers*, vol. VIII, pp. 196, 197.

39 *Ibid.*, p. 612.

40 *Ibid.*, pp. 721, 802.

41 T. C. Amory, *The Military Services and Public Life of Major General John Sullivan*, p. 9.

42 *N. H. State Papers*, vol. VIII, p. 777.

43 Metcalf, *Laws of New Hampshire*, vol. IV, p. 367.

44 *N. H. Provincial Papers*, vol. VII, p. 579.

45 *Ibid.*, p. 642.

46 *Ibid.*, p. 706.

47 *Ibid.*, p. 709.

48 *N. H. State Papers*, vol. VIII, p. 102.

49 Metcalf, *Laws of New Hampshire*, vol. IV, p. 37.

50 *N. H. State Papers*, vol. VIII, p. 413.

51 Metcalf, *Laws of New Hampshire*, vol. IV, p. 726.

52 *N. H. State Papers*, vol. VIII, p. 194.

53 Metcalf, *Laws of New Hampshire*, vol. IV, pp. 184 ff.

54 *Ibid.*, p. 289.

55 Hunt, *Journals of the Continental Congress*, vol. XIX, p. 112.

56 Metcalf, *Laws of New Hampshire*, vol. IV, p. 379.

57 *N. H. State Papers*, vol. VIII, pp. 971, 972.

58 Metcalf, *Laws of New Hampshire*, vol. IV, p. 562.

59 New Hampshire Historical Society, *Collections*, vol. II, p. 70.

60 *New England Historical and Genealogical Register*, vol. XXII, p. 342.

61 *N. H. State Papers*, vol. XVIII, pp. 721, 722.

62 Belknap, *History of New Hampshire*, vol. II, p. 328.

63 Burnett, *Letters of Members of the Continental Congress*, vol. III, p. 507.

64 Record of the proceedings of the convention, *Weare Manuscripts*, vol. IV, p. 16.

65 Journal of the convention, New Hampshire Historical Society, *Collections*, vol. IX, pp. 245-271.

66 Metcalf, *Laws of New Hampshire*, vol. IV, pp. 78 ff.

67 *Ibid.*, p. 88.

68 *N. H. State Papers*, vol. VIII, pp. 629, 690, 691.

69 Metcalf, *Laws of New Hampshire*, vol. IV, p. 115.

70 *Ibid.*, p. 139.

71 Sketch of John Langdon, *N. H. State Papers*, vol. XXI, p. 805.

72 *Ibid.*, vol. VIII, p. 500 n.

73 New Hampshire Historical Society, *Collections*, vol. IX, p. 245.

74 *N. H. State Papers*, vol. VIII, p. 837.

75 Letter dated November 17, 1779, New Hampshire Historical Society, *Collections*, vol. II, pp. 68, 69.

76 *Ibid.*, vol. IX, p. 245.

Chapter 12. The Revolution and Land Tenure

1 *New Hampshire Town Charters*, vol. XXIV, pp. 31, 32.

2 Adams, *Revolutionary New England*, p. 125.

3 For a detailed account of the Masonian controversy, see O. G. Hammond, *The Mason Title and Its Relation to New Hampshire and Massachusetts;* Fry, *New Hampshire as a Royal Province*, chap. IV.

4 Adams, *Revolutionary New England*, p. 125. (Quoted by courtesy of Little, Brown and Co.)

Notes

5 Greene and Harrington, *American Population Before the Federal Census of 1790*, p. 71.

6 To "dock" an entail was to bar it. By the Statute of De Donis (1285) grants or devises of land upon condition that it descend to certain heirs of the grantee or devisee were officially recognized and the conditions given the force of law. Out of this statute arose entailed estates. These estates were required by law to descend along the line of heirs designated in the grant or devise. Conveyance with good title to a person outside the line of heirs could only be accomplished by barring the entail.

John and Robert Mason, sons of Robert Mason, sought to bar the entail on the Masonian grant by a common recovery in the Court of King's Bench in England, using the fiction that New Hampshire was located in the parish of East Greenwich and thus within the court's jurisdiction. This common recovery was technically without force because it should have been obtained in a New Hampshire court which really had jurisdiction. Since the barring of the entail was ineffectual, John and Robert Mason in effect conveyed only a life estate to Samual Allen. The property, being still entailed, was required by law to descend to the lineal heirs of John and Robert Mason.

7 Greene and Harrington, *op. cit.*, p. 72.

8 Adams, *Revolutionary New England*, p. 124. (Quoted by courtesy of Little, Brown and Co.)

9 Mayo, *John Wentworth*, p. 21.

10 *Ibid.*, p. 73.

11 *N. H. Provincial Papers*, vol. VII, p. 320.

12 Fry, *New Hampshire as a Royal Province*, p. 281.

13 *Ibid.*, pp. 283, 284.

14 *Ibid.*, p. 293.

15 Mayo, *op. cit.*, pp. 40, 41.

16 *Laws of New Hampshire* (edited by A. S. Batchellor), vol. II, p. 82.

17 See commission of Governor Benning Wentworth, *ibid.*, pp. 620-622.

18 *Letter Book.*

19 Boylston, *Historical Sketch of the Hillsborough County Congresses*, pp. 12, 13.

20 L. Sabine, *The American Loyalists*, p. 2.

21 Claims of New Hampshire Loyalists; five volumes of transcripts from London Record Office out of *Records of the Committee for Enquiring into the Losses and Services of the American Loyalists*. Transcripts in New Hampshire Historical Society.

22 Belknap, *History of New Hampshire*, vol. III, p. 177.

23 Bean, *Laws of New Hampshire*, vol. VII, pp. 539, 621.

24 Batchellor, *Laws of New Hampshire*, vol. II, p. 295.

25 Metcalf, *Laws of New Hampshire*, vol. V, p. 384.

26 Batchellor, *Laws of New Hampshire*, vol. II, p. 85.

27 Such a fictitious suit was a collusive action recognized by the courts for the purpose of barring an entail.

28 For a concise description of different types of land tenure and methods of conveyance, see J. Bouvier, *Law Dictionary and Concise Encyclopedia*.

29 J. Kent, *Commentaries on American Law*, vol. IV, p. 15.

30 *Laws of the State of New Hampshire*, passed at June session, 1837, p. 316.

In 1857 the Supreme Court of New Hampshire decided in the case of *Jewell v. Warner* (35 N. H. 176) that entailed estates had in effect been abolished by the equal descent laws of 1789 and that hence the statute of 1837 was unnecessary although it served to remove doubts.

Chapter 13. The Evolution of State Government

1 *N. H. Town Papers*, vol. IX, p. 896.

2 Belknap, *History of New Hampshire*, vol. III, pp. 193, 194.

3 Letter dated December 11, 1775, *N. H. Provincial Papers*, vol. VII, p. 686.

4 Ford, *Journals of the Continental Congress*, vol. III, p. 319.

5 Batchellor, *Laws of New Hampshire*, vol. II, p. 402.

6 *N. H. Provincial Papers*, vol. VII, p. 644.

7 *Ibid.*, p. 657.

8 List of towns represented in the Assembly, *ibid.*, p. 370; census of 1775, *ibid.*, p. 780.

9 *Ibid.*, pp. 400, 401.

10 *Ibid.*, pp. 452-455, 468-470.

11 *Ibid.*, p. 645.

12 *Ibid.*, pp. 658, 659.

13 *N. H. Provincial Papers*, vol. VII, pp. 703, 704.

14 See Portsmouth's instructions to its representatives, *ibid.*, pp. 701, 702.

15 *N. H. State Papers*, vol. VIII, pp. 2, 3.

16 *Ibid.*, p. 33.

17 Metcalf, *Laws of New Hampshire*, vol. IV, p. 10.

18 *Ibid.*, pp. 34 ff.

19 *Ibid.*, p. 37.

20 *N. H. State Papers*, vol. VIII, pp. 341, 342.

21 Metcalf, *Laws of New Hampshire*, vol. IV, p. 87.

22 *N. H. Provincial Papers*, vol. VII, pp. 658, 659.

23 *N. H. State Papers*, vol. VIII, pp. 774, 775.

24 I have been unable to determine the exact reason for the absence of the western delegates.

25 Letter dated June 17, 1778, *Bartlett Manuscripts*.

26 Text of constitution, *N. H. Town Papers*, vol. IX, pp. 837-842.

27 Adams, *New England in the Republic*, pp. 84, 85.

28 *N. H. State Papers*, vol. VIII, p. 897.

29 *N. H. Town Papers*, vol. IX, pp. 852-858.

30 *Ibid.*, p. 851.

31 *Ibid.*, p. 847.

32 *Ibid.*, pp. 859-866.

33 *Ibid.*, pp. 866-871.

34 *Ibid.*, pp. 871, 872.

35 *N. H. State Papers*, vol. VIII, p. 422.

36 *Plumer Biographies*, vol. IV, p. 319.

37 *Concord Town Records*, pp. 198, 199.

38 Text of revised constitution, *N. H. Town Papers*, vol. IX, pp. 882-895.

39 *Concord Town Records*, p. 208.

40 Text of revised constitution, *N. H. Town Papers*, vol. IX, pp. 896-918.

41 C. E. Stevens, *Sources of the Constitution of the United States*, p. 38.

42 *Ibid.*, p. 77.

43 J. Bryce, *American Commonwealth*, vol. I, p. 300. (Quoted by courtesy of the Macmillan Co.)

Chapter 14. Secession Movement in the West

1 Beard, C. A. and Mary R., *Rise of American Civilization*, vol. I, pp. 266, 267.

2 The political differences were not, in the main, a reflection of the economic differences between the Connecticut Valley region and the seacoast. Curiously the Connecticut Valley was not the radical section of the state. The small-farming district from which emanated the paper money demands and

the opposition to the Federal Constitution of 1787 was the central portion of the state. It was the seacoast region and the Connecticut Valley towns which supported ratification of the Constitution of 1787. Libby, *Geographical Distribution of the Vote of the Thirteen States on the Federal Constitution*, pp. 7-11.

3 The Masonian controversy is discussed in more detail in chapter XII.

4 *N. H. Provincial and State Papers*, vol. x, pp. 197-500. Full and documented account of the entire controversy over the New Hampshire Grants.

5 Text of the address, *ibid.*, pp. 229-235. This address was a very clever argument. Meshech Weare wrote to New Hampshire's delegates in the Continental Congress, voicing the suspicion that the document had been "fabricated at Dartmouth College." Letter dated December 16, 1776, *ibid.*, p. 228.

6 *Ibid.*, p. 233.

7 *N. H. State Papers*, vol. VIII, pp. 421-426.

8 *N. H. Town Papers*, vol. XIII, pp. 760-765.

9 *Ibid.*

10 L. B. Richardson, *History of Dartmouth College*, vol. I, pp. 180-185.

11 *N H. Provincial and State Papers*, vol. x, pp. 288 n., 291, 292 n.

12 *Ibid.*, pp. 279-281.

13 Burnett, *Letters of Members of Continental Congress*, vol. III, p. 427.

14 Richardson, *op. cit.*, vol. I, pp. 180-185.

15 *N. H. Provincial and State Papers*, vol. x, p. 288.

16 Proceedings of the convention, *N. H. State Papers*, vol. VIII, pp. 817, 818.

17 Letter dated December 8, 1778, Burnett, *Letters of Members of Continental Congress*, vol. III, p. 522.

18 See attitude of delegate John Sullivan on this question, *N. H. Town Papers*, vol. XIII, pp. 765, 766.

19 Metcalf, *Laws of New Hampshire*, vol. IV, pp. 233-236.

20 Richardson, *History of Dartmouth College*, vol. I, pp. 181, 184.

21 *Ibid.*, pp. 181, 182.

22 These towns were Hinsdale, Surry, Gilsum, Alstead, Richmond, Chesterfield, Westmoreland, Marlow, Charlestown, Acworth, Newport, Lempster, Saville, Claremont, Cornish, Croydon, Plainfield, Grantham, Enfield, Grafton, Cardigan, Dorchester, Lebanon, Gunthwaite, Lancaster, Bath, Lyman, Morristown, and Lincoln. *N. H. Provincial and State Papers*, vol. x, pp. 398-400.

23 *Ibid.*, pp. 226-228.

Notes

24 *N. H. State Papers*, vol. VIII, pp. 925 ff.

25 *N. H. Provincial and State Papers*, vol. X, p. 462.

26 Richardson, *op. cit.*, vol. I, pp. 183, 184.

27 Amory, *Military Service and Public Life of Major General John Sullivan*, pp. 193-197.

28 Richardson, *op. cit.*, vol. I, pp. 184, 185.

29 *N. H. Town Papers*, vol. IX, p. 917.

30 Richardson, *op. cit.*, vol. I, p. 342.

Chapter 15. New Hampshire and the Peace Settlement

1 C. W. Alvord, *Lord Shelburne and the Founding of British-American Good Will*, p. 26.

2 Text of treaty, Hunt, *Journals of the Continental Congress*, vol. XXIV, pp. 243-251.

3 *Ibid.*, pp. 238-240, 242.

4 Burnett, *Letters of Members of Continental Congress*, vol. VII, p. 72.

5 *New Hampshire Gazette*, March 29, 1783.

6 Adams, *Annals of Portsmouth*, pp. 276-278.

7 *N. H. State Papers*, vol. VIII, p. 978.

8 New Hampshire Historical Society, *Collections*, vol. II, pp. 267-290.

9 *Ibid.*, vol. XI, *passim*.

10 J. H. Latané, *History of American Foreign Policy*, p. 212.

11 Adams, *Annals of Portsmouth*, p. 268.

12 Metcalf, *Laws of New Hampshire*, vol. V, p. 195.

13 Latané, *op. cit.*, p. 91.

14 Metcalf, *Laws of New Hampshire*, vol. IV, p. 191.

15 Mayo, *John Wentworth*, pp. 168-170.

16 Metcalf, *Laws of New Hampshire*, vol. IV, p. 456.

17 *New Hampshire Gazette*, August 2, 1783.

18 Metcalf, *Laws of New Hampshire*, vol. V, p. 195; *N. H. State Papers*, vol. XX, pp. 697-699.

19 See opinion of the Supreme Court of New Hampshire in Dow v. Northern Railroad, *New Hampshire Reports* (edited by C. B. Hibbard), vol. LXVII, p. 59.

20 *N. H. Town Papers*, vol. IX, p. 917.

21 *N. H. State Papers*, vol. VIII, pp. 967, 970.

22 Metcalf, *Laws of New Hampshire*, vol. V, pp. 42, 445, 447.

23 *Ibid.*, p. 129.

24 *Ibid.*, p. 135.

25 L. Einstein, *Divided Loyalties*, pp. 226-245.

26 Claims of New Hampshire Loyalists; five volumes of transcripts from London Record Office, from *Records of the Committee for Enquiring into the Losses and Services of American Loyalists*.

27 Latané, *op. cit.*, pp. 159, 160, 455-460.

Chapter 16. Advance in Liberal Ideas

1 Mill, *On Liberty*.

2 Batchellor, *Laws of New Hampshire*, vol. II, p. 143.

3 Worthington, *New Hampshire Churches and the American Revolution*, appendix A, p. XVII.

4 E. D. Sanborn, *History of New Hampshire*, pp. 196, 197.

5 *N. H. Town Papers*, vol. IX, pp. 898, 899.

6 A. Nevins, *American States During and After the Revolution, 1775-1783*, p. 184; E. D. Sanborn, *op. cit.*, pp. 287-289.

7 William Plumer, a contemporary observer, wrote in his biography of the Reverend Paine Wingate, a Congregational minister who later became a judge, that when Wingate was on the bench he was particularly prejudiced against litigants seeking exemptions from the Congregational tithes. *Plumer Biographies*, vol. V, p. 605.

8 Bean, *Laws of New Hampshire*, vol. VIII, pp. 820, 821.

9 E. D. Sanborn, *op. cit.*, p. 289.

10 Batchellor, *Laws of New Hampshire*, vol. II, p. 85.

11 *Ibid.*, pp. 336, 337.

12 *Ibid.*, p. 358.

13 Belknap, *History of New Hampshire*, vol. III, pp. 217 ff.

14 *N. H. Provincial Papers*, vol. VII, p. 287.

15 *New Hampshire Gazette*, April 12, 1765.

16 Batchellor, *Laws of New Hampshire*, vol. II, p. 627.

Notes

17 Metcalf, *Laws of New Hampshire*, vol. III, p. 447.

18 Nevins, *American States During and After the Revolution*, pp. 465 ff.

19 Attendance at the College declined, however, and funds were sorely needed. Richardson, *History of Dartmouth College*, vol. I, p. 174.

20 Metcalf, *Laws of New Hampshire*, vol. IV, p. 370.

21 *N. H. Town Papers*, vol. IX, p. 915.

22 Metcalf, *Laws of New Hampshire*, vol. V, p. 449.

23 Bean, *Laws of New Hampshire*, vol. VII, p. 467.

24 List of newspapers has been taken from newspaper index in New Hampshire Historical Society.

25 *N. H. Town Papers*, vol. IX, p. 901.

26 Fry, *New Hampshire as a Royal Province*, pp. 431, 432.

27 Adams, *Annals of Portsmouth*, p. 172.

28 *Ibid.*, p. 224.

29 *New Hampshire Gazette*, November 28, 1766.

30 Metcalf, *Laws of New Hampshire*, vol. IV, p. 87.

31 Belknap, *History of New Hampshire*, vol. III, p. 207.

32 *N. H. Town Papers*, vol. IX, pp. 900, 901.

33 Metcalf, *Laws of New Hampshire*, vol. V, p. 596.

34 *Ibid.*, p. 718.

35 Bean, *Laws of New Hampshire*, vol. VIII, p. 129.

36 Metcalf, *Laws of New Hampshire*, vol. IV, p. 467.

37 *N. H. Provincial Papers*, vol. IV, p. 617.

38 Greene and Harrington, *American Population Before the Federal Census of 1790*, pp. 72, 73.

39 *N. H. Provincial Papers*, vol. VII, pp. 724-779.

40 Worthington, *New Hampshire Churches and the American Revolution*, p. 65.

41 *Bartlett Manuscripts*.

42 I. Hammond, "Slavery in New Hampshire," in *Granite Monthly*, vol. IV, pp. 108-110.

43 *N. H. State Papers*, vol. VIII, pp. 861, 862.

44 *N. H. Town Papers*, vol. IX, pp. 896, 897.

45 Greene and Harrington, *op. cit.*, p. 73.

46 Beard, C. A. and Mary R., *Rise of American Civilization*, vol. I, p. 296. (Quoted by courtesy of the Macmillan Co.)

FINIS

Bibliography

Manuscript Sources

Dartmouth College Library

Bartlett Manuscripts. Include correspondence of Dr. Josiah Bartlett of Kingston. This collection consists for the most part of letters received by Bartlett, many of which were written by William Whipple of Portsmouth. Most of these letters discuss the politics and public affairs of the period.

Wheelock Manuscripts. Include correspondence of Dr. Eleazar Wheelock, founder and President of Dartmouth College. There are also included in this collection many miscellaneous papers relating to political developments of the period. Dr. Wheelock's attitude was an unusual combination of a universal outlook combined with sectional interests.

New Hampshire Historical Society

Bartlett Manuscripts. One folio of miscellaneous papers of Dr. Josiah Bartlett.

Langdon Manuscripts. One folio of miscellaneous papers of John and Woodbury Langdon. Most of these papers are of a commercial character and illustrate the so-called triangular trade in which the New England colonies participated.

Bibliography

Letterbook of Governor John Wentworth. Transcripts of Wentworth correspondence in Halifax, N. S., Record Office. The collection gives a most interesting and vivid account of the period from the viewpoint of this able conservative.

Livermore Papers. Transcripts of the correspondence of Samuel Livermore while a delegate to the Continental Congress. Much of this correspondence relates to the Vermont question.

Plumer Biographies. Five volumes of manuscript biographies by William Plumer, an observer of the post-Revolutionary period. These biographies deal with the leading politicians and statesmen of New Hampshire during the latter half of the eighteenth century. Plumer was exceedingly critical but also quite accurate in his estimate of men.

Provincial and Revolutionary Papers. Include two volumes of miscellaneous manuscripts, many of which relate to New Hampshire privateers.

Stark Manuscripts. Include two volumes of the correspondence of Brigadier-General John Stark. These papers relate principally to military affairs and reveal a keen sense of the practical on the writer's part.

Stark and Morris Papers. Miscellaneous correspondence of the Stark and Morris families.

Waldron Papers. Include two volumes of the manuscript papers of the Waldron family of Dover covering the period 1713 to 1782.

Weare Manuscripts. Include fourteen volumes of the papers of Meshech Weare and others of the Weare family. This collection covers a long period of New Hampshire colonial history and contains many important official documents, which members of the Weare family acquired in their various official capacities.

New Hampshire State Library

Claims of New Hampshire Loyalists. Include five volumes of transcripts from the Public Record Office in London, selected from *Reccords of the Committee for Enquiring into the Losses and Services of the American Loyalists.* These transcripts reveal in dramatic fashion the experiences of New Hampshire's Loyalist refugees.

Revolutionary New Hampshire

Itineraries of Josiah Bartlett, 1775-1779. A record of the travels and expenses of Josiah Bartlett while a delegate to the Continental Congress.

New Hampshire State Treasurer's Office

Account Books of the First, Second and Third New Hampshire regiments in the Continental army. Include three volumes of balance sheets relating to individual soldiers and officers. The credits and debits of each soldier and officer are recorded therein.

Orders on the Treasurer. There are ten volumes of orders drawn on the treasurer during the War of the Revolution. This material lacks any semblance of organization and is difficult of analysis.

Treasurer's Account Book, 1775-1791. Includes a statement of the total receipts and expenditures for each year of this period. The system of accounting is rudimentary and easily followed.

Treasurer's Tax Books. Include three volumes of state tax records for the years 1775 to 1783. These records present an interesting picture of a little known field. The large defaults in tax payments are particularly illuminating.

War Accounts of the State. Include three volumes of records of military expenditures and accounts owed to the Continental government.

Private Papers

Record and Journal of Robert Stinson. This item is in the possession of Mrs. George H. Gould of George's Mills, New Hampshire. It is particularly enlightening in regard to the popular resentment against the Loyalists.

Bibliography
Published Sources

ADAMS, SAMUEL, *Writings of Samuel Adams*. Edited by Harry A. Cushing. 4 vols. New York, 1904-1908.

American Archives: . . . . *a documentary history of the origin and progress of the North American colonies; of the causes and accomplishment of the American Revolution; and of the constitution of government for the United States, to the final ratification thereof*. Edited by Peter Force. 4th series, 6 vols. Washington, 1837-1846. This source contains much New Hampshire material in the form of official correspondence.

American State Papers. Documents, legislative and executive, of the congress of the United States, from the first session of the first to the third session of the thirteenth congress, inclusive. 38 vols. Washington, 1832-1861. The two series designated *Military Affairs* and *Finance* have been used.

Collections of the New Hampshire Historical Society. 11 vols. Concord, 1824-1915. A collection of essays on New Hampshire history of varying degrees of accuracy together with invaluable source material.

Collections, topographical, historical and biographical relating principally to New Hampshire. Edited by J. B. Moore and J. Farmer. 3 vols. Concord, 1822-1824. A collection of miscellaneous data concerning eighteenth century New Hampshire.

Compilation of the Messages and Papers of the Presidents, 1789-1897. Edited by James D. Richardson. 10 vols. Washington, 1900.

Concord Town Records, 1732-1820. Concord, 1894.

Correspondence of the American Revolution. Edited by Jared Sparks. 4 vols. Boston, 1853.

Documents and Readings in American Government. Edited by John M. Mathews and Clarence A. Berdahl. New York, 1930.

Documents Relative to the Colonial History of the State of New York. Edited by E. B. O'Callaghan and B. Fernow. 15 vols. Albany, 1856-1887. A valuable source for instructions issued by the British government to the colonial governors.

Facsimiles of Manuscripts in European Archives Relating to America, 1773-1783. Edited by B. F. Stevens. 25 vols. London, 1889-1898. The New Hampshire material is scanty.

FRANKLIN, BENJAMIN, *Complete Works.* Edited by John Bigelow. 10 vols. New York, 1887-1888.

——————————, *Writings of Benjamin Franklin.* Edited by Albert H. Smyth. 10 vols. New York, 1905-1907.

GEORGE III, *Correspondence of King George the Third from 1760 to December, 1783.* Edited by Sir John W. Fortescue. 6 vols. London, 1927-1928. The Tory viewpoint is well presented.

JEFFERSON, THOMAS, *Writings of Thomas Jefferson.* Edited by Paul Leicester Ford. 10 vols. New York, 1892-1899.

Journals of the Continental Congress, 1774-1789. Edited by Worthington C. Ford. 31 vols. published. Washington, 1904-1931. (Volumes XVI-XXVII edited by Gaillard Hunt, volumes XXVIII-XXXI by John C. Fitzpatrick.)

Letters by Josiah Bartlett, William Whipple and others, written before and during the Revolution. Philadelphia, 1889.

Letters of Members of the Continental Congress. Edited by Edmund C. Burnett. 7 vols. published. Washington, 1921-1934. The value of this source is enhanced by its excellent index.

New England Historical and Genealogical Register. 88 vols. Boston, 1847-1934.

New Hampshire Gazette. A weekly newspaper published at Portsmouth beginning in 1756. The files in the Dartmouth College Library and the New Hampshire Historical Society have been used.

Bibliography

NEW HAMPSHIRE. *Documents and Records Relating to the Province, Towns and State of New Hampshire.* Published by the state, 1867-1933. The entire collection includes the following series: *Provincial Papers,* vols. I-VII, X; *Town Papers,* vols. IX, XI-XIII; *Revolutionary Rolls,* vols. XIV-XVII; *State Papers,* vols. VIII, XVIII-XXIII; *Town Charters,* vols. XXIV-XXIX; *Revolutionary Documents,* vol. XXX; *Probate Records,* vols. XXXI-XXXIV. Cited as *New Hampshire Provincial Papers, New Hampshire State Papers* and *New Hampshire Town Papers,* etc., followed by the number of the volume in the series as a whole. This collection includes legislative journals and other government records as well as official and semiofficial correspondence. The material is poorly organized and incomplete, yet the best single source.

NEW HAMPSHIRE. *Journals of the Senate and House of Representatives, 1794.* Portsmouth, 1795.

NEW HAMPSHIRE. *Laws of New Hampshire.* Edited by A. S. Batchellor, H. Metcalf, and E. Bean. 8 vols. Published by the state, 1904-1920. An accurate and well-indexed compilation.

NEW HAMPSHIRE. *Laws of the State of New Hampshire, June session, 1837.* Concord, 1837.

PATTEN, MATTHEW, *Diary of Matthew Patten of Bedford, N. H., 1754-1788.* Concord, 1903. A farmer's viewpoint of the Revolution.

Reports of Cases Ruled and Adjudged in the Several Courts of the United States and Pennsylvania, held at the seat of the Federal government. Edited by A. J. Dallas. Vol. III. Philadelphia, 1799.

ROCKINGHAM, MARQUIS OF, *Memoirs of the Marquis of Rockingham and his Contemporaries.* Edited by G. T. K. Albemarle. 2 vols. London, 1852. An excellent cross-section of English attitudes toward the American colonies.

Select Charters and Other Documents Illustrative of American History, 1606-1775. Edited by William MacDonald. New York and London, 1906.

Songs and Ballads of the American Revolution. Edited by Frank Moore. New York, 1856.

Revolutionary New Hampshire

Sources and Documents Illustrating the American Revolution 1764-1788 and the Formation of the Federal Constitution. Edited by S. E. Morison. Oxford, 1929.

Statement of the cause of the McClary owners and Doane and Doane's Administrators from its Commencement in 1777 to its close in the Supreme Court of the United States, February, 1795. Portsmouth, 1795. Anonymous pamphlet in New Hampshire Historical Society.

SULLIVAN, JOHN, *Letters and Papers of Major-General John Sullivan, Continental Army.* Edited by Otis G. Hammond. 2 vols. published. Concord, 1930, 1931. A third volume awaits publication. A valuable collection of the correspondence of a typical American Revolutionist.

WASHINGTON, GEORGE, *Writings of George Washington from the Original Manuscript Sources, 1754-1799.* Edited by John C. Fitzpatrick. 11 vols. published. Washington, 1931-1934.

WHIPPLE CORRESPONDENCE, in *Historical Magazine and Notes and Queries concerning the Antiquities, History and Biography of America.* Vol. VI, pp. 74, 75. Boston, 1862. Whipple's absolute integrity and keen mind make all his letters interesting.

Secondary Works

ADAMS, JAMES TRUSLOW, *The Founding of New England.* Boston, 1921. The best comprehensive study of this period.

——————————, *New England in the Republic, 1776-1850.* Boston, 1926.

——————————, *Revolutionary New England, 1691-1776.* Boston, 1923. The author displays a good understanding of the fundamentals of Revolutionary psychology.

ADAMS, NATHANIEL, *Annals of Portsmouth, comprising a period of two hundred years from the first settlement of the town.* Portsmouth, 1825. This work might easily be classed as a primary source, since its author was town clerk and a near contemporary.

Bibliography

AGAR, HERBERT, *The People's Choice, from Washington to Harding.* Boston and New York, 1933.

ALVORD, CLARENCE W., *The Mississippi Valley in British Politics; a study of the trade, land speculation, and experiments in imperialism culminating in the American Revolution.* 2 vols. Cleveland, 1917. A scholarly dissertation on the western problem as it affected the Revolution.

——————————, *Lord Shelburne and the Founding of British-American Goodwill.* London, 1926.

AMORY, THOMAS C., *The Military Services and Public Life of Major-General John Sullivan, of the American Revolutionary Army.* Boston, 1868. There is a great need for a better treatment of Sullivan, more accurate and devoid of hero-worship.

ANDREWS, CHARLES M., *Colonial Background of the American Revolution.* New Haven, 1924. The author considers the colonies in their broader relation to British colonial policy.

BARSTOW, GEORGE, *The History of New Hampshire, from its discovery, in 1614, to the passage of the Toleration Act, in 1819.* Concord, 1853. A work of mediocre quality in the Bancroft style.

BEARD, CHARLES A. AND MARY R., *Rise of American Civilization.* 2 vols. New York, 1927.

BECKER, CARL L., *The Beginnings of the American People.* Boston, 1915.

BELKNAP, JEREMY, *History of New Hampshire.* 3 vols. Boston, 1791-1792. This work is the best history of New Hampshire during the colonial era yet written. Belknap's accuracy, impartiality, and sound interpretation are refreshing.

——————————, *History of New Hampshire,* one volume edition published by John Farmer. Dover, 1831.

BELL, CHARLES, *Facts Relating to the Early History of Chester, N. H., from the settlement in 1720, until the formation of the state constitution in the year 1784.* Concord, 1863.

BELL, CHARLES H., *History of the Town of Exeter, New Hampshire.* Boston, 1888.

BOGART, ERNEST L., *Economic History of the American People.* New York and London, 1934. Gives an excellent treatment of the economic aspects of the Revolution.

BOUTON, NATHANIEL, *The History of Concord, from its first grant in 1725, to the organization of the city government in 1853, with a history of the ancient Penacooks.* Concord, 1856.

BOUVIER, JOHN, *Law Dictionary and Concise Encyclopedia.* 2 vols. St. Paul, 1914.

BOYLSTON, EDWARD D., *Historical Sketch of the Hillsborough County Congresses, held at Amherst, (N. H.) 1774 & 1775.* Amherst, 1884.

BREWSTER, CHARLES W., *Rambles about Portsmouth.* First Series. Portsmouth, 1873. The author has assembled hundreds of anecdotes relating to the colonial period. His accuracy must always be questioned, however.

——————————, *Rambles about Portsmouth.* Second Series. 2 vols. Portsmouth, 1859-1860.

BRYCE, JAMES, *American Commonwealth.* 2 vols. New York, 1889.

BULLOCK, CHARLES J., *Essays on the Monetary History of the United States.* New York and London, 1900. The third part of this work is an essay on paper money in New Hampshire. The author, however, lacked access to many newly discovered sources, and his work is incomplete.

BURNS, JOHN F., *Controversies Between Royal Governors and Their Assemblies in the Northern American Colonies.* Boston, 1923. An able treatment of this subject for New Hampshire.

Cambridge History of the British Empire. Edited by J. H. Rose, A. P. Newton and E. A. Benians. New York and Cambridge, 1929-1933. Volume I, entitled *The Old Empire from the Beginnings to 1783* has been used. The discussion of the British trade regulations is the best that has been examined.

Bibliography

CHANNING, EDWARD, *A History of the United States.* 6 vols. New York, 1905-1925. The third volume is a standard text on the Revolution in general.

EINSTEIN, LEWIS D., *Divided Loyalties; Americans in England during the War of Independence.* London, 1933. The Loyalist problem as viewed from England

FAULKNER, HAROLD U., *American Economic History.* New York and London, 1924. Excellent chapters on colonial industry, agriculture, and commerce.

FISKE, JOHN, *The American Revolution.* 2 vols. Boston and New York, 1891.

FROTHINGHAM, RICHARD, *The Rise of the Republic of the United States.* Boston, 1872.

FRY, WILLIAM H., *New Hampshire as a Royal Province* in Columbia University, *Studies in History, Economics and Public Law,* vol. XXIX. New York, 1908. An accurate interpretation of an impressive collection of facts from the viewpoint of a political scientist.

GREENE, EVARTS B. AND HARRINGTON, VIRGINIA D., *American Population before the Federal Census of 1790.* New York, 1932. The best treatise on colonial population which has appeared.

HALE, SALMA, *Annals of the Town of Keene, from its first settlement, in 1734, to the year 1790.* Keene, 1851.

HALL, BENJAMIN H., *History of Eastern Vermont, from its earliest settlement to the close of the eighteenth century.* New York, 1858.

HAMMOND, ISAAC W., "Slavery in New Hampshire in the Olden Time," in *Granite Monthly,* vol. IV, pp. 108-110. Concord, 1881.

HAMMOND, OTIS G., *The Mason Title and Its Relations to New Hampshire and Massachusetts.* Worcester, 1916. An excellent summary of a complex problem.

——————————, *Tories of New Hampshire in the War of the Revolution.* Concord, 1917.

HARLOW, RALPH V., "Aspects of Revolutionary Finance, 1775-1783," in *American Historical Review*, vol. XXXV, pp. 46-68. New York, 1930. The writer in a brilliant essay criticizes the viewpoint of the orthodox economists on Revolutionary finance.

HARRIMAN, ARTHUR I., *Praises on Tombs, Eulogies, Epitaphs, Inscriptions, and Historical Facts of the American Struggle for Independence.* Portsmouth, 1932.

HATCH, LOUIS C., *The Administration of the American Revolutionary Army.* New York and London, 1904. This work is the best available on the subject but it leaves much to be desired as to organization and completeness.

HAWK, EMORY Q., *Economic History of the South.* New York, 1934.

HUNT, AGNES, *The Provincial Committees of Safety of the American Revolution.* Cleveland, 1904. A dull treatment of an interesting subject.

JAMESON, J. FRANKLIN, *The American Revolution Considered as a Social Movement.* Princeton, 1926. Dr. Jameson's generalizations are rather broad in some instances, but his interpretation is brilliant.

KENT, JAMES, *Commentaries on American Law.* 4 vols. New York, 1840.

KIDDER, FREDERIC, *History of the First New Hampshire Regiment in the War of the Revolution.* Albany, 1868.

LATANÉ, JOHN H., *History of American Foreign Policy.* Garden City, 1927.

LEONARD, LEVI W., *History of Dublin, New Hampshire.* Dublin, 1919.

LIBBY, ORIN G., *The Geographical Distribution of the Vote of the Thirteen States on the Federal Constitution, 1787-1788.* Madison, 1894. An accurate and scientific treatise to be considered in connection with F. J. Turner's essays.

McCLINTOCK, JOHN N., *Colony, Province, State, 1623-1888; History of New Hampshire.* Boston, 1888. As too often happens, the writer has confused history with genealogy, the result being poorly organized, inaccurate, and incomplete.

Bibliography

MAHAN, ALFRED T., *The Major Operations of the Navies in the War of American Independence*. London, 1913.

MATHEWS, LOIS K., *The Expansion of New England: the spread of New England settlements and institutions to the Mississippi river, 1620-1865*. Boston and New York, 1909.

MAYO, LAWRENCE S., *John Wentworth, Governor of New Hampshire, 1767-1775*. Cambridge, 1921. A fine interpretation of the life of an honest and intelligent executive.

————————, "Colonel John Stark at Winter Hill, 1775," in Massachusetts Historical Society, *Proceedings*, vol. LVII, pp. 328-336. Boston, 1924.

NEVINS, ALLAN, *The American States During and After the Revolution, 1775-1789*. New York, 1924. Certain inaccuracies detract from the value of the author's interesting conclusions.

New England Quarterly; an historical review of New England life and letters. 7 vols. 1928-1934.

PARKER, EDWARD L., *The History of Londonderry, comprising the towns of Derry and Londonderry, N. H.* Boston, 1851.

PARSONS, CHARLES L., "The Capture of Fort William and Mary, December 14 and 15, 1774," in New Hampshire Historical Society, *Proceedings*, vol. IV, pp. 18-47. Concord, 1906.

PILLSBURY, HOBART, *New Hampshire; resources, attractions, and its people; a history*. 5 vols. New York, 1927-1929. This work can scarcely be called history. It is a disjointed collection of facts and genealogies, often inaccurate and confusing.

POTTER, CHANDLER E., *Military History of the State of New Hampshire, from its settlement, in 1623, to the rebellion in 1861*. Concord, 1866. A source of valuable information on the military problem but difficult to use because it is not indexed.

RICHARDSON, LEON B., *History of Dartmouth College*. 2 vols. Hanover, 1932. A sympathetic and scholarly treatment of the subject with ample consideration of the historical background. The author's interpretation of the Vermont question is excellent.

ROBINSON, MAURICE H., *History of Taxation in New Hampshire*. New York, 1903. The writer apparently failed to use the manuscripts in the State Treasurer's Office. The value of his work is therefore limited.

SABINE, LORENZO, *The American Loyalists*. Boston, 1847.

SANBORN, EDWIN D., *History of New Hampshire, from its first discovery to the year 1830*. Manchester, 1875. Excellent chapters on the question of religious toleration.

SANBORN, FRANKLIN B., *New Hampshire, an epitome of popular government*. Boston and New York, 1904. The hornbook of New Hampshire history.

SANDERS, JENNINGS B., *The Evolution of the Executive Departments of the Continental Congress, 1774-1789*. Chapel Hill, 1935. An excellent piece of research into an unexplored field.

SAUNDERSON, HENRY H., *History of Charlestown, New Hampshire*. Claremont, 1876.

SCHLESINGER, ARTHUR M., *The Colonial Merchants and the American Revolution, 1763-1776* in Columbia University, *Studies in History, Economics and Public Law*, vol. LXXVIII. New York, 1918. A scholarly treatise, the completeness of which testifies to the tremendous amount of research it must have involved.

SIEBERT, W. H., *"The Loyalist Refugees of New Hampshire,"* Ohio State University Bulletin, vol. XXI. Columbus, 1916.

SMITH, JONATHAN, *Peterborough, New Hampshire, in the American Revolution*. Peterborough, 1913.

STACKPOLE, EVERETT S., *History of New Hampshire*. 4 vols. New York, 1917. Next to Belknap's, the best history, but the writer mentions few sources and tends too frequently to accept the popular version without reservation.

STARK, F. R., *The Abolition of Privateering and the Declaration of Paris*, in Columbia University, *Studies in History, Economics and Public Law*, vol. VIII. New York, 1897. The author in convincing fashion explains the effect of American privateering upon the British policy of the final years of the Revolution.

Bibliography

STEVENS, CHARLES E., *Sources of the Constitution of the United States, Considered in Relation to Colonial and English History*. New York and London, 1894. A little known source which was found to contain many stimulating suggestions concerning the evolution of the state constitutions during the Revolution.

TURNER, FREDERICK J., *The Frontier in American History*. New York, 1920.

TYLER, M. C., *Literary History of the American Revolution, 1763-1783*. 2 vols. New York and London, 1897.

VAN TYNE, CLAUDE H., *The American Revolution, 1776-1783*. New York and London, 1905.

——————————, *Causes of the War of Independence*. Boston and New York, 1922. This work is generally considered to be by far the best study of the subject, from the viewpoint of literary quality as well as historical excellence.

——————————, *The Loyalists in the American Revolution*. New York and London, 1902.

——————————, *The War of Independence*. Boston and New York, 1929.

WALKER, JOSEPH B., "The New Hampshire Covenant of 1775" in *Granite Monthly*, vol. XXXV, pp. 188-197. Concord, 1903. An interesting article concerning this unique covenant, the significance of which historians have too often ignored.

WEEDEN, WILLIAM B., *Economic and Social History of New England, 1620-1789*. 2 vols. New York, 1890.

WINGATE, CHARLES E. L., *Life and Letters of Paine Wingate*. 2 vols. Winchester, 1930. Wingate's career is interesting because he was a moderate in politics. His correspondence reveals his inner doubts in the years 1774-1775 as to the wisdom of the Revolution.

WINSOR, JUSTIN (editor), *Narrative and Critical History of America*. 8 vols. Boston and New York, 1884-1889.

WORTHINGTON, HARRIET, *The New Hampshire Churches and the American Revolution*. Manuscript thesis, University of Chicago, 1924. Contains the results of important and accurate research.

Index

INDEX

Acworth, 190.
Adams, John, 14, 85, 182.
Adams, Samuel, 6, 12, 14, 33, 186.
Agriculture, effect of Revolution on, 152-153.
Alarm list, 94.
Allen, Ethan, 189; *and the union of western New Hampshire towns with Vermont, 193-194.*
Allen, Ira, 189, 195-196.
Allen, Samuel, 164-165.
Alstead, 190.
AMERICA (ship), 112.
AMERICANUS, pseud., 6.
Amherst, N. H., 123.
AMHERST JOURNAL, 212.
Annapolis Trade Convention, 161-162.
Apthorp, 192.
Articles of War, 100-101.
Assembly, *fails to act on Massachusetts circular letter, 7, 9; petitions king against taxes, 7, 9; answers Virginia Resolves, 7-8; petitions Lord Dartmouth, 12; appoints Committee of Correspondence, 13, 19; adjourned, 13; refuses to garrison Fort William and Mary, 19; dissolved, 19; holds extra-legal meeting, 19-20, 35; convenes for last time, 25-26; excludes Grafton County members, 25-26, 28; representation in, 1775, 26, 28, 177; passes bankruptcy law, 133.*
"Associated Refugees," 128.
Association Test, 50ff., 121-122; *text, 50-51; signers, 51-52, 61.*
Assumption Bill, 143.
Atherton, Joshua, 54, 56, 120, 128, 130.
Atkinson, George, 54, 182.
Atkinson, Theodore, 22, 42, 56, 166.
Atkinson Academy, 211.
Auctions, forbidden by Legislature, 160.
Austin, Nicholas, 21-22.
Ayer, John, 144.

Bankruptcy laws, 133, *effect of Revolution on, 214.*
Baptist Church, 208, *attitude toward the Revolution, 61.*
Barkley, Capt., 29-30.
Barran, William, 124.
Barrington, 14, 34.
Bartlett, Josiah, 44, 55; *loses royal commissions, 24; chosen delegate to Continental Congress, 36, 87; on Paine's "Common Sense," 70; signs Declaration of Independence, 71; member of committee*
to draft a confederation, 72; signs Articles of Confederation, 75; on inefficiency of Continental Congress, 78-79; tribute to, 84-85; on privateering, 110, 116; on paper money, 139; represents New Hampshire in Providence convention, 159; and the secession movement, 193-194; letters to, 40, 72, 77, 79, 80, 81, 82, 89, 109, 110, 119, 135, 137, 153, 155, 181, 215.
Bartlett, Richard, 124.
Barton, Robert, 156.
Bath, 190, 192.
Bedel, Timothy, 102.
Belknap, Jeremy, 60; *on Catholicism, 20; on agriculture, 152; on economic situation, 158-159; on criminal trials, 213; on slavery, 214-215.*
Bellows, Benjamin, 196.
Blaisdell, Michael, 111.
Blay, Ruth, 213.
Boston, *first British troops arrive, 7; harbor closed by British, 17; gets relief from New Hampshire, 20-21; barracks built by New Hampshire carpenters, 21-22; economic conference, 1780, 161.*
Boston Massacre, 9
Boston Port Act, 17, 18-19, 20.
Boston Tea Party, 14.
Bounty system of enlistment, 94-95.
Brackett, Joshua, 55, 114.
Brentwood, 28, 39, 58, 68, 177, 179.
Brewster, Nero, 215.
British navy, bombards coast, 66.
Bunker Hill, Battle of, 65.
Bunten, John, 111.
Burke, Edmund, 17, 32.

Canaan, 2, 184, 190, 192.
CANCEAUX, Lieut. Mowat, 23.
Candia, 21.
Cardigan, 184, 190, 192.
Carleton, Sir Guy, 200.
Carr, Mr., 33.
Catholicism, New Hampshire's attitude toward, 20, 181, 182.
Charles II, 164.
Charlestown, 195.
Charlestown Academy, 211.
Chase, Samuel, 81.
Chatham, William Pitt, 1st earl, 5.
Cheshire County, 10, 44; *representation in Assembly, 11; lawlessness, 23; holds Congress, 37; Loyalists, 52, 126; representation in Legislature, 190; and secession movement, 195-196, 197.*

[268]

Index

Chester, 21, 41, 170.
Chesterfield, 190, 196.
Chesterfield Academy, 211.
Chittenden, Thomas, 193, 197.
Chivers, Capt., 38-39.
Christian Church, 209.
Cilley, Joseph, 92, 93.
Cincinnati, Society of the, 103.
Claggett, Wyseman, 45, 54.
Clap, Supply, 21, 109, 159.
Claremont, 126-127, 211.
Claremont Episcopal Church, 59-60, *persecution of, 122-123, 128.*
Clergy, importance in Revolution, 58.
Cochran, Capt. John, 22, 23.
Colden, Cadwallader, 11.
Commerce, *injured by New England Restraining Act, 29; effect of Revolution on, 149-150; state regulates exports and imports, 156-158.*
Committee of Correspondence, *established, 13, 34; origin, 33-34; membership, 19, 39; and Boston Port Bill, 34-35; calls Provincial Congress, 35-36, 177; urges towns to adopt Continental Association, 38.*
Committee of Correspondence (local organizations), 34.
Committee of Safety, 90; *powers, 43-44, 45; membership, 44-45; sends Association test to towns, 121-122; and suppression of Loyalists, 123-124; tries Fowle for counterfeiting, 145; regulates exports and imports, 156-157; appoints rum appraisers, 160.*
Committee of Safety (local organizations), *Provincial Congress urges establishment of, 42; investigates Loyalists, 121; empowered to enforce price-fixing, 159.*
Concord, 2, 21; *not represented in Assembly, 28, 177; adopts non-importation agreement, 36; objects to Constitution of 1781, 184, 185; newspapers, 212.*
CONCORD HERALD, 212.
Confederation, Articles of, 73-75, 115; *New Hampshire's attitude toward, 72-74, 82; approved by New Hampshire Legislature, 74-75; affected by sectional politics, 81-82.*
Confiscation Act, 125-126, 202-203.
Congregational Church, 208, 209, *attitude toward Revolution, 56, 60.*
Connecticut River, dispute over northernmost head, 201-202.
Connecticut Valley, 2-3; *protected by ranger service, 42, 101-102; Loyalist activity in, 126; lumbering, 151; representation in Legislature, 178, 198; towns object to state government, 189-192; secession movement in, 190, 192-198.*
Constitution of 1776, 43, 68, 178-180.
Constitution of 1779, 181-182.
Constitution of 1781, 182-185.
Constitution of 1784, 209, 211, 212, 213, 216.
Constitutional Convention, 1778-79, 180-181.
Constitutional Convention, 1781-83, 182-186.
Continental Army, *inefficiency of Congress' regulation of, 80; organization, 90, 92-93; size fluctuates, 93-96, 104-105; officers' salaries, 97, 102-103; clothing, 98, 100; rations, 98-100.*
Continental Army (New Hampshire contingent), 102; *organization, 90, 92, 94-95; clothing and equipment, 96; mutiny of Gen. Poor's brigade, 97-98; size, 105, 148.*
Continental Association, 37-39, 215.
Continental Congress, 19; *origin, 35; New Hampshire delegates, 35-36, 84, 183; first meeting, 37-38; recommends New Hampshire's establishing a government, 67-68, 176; assumes governmental powers, 70-71; adopts Articles of Confederation, 72-73; difficulties facing Congress, 76-79; standing committees vs. executive departments, 79-80, 100, 161; regulation of the army, 80-81, 97-103; sectional politics, 81-84; levies on states for supplies, 83, 136; establishes pension system, 103-104; authorizes privateering, 107; recommendations on treatment of Loyalists, 121, 125; levies taxes on New Hampshire, 135-137, 142; and dispute over New Hampshire Grants, 193, 195-197; ratifies Treaty of 1783, 200; sends Olive Branch Petition, 65-66.*
Continental Loan Office, 145.
Cooke, Nicholas, 144.
Cooper, William, 20.
Coös County, 202.
Cornish, 192, 195.
Cossitt, Rana, 59-60, 122.
Council, *established, 68, 179; issues commissions to privateers, 108.*
Counterfeiting, 143-144.
Counties, established, 10-11.
County congresses, 37.
Currency, *before the Revolution, 133, 135; inflation, 138-143, 145-147, 158-160; depreciation, 142, 145-147; attitude of states toward inflation, 83-84.*
Customs duties, 12.
Cutter, Ammi Ruhamah, 55.
Cutts, Samuel, 22, 44, 54.

[269]

Dartmouth, William Legge, 2d earl, 12, 16, 18, 20, 36, 38, 40, *on firearms law, 22.*

Dartmouth College, 20, 193, 198, 211.

Dearborn, Henry, 55, 92, 93, 99.

Debts, British-American, collection under Treaty of 1783, 200, 202.

Declaration of the Causes, 65.

Declaratory Act, 4.

Dent, Elizabeth, 213.

Derrick, Peter, 111.

Dickinson, John, *Letters from a Farmer,* 6, 47.

Disenfranchisement Act, 127, 128.

Doane, Elisha, 114-116.

Doane, Isaiah, 114.

Dominy, John, 213.

Dover, 14, 51, 58; *establishes Committee of Correspondence, 34; criticizes state government, 68, 179; receives custody of New York State Loyalists, 123.*

DOVER PHOENIX, 212.

Dracut Convention, 1776, 159.

Draft laws, 95.

DRESDEN MERCURY, 212.

Dublin, 40.

Duché, Rev. Jacob, 79.

Dudley, John, 45.

Durham, 21.

Durham Company, 40.

East India Company, 13, 15, 17.

Economic conferences, 159-161.

Education, effect of Revolution on, 209-211.

Enfield, 2, 192.

Enlistments, bounty system of, 94-95.

Entails, 173-174.

Episcopal Church, 208, *attitude toward Revolution, 59-60.*

Epping, 28, 177.

Epsom, 39.

Exeter, 23, 40; *joins non-importation agreement, 9; passes "tea resolves," 14; establishes Committee of Correspondence, 34; establishes Committee of Safety, 38; resolves against peddlers, 39; receives custody of New York Loyalists, 123; newspapers, 212.*

EXETER JOURNAL, 212.

Falmouth, Dist. of Maine, burned, 66.

Farmers, attitude toward Revolution, 55.

Fenton, John, 25-26, 56, 130, 204.

Finance, *Provincial Congress seizes royal treasury, 42; Provincial Congress votes to borrow money, 42; government costs during Revolution, 138; war debt, 143.*

Finance (Continental), negligence of Continental Congress, 79-80.

Firearms, *import forbidden by British, 22; New Hampshire's reaction, 22-24.*

Fisher, John, 166, 204, 205.

Fishing, *effect of Revolution on, 151; American rights restored by Treaty of 1783, 84, 200, 205-206.*

Folsom, Nathaniel, 44, 54; *and loot of Fort William and Mary, 23, 24; delegate to Continental Congress, 36, 87; commands New Hampshire forces, 41, 43, 90; on Declaration of Independence, 72; objects to 8th Article of Confederation, 73; on his duties in Congress, 77; on Rev. Duché, 79; on Congress' regulation of the Army, 80; sketch of, 85; loses high command in Army, 92; represents New Hampshire at Providence convention, 159.*

Folsom, Samuel, 155.

Fort William and Mary, 19; *military stores seized by mob, 22-23, 40.*

Foster, Abiel, 60, 87.

Fowle, Daniel, 69.

Fowle, Robert Lewis, 128, 144-145.

Francestown, 38.

Franklin, Benjamin, 14, 72, 145.

FREEMAN'S JOURNAL, 69, 70.

Freewill Baptist Church, 209.

Frost, George, 87.

Frye, Ebenezer, 124.

Gage, Gen. Thomas, 18, 21, 24, 29, 64.

Gains, George, 45, 54, 109.

Gamble, Capt., 24.

Gambling, 39.

GASPÉE (British patrol boat), 12, 33.

Gates, Horatio, 80.

GENERAL SULLIVAN (privateer), 109, 113.

George III, 17; *ignores Olive Branch Petition, 65-66; declares colonies in state of rebellion, 66.*

Germain, Lord George, 150, 197.

Gerrish, Caesar, 215.

Giddinge, John, 40, 55.

Gidney, Joshua, 123.

Gilman, John Taylor, 45, 54, 116; *on sectional politics, 82-83; delegate to Continental Congress, 87; appointed pension agent, 104; on Treaty of 1783, 200-201.*

Gilman, Nicholas, 42, 45, 54, 134, 145.

Gilman, Peter, 7.

Gilmanton, 170.

Gilmanton Academy, 211.

Gosport, 31.

Governor, powers, 1767, 3.

Index

Grafton County, 10, 44; *representation in Assembly, 11, 25, 26, 28; no Loyalists in, 52; representation in Legislature, 178, 179, 190; not represented in Constitutional Convention, 1778, 180; and secession movement, 196, 197.*
Graves, Admiral Samuel, 23.
Great Bay Region, 2, 151.
Greene, Jacob, 25.
Greenland, 68, 179.
GROSVENOR (ship, Capt. Brown), 15.
Gunthwait, 190, 192.

Hale, Enoch, 196.
Hale, Nathan, 92, 93.
Hale, Samuel, 54.
Hall, Seneca, 215.
Hall Stream, 201, 202.
Hamilton, Alexander, 137, 143, 147.
HAMPDEN (privateer), 110-111.
Hampton, 14, 28, 34, 177.
Hanover, 26, 144, 184, 190, 192, 212.
Hart, John, 110.
Haven, Samuel, 60, 201.
Haverhill, 14, 26, 34, 190, 192.
Haverhill Academy, 211.
Hawke, N. H., 74.
Heath, William, 102.
Henniker, 121.
Henry, Patrick, 7, 33.
Hewes, Robert, 155.
Hillsborough, Lord, 7, 9, 10.
Hillsborough County, 10, 44, 179; *lawlessness, 23; County Congress recommends formation of military companies, 37; Loyalists, 51-52, 121, 145; and currency inflation, 142-143, 158.*
Holderness, 59.
Holland, Stephen, 56, 127, 129, 166, 172, 203, 205.
Hollis, 38, 204.
Hopkinton, 28, 177.
Hunter, Hugh, 111.

Independence, *New Hampshire sentiment against, 68-69, 179; New Hampshire declares its independence, 71.*
Independence, Declaration of, 71-72, 180.
Indian Stream, 201.
Indian Stream Republic, 202.
Inheritance laws, 172-174.
Intolerable Acts, 17-18, 49.

Jackson, Daniel, 107.
Jackson, Hall, 55.

Jaffrey, George, 42, 166.
Jefferson, Thomas, 33-34, 71, 80, 174.
Jones, John Paul, 112.
Jordan, Richard, 155.
Judiciary, *before Revolution, 10-11; courts established by Legislature, 179-180; under the Constitution of 1781, 183.*

Keene, 36-37, 126, 212.
Kenny, Penelope, 213.
Kensington, 58, 68, 179.
Kimball, Joseph, 121.
KING FISHER (sloop), 29.
Kingston, 39, 40.

Laboring classes, attitude toward Revolution, 55-56.
Ladd, Eliphalet, 156.
Ladd, Jewett & Osgood, Exeter, 109.
Land, *insecurity of title, 164-167, 189; quitrents, 170; confiscation of Loyalists' estates, 172, 204; primogeniture, 172-173, 174; entails, 173-174.*
Landaff, 190, 193.
Langdon, John, 45, 54, 149; *frames resolves against Wentworth, 21; and loot of Fort William and Mary, 22, 24; delegate to Continental Congress, 39, 87; on the Confederation, 72; owns privateers, 109; becomes Continental naval agent, 113; on paper money, 139; benefits by Revolution, 150, 160; letters to, 63, 70, 72, 78, 79.*
Langdon, Samuel, 211.
Langdon, Woodbury, 21, 87.
Laws, Legislature re-establishes provincial system, 180.
Lawyers, attitude toward Revolution, 54.
Lebanon, 2, 26, 190, 192.
Lee, Francis L., 33.
Lee, Richard Henry, 33, 71, 80.
Legislature, *under Constitution of 1776, 68, 178-179; approves Articles of Confederation, 74-75; supervises supplies and equipment of state levies, 96; draws up Articles of War, 100-101; awards pensions to disabled soldiers, 104; laws for the suppression of Loyalists, 123-127; legal tender laws, 140, 142-143; passes law against counterfeiting and forging, 144; encourages manufacturing, 155; cedes Congress the right to impose tariff, 157-158; laws fixing prices and regulating sales, 159-160; property qualifications for membership, 176-177, 181, 183, 184, 185; establishes judiciary and legal system, 179-180; calls Constitutional Conventions, 180, 182; under the Constitution*

of *1781, 183-185; and secession movement in western towns, 192, 196, 197;* empowers English citizens to sue in New Hampshire courts, 202; repeals Confiscation Act, 204; refuses slaves' petition for freedom, 215.

Lexington, Battle of, 63-64.

Lincoln, Gen. Benjamin, 81.

Livermore, Samuel, 45, 49, 54, 85, 195; *delegate to Continental Congress, 87; on taxation, 137.*

Livius, Peter, 168.

Loans, 42, *floated to finance Revolution, 142, 145.*

Londonderry, 2, 21, 28, 154, 177.

Long, Pierce, 44, 155.

Lovell, James, 75.

Loyalists, *definition, 48-49; numbers, 51, 61; geographical distribution, 51-52; occupational distribution, 52-58; religious distribution, 58-61; persecution of, 119-124, 127, 128, 130-131; Association Test, 121-122;* trial by Committee of Safety, 123-124; New York State Loyalists imprisoned in New Hampshire, 123; disarmament of, 124; confiscation of property, 124-127, 172, 202-204; deprived of legal rights, 127; disenfranchised, 127, 128; in British Army, 127-128; emigration of, 128; unconfiscated property protected by Treaty of 1783, 200, 203-204; compensated for losses by British government, 204-205.

Lumbering, *effect of Revolution on, 151-152; mast trees reserved for the Crown, 170-172.*

Lutwyche, Edward Goldstone, 54.

Lyman, 190, 192.

Lyme, 2, 190, 192, *represented in last Assembly, 25, 26, 29, 177.*

McClary, Andrew, 90, 92.

McClary, John, 45.

MCCLARY (privateer), 114-116.

McClure, David, 70

McDonough, Thomas, 130.

MacGregore, David, 60.

Mack, Elisha, 126.

McMasters, James, 9.

Madbury, 51.

Manufacturing, 11; *effect of Revolution on, 153-156; state aid to, 154-155.*

Maritime Office, established, 134, 156-157.

Marlboro, 74.

Marlow, 190.

Mason, Capt. John, 163, 164.

Mason, John Tufton, 165.

Mason, Robert Tufton, 164.

Masonian Curve, 188.

Masonian Grant, 163-167.

Masonian Proprietors, 166-167.

Massachusetts, *urges colonies to unite against Townshend Acts, 6-7; grants lands north of Merrimack, 164-165.*

Massachusetts Committee of Correspondence, 13; *established, 12;* on Battle of Lexington, 64.

Massachusetts Government Act, 17-18, 20.

Mast trees, reserved for the Crown, 170-172.

Matrons of Liberty, 15.

Merchants, attitude toward Revolution, 54.

Merrimack Valley, 2, 151.

Meserve, George, 12, 166, 204.

Methodist Church, 209.

Military preparation, 1774-75, 40-42, 43, 64, 65.

Militia, *reorganized by Provincial Congress, 43, 94;* organization, 88-90; before Revolution, 89; *permanent system established, 94;* regulated by Articles of War, 100-101; inefficiency of, 101.

Minute Men, 41.

MIRROUR (newspaper), 212.

Mississippi River, free navigation of, 84.

Morey, Israel, 25, 45.

Morris, Robert, 78, 100.

Morristown, 190, 193.

Moulton, Jonathan, 45.

Munitions, manufacture of, 154-155.

Nate, Alexander, 111.

Navy, Continental, 106-107, 116; *size, 112;* organization, 112-113; *salaries of officers and crew, 113;* equipment, 113-114.

New Boston, 38.

New Connecticut, State of, 192.

New England Restraining Act, 29-30, 151.

New Hampshire, *sectionalism, 1-2;* population, 1, 172; prosperity, 1774, 18; *settlement of, 164-165, 167-168, 172;* boundaries, 163-164, 165, 167-168, 188-189, 194-196; *boundaries under the Treaty of 1783, 200, 201-202.*

New Hampshire Agricultural Society, 153.

NEW HAMPSHIRE GAZETTE, 69, 212.

New Hampshire Grants, 126, 168; *settlers west of Connecticut River revolt against New York government, 189, 192; towns west of river declare themselves State of Vermont, 192; towns east of river unite*

Index

with Vermont, *192-197; New Hampshire renews her claim to, 194-195.*
NEW HAMPSHIRE JOURNAL, 212.
NEW HAMPSHIRE MERCURY, 212.
NEW HAMPSHIRE RECORDER, 212.
NEW HAMPSHIRE SPY, 212.
New Haven, Conn., economic conference, 1778, 160-161.
New Ipswich, 9.
New Ipswich Academy, 211.
New York, *sends Loyalists to New Hampshire for custody, 123; disputes boundary with New Hampshire, 168, 189, 194-195.*
Newburg Addresses, 103.
Newcastle, 14, 22, 34.
Newington, 68, 179.
Newmarch, Cato, 215.
Newmarket, 21, 39, 68, 179.
Newspapers, effect of Revolution on, 211-212.
Non-exportation Agreement, 37, 38-39.
Non-importation Agreement, 36-37.
Non-importation of English goods, 8-11, 37-39.
North, Lord, 9, 17, 25, 26, 66.
North Hampton, 68, 179.
Nottingham, 170.

Official class, attitude toward Revolution, 53-54.
Olcott, Peter, 195.
Olive Branch Petition, 65-66.
Orford, 25, 26, 29, 177, 192.

Paine, Tom, 174; *Common Sense*, 69-70.
Paper money, *issued to finance Revolution, 42, 138-142; redeemed by New Hampshire, 142, 143.*
Parker, John, 19.
Parker, Robert, 109.
Parry, Edward, 15-16.
Patten, Matthew, 120.
Payne, Elisha, 193, 196.
Peabody, Nathaniel, 45, 55, 85, 158; *on office-seekers, 79; on Continental Congress, 85; delegate to Continental Congress, 87.*
Pearne, William, 38, 156.
Pearse, Peter, 166.
Pedlers, make enforcement of Continental Association difficult, 39.
Peltier, Mr., 111.
Penal code, effect of Revolution on, 185, 212-214.
Penhallow, John, 115.
Pension system, 102-104, *New Hampshire opposition to, 83, 185.*

Peters, John, 122.
Peverly, Kinsman, 111.
Phelps, Bezaleel, 144.
Philadelphia, price-fixing conference, 1780, 161.
Philbrick, Samuel, 181.
Phillips, John, 20, 146, 211.
Phillips Exeter Academy, 211.
Physicians, attitude toward Revolution, 55.
Pickering, John, 36, 54, 63.
Pickering, Thomas, 22, 110-111.
Pierce, John, 167.
Piermont, 192.
Piscataqua River, 151.
Pitkin, Timothy, 143.
Pittsburg, 202.
Plainfield, 190.
Plumer, William, 54, 184.
Plymouth, 25, 26, 29, 177.
Poor, Enoch, 80, 89, 92, 93, 97.
Port duties, 134, 157.
Porter, Asa, 122.
Portsmouth, 1-2, 72; *petitions king, 6; merchants refuse to boycott English goods, 8-9; boycotted by Boston, 9-10; condemns Tea Act, 14; Matrons of Liberty denounce Tea Resolves, 15; boycotts tea, 15-16; grants money for relief of Boston, 20-21; votes to protect Wentworth, 24-25; harbor blockaded, 29-30; builds forts at entrance of harbor, 66; protests against state constitution, 68, 179; approves Articles of Confederation, 73; privateers operating from, 108; naval vessels built in, 112; receives custody of New York State Loyalists, 123; powder mill, 155; celebrates peace, 201; harbor opened to British ships, 201; newspapers, 212; slaves petition Legislature for freedom, 215.*
Portsmouth Committee of Correspondence, *established, 34; on Boston Port Act, 19.*
Portsmouth Committee of Safety, *resolves against Wentworth, 21; arouses mob against Fort William and Mary, 22-23; boycotts The Scarborough and Fort William and Mary, 30; enforces Continental Association, 38-39; closes gambling establishments, 39; forbids profiteering, 39; requests aid of Washington, 66-67.*
Portsmouth Committee of Ways and Means, see Portsmouth Committee of Safety.
Portsmouth Episcopal Church, 59-60.
PORTSMOUTH MERCURY, 212.
Portsmouth Volunteers, 40.

Postoffice, established by Provincial Congress, 42.

Prentice, Nathaniel, 196.

Presbyterian Church, 208, *attitude toward Revolution*, 60-61.

President, office established by Constitution of 1781, 185.

Press, Censorship of, 69.

Prices, *fixed by Continental Congress, 83; during Revolution, 110, 153, 158; fixed by Legislature, 159-160.*

Primogeniture, 172-173, 174.

Privateering, *laws for regulation of, 107-108, 114-115; profits of, 108-109, 113; extent of, 108-109, 116-117; desperate character of, 109-112.*

Profiteering, 39, 138, 160-161.

Proscription Act, 51ff., 125, 128.

Providence, currency convention, 1776, 159.

Provincial Congress, 19-20, 21, 25; *first meeting, 35-36; instructs delegates to Continental Congress, 35-36.*

Provincial Congress (2d), first meeting, 39-40.

Provincial Congress (3d), *emergency session to discuss military organization, 41, 64; representation in, 177.*

Provincial Congress (4th), 41-42; *issues paper money, 42, 138-139; reorganizes militia, 43; votes to raise first troops, 65; reapportions representation of towns, 43, 67, 178; offers bounty for manufacture of saltpetre, 154-155; forbids exportation of fish, 156; representation in, 177; alters the franchise system, 177.*

Provincial Congress (5th), *resolves itself into House of Representatives, 43, 68, 178-179; votes to establish a form of government, 43, 68, 178-179; chooses a committee to plan for sinking the Colony debt, 139.*

Provincial government, in 1767, 2-3.

Putnam, Israel, 97-98.

Quakers, 208, *attitude toward Revolution, 58-59.*

Quartering Act, 18, 20.

Quebec Act, 18, 20.

Queen's Chapel, Portsmouth, 59-60.

Quitrents, 170.

RALEIGH (ship), 112, 114.

RANGER (ship), 112.

Reed, James, 80, 89, 92, 93.

Reid, George, 92, 93.

Religious tolerance, contribution of Revolution to, 208-209.

Representation, *in Assembly, 1775, 26, 28, 177; reapportioned by 4th Provincial Congress, 43, 67, 178; under Constitution of 1776, 43, 67-68, 178-179; in 3d and 4th Provincial Congresses, 177; according to Constitution of 1781, 183-185.*

Representatives, House of, *protests against organization of state government, 68; tries Asa Porter for conspiracy, 122; under Constitution of 1781, 183-185.*

RESOLUTION (brigantine), 12.

Revere, Paul, 22.

Revolutionists, definition, 48-49.

Richmond, 59.

Rindge, Daniel, 56, 166-167.

Roads, built by quitrents, 170.

Robertson, Robert, 127.

Rochester, 58, 170; *Committee of Correspondence condemns Nicholas Austin, 21; establishes Committee of Correspondence, 34; remonstrates against state government, 68, 179.*

Rockingham, Marquis of, 4, 5, 10.

Rockingham County, 10; *controls Revolutionary government, 44, 178, 179, 180, 183; Loyalists, 51, 52; and currency inflation, 142, 158; rum appraisers, 160; slavery in, 214.*

Rogers, Pharaoh, 215.

Royse, Vere, 210.

Ryan, James, 144.

Rye, 22, 68, 179.

Sales laws, 159-160.

Salisbury Academy, 211.

Sanderson, Mr., 124.

Sanger, Abner, 124.

Scammell, Alexander, 92, 93.

SCARBOROUGH, Capt. Barkley, 23, 26, 29-30, 43.

Schuyler, Philip John, 81.

Seamen, impressment of, 29.

Sectionalism in colonies, 46-47, 81-84.

Senate, under Constitution of 1781, 182-183, 184.

Shakers, 209.

Sheafe, James, 130.

Shelburne, Lord, 18, 133, 199, 200, 204.

Shepard, Samuel, 61.

Sheppard, James, 114.

Shipbuilding, effect of Revolution on, 150-151.

Shoals, Isle of, 156.

Shortridge, Samuel, 111.

Simpson, Sarah, 213.